New Irish Storytellers

For Declan

New Irish Storytellers
Narrative Strategies in Film

Díóg O'Connell

intellect Bristol, UK / Chicago, USA

First published in the UK in 2010 by
Intellect, The Mill, Parnall Road, Fishponds, Bristol, BS16 3JG, UK

First published in the USA in 2010 by
Intellect, The University of Chicago Press, 1427 E. 60th Street,
Chicago, IL 60637, USA

A catalogue record for this book is available from the
British Library.

Cover photo by David Cleary from the motion picture *Once*.
Back cover photo (from top to bottom): Still from *Disco Pigs*, courtesy
of Patrick Redmond, Photographer and Element Films; Still from
Garage, courtesy of Lenny Abrahamson; Still from *Adam & Paul*,
courtesy of Lenny Abrahamson

Cover designer: Holly Rose
Copy-editor: Heather Owen
Typesetting: Mac Style, Beverley, E. Yorkshire

ISBN 978-1-84150-312-7

Printed and bound in the UK by 4edge Ltd, Hockley. www.4edge.co.uk

FSC Mixed Sources
SA-COC-001695
© 1996 FSC A.C.

Contents

Acknowledgements

I owe a debt of gratitude to many people in completing the work of this book, which grew out of a doctoral study entitled 'Narrative Strategies in Contemporary Irish Film', completed in 2005. I acknowledge the huge support, advice, help and encouragement of my PhD supervisor at DCU, Dr. Pat Brereton, during this time and since. The Institute of Art, Design & Technology and Dr. Josephine Browne, Head of School of Business and Humanities, supported me during my doctoral studies, particularly with research-friendly teaching timetables and by providing financial assistance to attend many conferences on Irish film and screenwriting. Chapter 3 and Chapter 4 are based on pieces presented at the Irish Postgraduate Film Seminar (2003–05) when researching my doctorate. I am grateful to Dr. John Hill and Prof. Kevin Rockett for organizing these seminars and subsequent publications, an invaluable opportunity for research students. I would like to recognize the contributions my students at IADT make in class by providing new insights and interpretations of Irish cinema in discussions about narrative themes, forms and styles which are often provocative and insightful.

Since embarking on this book project, which involved updating existing research and carrying out new work, many people have provided support in many different ways. Special thanks to the staff at the Irish Film Institute and the Irish Film Archive, particularly Rebecca Grant, Karen Wall and Sunniva O'Flynn, who provide an excellent service and resource for researchers of Irish film, without which this study would not have been possible. Thanks also to the people working in the Irish Film Industry who provided information and assistance for my research, including Lenny Abrahamson, Nichola Bruce, David Cleary, Anna Devlin, Martin Duffy, Janine Marmot, Pat Murphy, Rebecca O'Flanagan, Mark O'Halloran, Liam O'Neill, Steve Pyke, Rod Stoneman and Enda Walsh.

Many other people helped with this project by providing critical engagement, sharing outings to the cinema, proof reading and much-needed support that I am truly grateful for: Steven Benedict, Anne Bourke, Stephen Boyd, Dara Cassidy, Seán Crosson, Siobhán Flanagan, Roddy Flynn, Michael Patrick Gillespie, Selina Guinness, Ed Hatton, Barbara Hughes, Máire Kearney, Deirdre Kerins, Carol MacKeogh, Gráinne Mallon, Cathy McGlynn, Conor McHale, Deirdre O'Connell, Niamh Reilly, Elaine Sisson, Tony Tracy and Séamus White.

Finally, the enduring support and patience of my husband Declan and my children Aoife (10), Ailíse (8) and Clíona (2) cannot go unmentioned, without their love, fun and friendship this book would never have reached completion.

Introduction: Reclaiming the Notion of Story

Storytelling is essentially a social – a co-operative – activity; to narrate is to act on listeners, and an audience's sense of sharing an experience and thus belonging together may be as valuable as individual imaginary release. The foundations of the art belong to a common heritage of mankind, but some formal details and performance patterns may be specific to a particular culture. People with a common set of stories (and ways of telling them) form a community; conversely, different repertoires may divide audiences – but stories can cross ethnic barriers. (Zimmermann, 2001: 9)

If you aren't telling a story, moving from one image to another, the images have to be more and more 'interesting' per se. If you *are* telling a story, then the human mind, as it's working along with you, is perceiving your thrust, both consciously and, more importantly, subconsciously. The audience members are going to go along with that story and will require neither inducement, in the form of visual extravagance, nor explanation in the form of narration. (Mamet, 1994: 384)

Recounting the life of folklorist Seán Ó hEochaidh, who collected fairy tales and stories particularly from the south west corner of Co. Donegal, Des Bell's documentary *The Last Storyteller?* (2002) focuses on the work from 1935 of the Irish Folklore Commission, the statutory body charged with recording Irish stories and preserving the act of storytelling. The parallels suggested here between folklore and film-making frames the approach adopted for this work: to reclaim the notion of story for the pursuit of a critical understanding of Irish film narrative. Long before the technological innovations allowing moving images to develop into narrative forms, the intrinsic need for storytelling was embedded in the culture of all ancient and modern societies, providing both a social outlet and entertainment role. 'Folklore', according to Zimmermann 'consists, among other things, of ready-made plots, of codified ways of putting together basic elements to produce partly new stories, and of manners of performing them in face-to-face communication' (Zimmermann, 2001: 11).This definition also captures many features of film narrative and storytelling in the visual medium, particularly in the way such 'traditional narratives' are said to have a 'collective' dimension (Zimmermann, 2001: 11). Many structural similarities exist between folklore and film-making: the means of putting together, *narrative construction*, follows parallel patterns, while the place of consumption and reception is similarly a very public affair.

Even though cinema is one of the most modern and technologically developed of narrative art forms, it is still concerned with the most ancient endeavour of storytelling, myth-making and fable creation. This study takes as its impetus the act of storytelling, now popularly received and expressed principally and predominantly in motion pictures, and through an analysis of strategy and form in recent Irish film, it 'creates new contexts for the older sets of concepts' (Benjamin quoted in Smith, 1988). Through the prism of narrative theory, this book examines storytelling techniques and narrative strategies in contemporary Irish film since the reactivation of the Irish Film Board in 1993. Focused accordingly, the study illuminates the craft and creative decisions that contribute to defining patterns, styles and tendencies within recent Irish cinema. By examining narrative structure, this book reveals how Irish film-makers appropriate devices from a range of sources – mainstream Hollywood, independent American cinema and/or European films – and then merges them with idiosyncratic and local approaches to telling stories, creating hybrids which define an evolutionary and developmental phase in contemporary Irish cinema. Examining the interstices between these different approaches to film-making and contextualizing in a new and original way, this study identifies similarities and differences at certain key moments and reveals narrative changes and developments spanning a decade and a half.

When David Mamet says 'a good writer gets better only by learning to *cut*, to remove the ornamental, the descriptive, the narrative, and *especially* the deeply felt and meaningful. What remains? The story remains' (Mamet, 1994: 346), he is emphasizing the *story* as the primary communicative objective of the writer. The transcendental nature of narrative is difficult to explain, concerning an action and a concept as concrete yet as illusory as the term story. For this reason, Mamet's definition of screenwriting as a 'craft based on logic' is useful. This logic is rooted in the 'assiduous application of several basic questions' (Mamet, 1994), generally applied to the goal-oriented main character that is a regular feature of the mainstream narrative structure. Theorists of narrative who are interested in how an infinite variety of stories may be generated from a limited number of basic structures often have recourse, like linguists, to the notions of deep and surface structure (Rimmon-Kenan, 1983). This strategy assumes a formalist approach, the position embodied here. The methodology devised incorporates ancient classical writers like Aristotle and early twentieth-century formalists such as Vladimir Propp, authors of scriptwriting manuals (Robert McKee and Christopher Vogler) as well as narratologists (David Bordwell and Edward Branigan), reflecting a return to formalist approaches within narrative studies in recent times, indicating a renewed interest and concern for the notion of story.

Far from being a regressive, romantic inclination, this approach finds support in the writings of Roy Foster when he states that the 'idea of narrative is back in the air' (Foster, 2001: 1) and by Richard Kearney when he suggests that 'the power of narrativity makes a crucial difference to our lives. Indeed, I shall go as far as to argue, rephrasing Socrates, that the unnarrated life is not worth living' (Kearney, 2002: 14). This study examines the contribution contemporary Irish film-makers make as storytellers in the way Walter Benjamin imagined. While not denying that some film-makers use the medium to comment on wider society, the approach appropriated here attempts to reveal, in storyworld terms, what is at work within the narrative at a universal and human level, principally through a formalist and narrative address, while revealing some local nuanced reflections. Revealing the complex styles and techniques of story that film-makers of the past fifteen years in Ireland have adopted and realized, this work is situated within a field that seeks to find a space whereby theory and practice can relate to each other.

This chapter sets out the approach adopted in this book: an examination of storytelling technique within contemporary Irish film through the lens of narrative theory, presenting an argument for adopting a framework which illuminates the practice of scriptwriting by rendering narrative theory in a user-friendly way. Outlined below is the methodology developed to explore narrative strategies predominating in new Irish cinema, illustrating how theory can have a practical application. The approach breaks narrative into three parts: story, plot and character, and presents the tools of analysis for each stage. In applying the method to specific Irish films, the various components are examined to reveal style and narrative tendencies of different writer/director teams, at different moments in the recent history of Irish film and storytelling.

Before applying a close reading in narratological terms to a range and sample of recent Irish films, Chapter 1 provides a brief overview of the various script-policy developments by the Irish Film Board and the thinking behind these initiatives and changes between 1993 and 2008. While it would be impossible to present a discussion on all films aided by the Film Board (over one hundred and forty in the period under examination), Chapters 2–7 explore, through close readings, a sample of the styles and structures of various narrative forms, some guided by generic boundaries, others pushing the limits, while a variety are genre-defiant. This book represents the eclectic nature of style and story that Irish film-makers have presented to Irish and foreign audiences during the past fifteen years, looking at both mainstream approaches and alternative forms, focusing on notable points of departure as a way of revealing the characteristics of recent Irish cinema, through a narrative analysis based on a specified methodology developed and described below.

Theorizing the storyworld

Narrative in film is an abstract in the sense that it is a creation of itself and of its own world; it is *hermetically sealed* and stands alone. It relates only to the real world by connection after the event. As Eliot states, the significance of poets and artists can only be read in relation to other 'dead poets and artists', an aesthetic rather than historical criticism (Eliot, 1999:15), reclaiming the study of poetry within the confines of poetry itself. Similarly, this study seeks to position the study of film within the world of *film* and evaluate filmic texts according to the narrative world that governs the activities of writers and directors. While clearly these writers and directors belong to a wider society, this study positions the work of film-makers within the world of film-making as an aesthetic principle.

Space and time define narrative and story. It is assumed that space and time are the boundaries and borders of diegetic and extra-diegetic space, central to theorizing the storyworld. According to narrative theory, 'there is no such thing as an objective, unchanging world … [D]ifferent societies carve up reality differently, and the most sensitive indicator of the co-ordinates that give shape to any culture's world picture is to be found in the characteristic arrangements of time and space in the texts that each society nominates as art' (Clark & Holquist, 1984: 294). In adapting V.I. Pudovkin's formula for constructing films, as outlined in *Film Technique and Film Acting*, now perceived by many scholars as formulaic, Noel Carroll (1988) presents a method for analysing narrative according to time and space. The theory uses the concept of a question as a starting point, that is, the spectator frames a question subconsciously (rather than unconsciously) and expects answers to it. While the position is problematic when the ambiguity of art is considered, it is a useful starting point in structural analysis, echoed in similar schema used by David Bordwell (1990) and Edward Branigan (1998). When following a narrative film, a spectator internalizes the whole structure comprising the elements depicted in the drama. This structure includes alternative outcomes to various lines of action that the spectator must keep track of, in some cases anticipating, but always recalling. One alternative is finally actualized so that the film can be received as intelligible (Carroll, 1988: 173).

> The ways in which a question is made salient by a scene or group of scenes is diverse … [a] great deal of work is done in the writing, not only the dialogue and/or inter-titles, but also in the choice of subject and the dramatic focus of given scenes. (Carroll, 1988: 174)

Carroll presents a basic appreciation of the skeleton of a sample of film structures which he describes as 'an idealized, erotetic, linear, movie narrative' (Carroll, 1988: 171).[1] An elaboration on Bordwell's cause/effect model, Carroll describes an event or scene in an erotetic narrative in the following way: an establishing scene; a questioning scene; an answering scene; a sustaining scene; an incomplete answering scene; an answering/questioning scene (Bordwell & Carroll, 1996), a schema very close to Branigan and Todorov's paradigms which are also based on a linear structure of progression (Branigan, 1998). Whether a scene or an event is part of the core plot of a linear movie narrative depends on whether it is one of these types of scenes, i.e. whether it is part of the circuit of questions and answers that powers the film. In summary, the erotetic model or question/answer model answers questions posed in earlier scenes. This model holds that the major connective between 'scenes and scenes', 'events and events', in movies is an internal process of questioning and answering. While the erotetic model is concerned with how the viewer makes sense of the movie, like most theories, there is potential in it for analysing how the writer makes sense of the story for the viewer.

In adopting the hypothesis that the narrative structure of a randomly selected movie is fundamentally a system of internally generated questions that the movie goes on to answer, you will find that you have hold of a relationship that enables you to explain what makes certain scenes especially key: they either raise questions or answer them, or perform related functions including sustaining questions already raised or incompletely answering a previous question, or answering one question and then introducing a new one. (Carroll, 1988:179)

While the hypothesis immediately concerns itself with linear narrative, Carroll acknowledges that it would also lend itself to analysis of alternative structures. Given the shifts in narrative form in recent times following technological development, particularly non-linear editing, putting the approach into practice is timely. Where it is most useful is by offering an alternative to the equilibrium model as an analytical tool for the dominant narrative form. As Carroll says, unlike those of real life, the actions observed in movies have a level of intelligibility due to the role they play in the erotetic system of questions and answers. He argues that it is not the realism of movies that compels us but rather this erotetic relationship embedded in the narrative; it supports the structure of dramatic conflict. The approach presents the story analyst with a way of intellectually engaging with an intuitive practice and dramatic form, in accordance with cognitive theory. The audience works with a logically-constructed model in Kantian terms, not a 'random string of events'. The schema assumes a proactive audience, anticipating and recalling, key cognitive activities involved in processing film narratives. Consequently, 'erotetic narration endows the movie with an aura of clarity while also affording an intense satisfaction of our human propensity for intelligibility' (Carroll, 1988: 181).

Without attempting to answer all questions relating to narrative, this discussion examines how Irish screenwriters construct stories within a universal application situated in the wider world of film both national and international, while also displaying a local resonance. It is the writers' and directors' approaches to their craft in a particular way, along certain lines that this book seeks to explicate. The method raises pertinent concerns and issues, particular to structure and aesthetics, in relation to recent Irish cinema as part of a global/international art form. A narrative analysis is also a way of exploring recent Irish film as it evolves over time and develops according to the infrastructure put in place and in relation to wider popular culture and modes of storytelling.

Theorizing plot

Plot as a focus of exploration has occupied an important position in the history of narrative theory and can be traced back to Aristotle's *Poetics*. Plot, the work of *mythos*, gives life to action, is fundamental to human existence. In Kearney's words, this action is given a grammar 'by transposing it into a telling; a fable or fantasy; and a crafted structure' (Kearney, 2002: 129). Structuralists and formalists, traditionally, have put the greatest degree of emphasis on plot in their analysis of narrative, primarily because plot is most closely associated with action. Character is then considered the *actant*[2] of action, agents of cause/effect, or the propellant of the plot. Along these lines, characters are made subordinate to fictional events even when initiated by them or when they are central to them (see Aristotle and Barthes, for example). Plot is intrinsically linked to space and time, and to cause and effect. Cause-effect is basic to narrative and takes place in time. Story-time is constructed on the basis of what the plot presents. The plot may reveal clues or withhold information and functions to increase suspense, to keep the viewer guessing or simply to raise expectations. Narration involves the plot's way of distributing story information in order to achieve specific effects. A theoretical approach to plot would ask how does something happen, pose a question and generate an answer, linked to the laws of verisimilitude but also to the structural needs of the plot.

Because narrative texts can be found in all periods of human history, all cultures and all levels of society, Roland Barthes concluded that narrative texts are based upon one common model, a model that causes the narrative to be recognizable as narrative. The studies that gave rise to structuralism are based on two assumptions, although applied to linguistics, usefully appropriated for film. Firstly, there exists a homology (similar state), a correspondence between the (linguistic) structure of the sentence or the (filmic) structure of the scene, and that of the whole text composed of various sentences and various scenes. Secondly, a homology exists between the 'deep structure' of the sentence and the 'deep structure' of the narrative text: the fabula. This Bordwell refers to as 'story', (Bordwell et al., 1985). The fabula, he elaborates, is a pattern 'which perceivers of narratives create through assumptions and inferences' (Bordwell et al., 1985: 49), recognizing and understanding the plot leads to the interpretation of story. The narrative makes sense by establishing connections, identifying similar states and structures: the homology. The plot, therefore, becomes familiar, is easily read and stimulates certain expectations as the viewer understands the story.

While there has been much criticism of this structuralist approach (modernism and postmodernism have traditionally found it 'meaningless'), it explains the existence of a logic and is useful in theorizing around plot. An argument follows that readers, intentionally or not, search for a logical line in texts (Bordwell et al., 1985: 176). They expend a great amount of energy in this search and, if necessary, they introduce such a line themselves (or when suspension of disbelief fails they might simply give up). Responses which are intrinsic to drama depend on it, such as emotional involvement, aesthetic pleasure, suspense and humour. While an audience does not always retain precise details of a plot, they maintain a sense or feeling for the story. Most plots, Bal argues, are constructed according to the demands of a human 'logic of events', provided that this concept is not too narrowly defined. 'Logic of events' is explained as 'a course of events … that is experienced by the reader as natural and in accordance with some form of understanding with the world' (Bal, 1999: 177). This draws parallels with the work of Vladimir Propp, Joseph Campbell and Christopher Vogler, as they also subscribe to the existence of a homology and consequently map it out. Propp's 'Call for Help' is analogous to Campbell's 'Separation or Departure' and Vogler's 'Call to Adventure'. 'Misfortune is announced' (Propp), 'The Road of Trials' (Campbell) is introduced or, in Vogler's term, the hero must 'Cross the First Threshold' (Vogler, 1999). The homology thus referred to is a state related to the storyworld, not the 'real world'. The process of narrative construction and reading involves an emotional response derived from a logical process. While Bal's intellectual loyalty is to structuralism, this definition can be appropriated for the purposes of this discussion. Tying in with the local/global debate, Bal believes that fabulas (which, unlike Bordwell, she distinguishes from story) are comparable transculturally and transhistorically.

In conclusion, a plot may be considered as a specific grouping of a series of events, as a whole that constitutes a process, while every event can also be called a process, or at least part of a process. Aristotle distinguishes three phases in every plot as follows: the possibility (or vitality); the event (or realization); the result (or conclusion). The initial situation will always be a state of deficiency in which one or more characters want to introduce change. The development of the plot reveals that, according to certain patterns, the process of change involves an improvement or deterioration with regard to the initial situation (Bal, 1999: 193). The situation brought about by the conclusion of the fabula and syuzhet[3] (story and plot) may be advancing to a higher plain, resolving conflict, gaining greater insight or simply solving the puzzle. Far from being formulaic, this approach offers a structure for the craft to work within and a framework by which to place and examine film. Distinguishing between these terms, plot and story, and applying them to close readings, sheds light of the narrative strategies employed.

Theorizing character

Even though for Aristotle and Barthes plot is paramount when analysing narrative, they both reveal an important function for character in their writings. Through the term *mimesis*, which is the imitation of action and life, not person and character, Aristotle explains this hierarchy. The goal of a narrative is action, which can lead to an emotional state such as happiness. The goal of tragedy is not a qualitative emotional state but, through behaviour, which is action, this state is reached. Yet, in referring to tragedy in terms of 'reversal and recognition', Aristotle is concerned directly with character and not only action. By giving character a category or code, Barthes is also specifically assigning a narrative function to character, despite his attachment to plot (Lothe, 2000: 77). When engaging at an emotional level with a narrative, it is through character identification that empathetic responses are formed. This position is given closer attention in more recent writings on film narrative, by Alex Neill (1993; 1996; 1999), Susan Feagin (1988) and Paisley Livingstone (1996), among others (see Chapter 4). Paisley Livingstone in *Post-Theory: Reconstructing Film Studies* (see Chapter 7) teases out character, linking it to the contentious position of 'intentionalism'. For the purpose of this study it is useful as a method for exploring characterization in narrative forms, revealing a process around how the reader is effectively guided in judging what happens in a story. This he links directly to a theory of intentionalism:

> A more promising alternative is the idea that the appropriate choice of background beliefs is underwritten by a complex intentionality principle. Competent readers and spectators do not make inferences about the implicit truths in a story by obeying the reality principle or by activating entire belief systems of bygone or alien communities. Instead, they do so by paying attention to the text's features and reasoning about the aims and attitudes of the actual storyteller. Yet this intentionality principle must be one that does not succumb to various familiar objections against intentionalism. (Livingstone, 1996: 163)

In probing character, one is not simply looking at 'the belief set of a fictional author who tells a story as known fact', but what the author intended in creating a storyworld. While intentionalism is contentious in film theory, it is an act performed by audiences viewing and critiquing films: assumptions are made, conclusions drawn. What Livingstone is proposing as an intentionality theory is one that concerns itself with the authorial – that the story is determined by authorial attitudes and the text's features. The story content is as a result of authorial intentions, principally, in the process of creating a storyworld. The intentionality principle implies that knowledge of authorial intentions with regard to a story can warrant a decision between, as Livingstone says, 'our interpretative alternatives, in other words, the intentions we want viewers to rely upon when they think about story content'. This is based on 'the authors' effective, communicative intentions, not idle musings or solitary imaginings' (Livingstone, 1996:167). This is achieved through the agents of drama, rather than in a plot device. Characterization, therefore, is a useful tool to reveal story intentions. As a theoretical approach to characterization, it is useful in deconstructing the narrative functioning of its main agents, at the point of source rather than consumption.

Livingstone presents a definition of characterization as

> a matter of someone's describing, depicting, or representing something … the something being represented must be an agent or agents … Agent can be defined broadly as referring to any entity capable of performing an intentional action. And intentional action can, in turn, be identified as behaviour produced and oriented by the agent's intention. (Livingstone, 1996: 150)

Thus, Livingstone reveals the problematic nature of defining character and characterization. For there to be an event of characterization, there must be an actual agent that performs the plot action; the agent is generally a character (although it can be something else), society in social realism films or natural phenomenon in adventure films. Defining character in this way continues the historical definition of character from Aristotle onwards, a definition that places characterization and character as intrinsic to plot or action. Aristotle's instruction for characterization was that they should be 'good, appropriate, consistent and life-like'. Historically, character tended to be viewed as necessary only as 'agents' or 'performers' of action (Todorov) or as agents of cause and effect (Bordwell). At times, some authors went as far as pronouncing character as 'dead'. Structuralists found that they could not accommodate character within their theories, because they embrace an ideology that 'decentres' man, running counter to the notions of individuality and psychological depth (Rimmon-Kenan, 1983: 30). At the same time, mimetic theories of character, presenting characters as people, equally sits uncomfortably with the storyworld posited here, giving undue credence to the notion of 'reality'. Semiotically, characters are perceived as 'dissolving into textuality' (Rimmon-Kenan, 1983: 32).

Philosophical definitions of character have the effect of theorizing character beyond a simple definition that positions this narrative feature as simply *actant*. A technique defined by Edward Branigan, focalization, will be usefully employed here (see Chapters 2 and 3). This is linked to Branigan's conception of character who 'may "tell" the story to us in a broad sense, but only through "living in" their world and speaking to other characters' (Branigan, 1998: 100). The narrative conditions, or restrictions, define what we mean by the concept of a 'character', giving the character several different ways in which characters may 'live in' their world'. Focalization is the means whereby the narrotologist isolates where a character actually experiences something through 'seeing and hearing'. In his writings on narratology, Branigan placed character on a similar footing to action when he states that each defines as well as limits each other's logical development. Introducing the narratological concept of focalization is meant to remind us that a character's role in a narrative may change from being an actual, or potential, focus of a causal chain to being the source of our knowledge of a causal chain. Focalization involves a character neither speaking nor acting, instead experiencing something through seeing and hearing. Focalization goes further: it involves 'thinking, remembering, interpreting, wondering, fearing, believing, desiring, understanding, feeling guilt' (Branigan, 1998: 101), replicating or imitating authentic human emotional states. It is the character that plunges to greater emotional depths of experience through desire, belief or thought that 'sees and hears'.

Branigan goes on to distinguish two types of focalization, each representing a different level of a character's experience. External focalization is the character's 'visual and aural awareness of narrative events', and internal focalization describes the character's private and subjective experiences, ranging from simple perception (optical vantage point) to deeper thoughts (dreams, hallucinations, memories) (Branigan, 1998: 103). While Bordwell's approach facilitates a linear reading, Branigan's methodology develops a horizontal and vertical reading, which can be used to reveal the complexity of an individual shot or scene (Branigan, 1998: 193) and/or sequence. Focalization is important in analysing characters in different settings, facilitating the theorizing of character beyond the position of *actant*. It reveals character as a fully-active participant of the storyworld, depending on their engagement internally and externally. Internal focalization displays a range from what the character is looking at (point of view shot) to their internal impressions, visually expressed in the out of focus or point of view shot, for example, depicting a character that is drunk, dizzy, confused, etc. (Branigan, 1998: 104). Bordwell distinguishes between characters that 'say and do' and those who 'see and hear': a direct link to range and depth of story information.

Narration not only manipulates the range of knowledge but also the degrees of knowledge. A question central to analysing character is 'how deeply does the plot plunge us into the characters' psychological state?': a spectrum which ranges from restricted to unrestricted and objective to subjective narrative (Bordwell, 1990).

The possibilities offered by focalization enable the exploration of character at a deeper level, revealing how the character performs in the overall narrative and what their role in the story is. It helps analyse what the writer created in a character and the level of skill and craft involved in creating diverse and curious characters. As an analytical tool, it can make statements about the characters' perceptions, feelings and thoughts. At the level of structure, it illustrates how the narrative presents or withholds story information. The approach places character in the centre of the narrative, not as 'something' which simply advances the plot forward but as 'someone' who is central to the storyworld that the writer and director created. The significance of this approach is the potential it provides for reclaiming the 'story' as a focus of analysis and facilitating an assessment of craft in scriptwriting. Narratology offers a flexible tool in revealing what is at work within contemporary Irish screen stories. It not only provides for a structural reading but also leads to an analysis of content through form.

Summary

The method devised here brings together a number of theoretical positions from narrative studies, principally around character, plot and story. The basic plot structure follows a logic of events and relies on a structure of questions and answers which sets up and enacts the situation in a dramatic, conflicting and tense way. Through this nuts-and-bolts approach, a deeper structure is revealed, but only by harnessing characterization. The characters are the conduit through which the story intentions are revealed, acted out in dramatic episodes. Depending on what level the characters engage with the plot, they have varied roles within the overall story, meaning and outcome. As a tool of analysis, focalization is pivotal to unearthing this relationship.

What most narratologists appear to agree on is that interpreters of stories draw on pre-stored knowledge representations, 'especially those involving stereotyped sequences of actions and events, to interpret action structured as narratively organised' (Herman, 2002: 6). Furthermore, the amount of narrativity a story has, that is the degree to which it is amenable to being processed as a narrative, is directly related to how it relates to what narratologists call 'canonicity and breach'. It is the combination of expectation and surprise that mainstream and counter narratives rely on in reaching their audience or, in David Herman's words, stereotypic and nonstereotypic knowledge (Herman, 2002: 7). Herman argues further that, although many narratologists have accentuated narratives' temporal properties, understanding narrative also requires spatializing or 'cognitively mapping' the storyworld it conveys (Chatman, 1999: 8).

Story analysts and spectators bring different evaluative criteria with them to the interpretation of these storyworlds, depending on how they are positioned. Narratives containing messages embedded in form or content require additional evaluative criteria – for example, ironic narratives are predicated on a combination of some viewers 'getting it' while others do not. Regardless of the intent or purpose of story, what narratives create are entities in themselves, at one level separate and distinct from the world beyond them. What bestows on narratives their strength is the immersiveness power they embody: the ability to transport the viewer into a place where they must go in order to comprehend and experience the storyworld.

Notes

1. The term erotetic is used to describe relationships in the narrative. 'The basic narrative connective – the rhetorical bond between the two scenes – is the question/answer. The importance of this relation, which I call "erotetic", can be seen in films more complex than two-shot narratives' (Carroll, 1988: 171).
2. *Actant* is a term developed by French structuralist A. J. Greimas referring to a fundamental role or fundamental function 'not only to characters but also to things (e.g. a magic ring) or to abstract quantities (e.g. fate)' (Lothe, 2000: 77).
3. Lothe defines *syuzhet* as 'an element of form which extends over into the text's content side ... the relationship between textual form and content and the reader's vital role in the understanding of narrative' (Lothe, 2000: 7–8). For Bordwell, *syuzhet* refers to 'plot', 'is the actual arrangement and presentation of the *fabula* in the film' (Bordwell et al. 1985: 49–50).

Chapter 1

Irish Film Board / Bord Scannán na hÉireann

Whenever wisdom was needed the fairy tale had it, and where the need was greatest ... its aid was nearest ...The more a story enters fully the memory of the listener, the more completely it becomes part of him. Soon his need to retell it to someone else, someday, grows and grows. (Quoted in *The Last Storyteller?* directed by Des Bell, 2002)

The cinema, like the detective story, enables us to experience without danger to ourselves all the excitements, passions, and fantasies which have to be repressed in a humanistic age. (Jung (1931) quoted in Hauke & Alister, 2001: 151)

When cinema was evolving throughout Europe and the United States in the first half of the twentieth century, the Irish Free State was dual-focussed: surprisingly censorious[1] towards film narratives while investing significantly in the tradition of oral storytelling, known in Ireland as *béaloideas*. Through the Irish Folklore Commission, locals were equipped with tape-recorders to record oral narratives and create an archive before the material was lost. As an exercise in nation building, the Irish Free State saw the value in this form of storytelling and the need for preservation. On the other hand, the new and developing, innovative form of storytelling, the cinema, was seen as a threatening force. Irish film production has had a sporadic state-support structure, characterized by a stop/go approach since 1958 with the setting up of Ardmore Studios. Rather than being a support for indigenous productions, the studios mainly facilitated foreign film at this time until going into liquidation in 1963. In 1968 a report advocating the support of low-budget and short-film production was released, chaired by Hollywood film-maker John Huston and published in Bill form in 1970. However, it would be ten years before the Irish Film Board was formally instituted and in its short existence (disbanded by Charles Haughey, Taoiseach at the time in 1987) went through a change of political masters on three different occasions.[2] Despite this period of instability aggravated by internal politics at Board level, between 1981 and 1987 the Irish Film Board provided production finance for ten features, numerous short films, some documentaries, experimental films and an animation. This was a period of experimental film, interrogative of many aspects of Irish identity (*Angel*, Neil Jordan, 1982; *The Outcasts*, Robert Wynne-Simmons, 1982; *Pigs*, Cathal Black, 1984; *Budawanny*, Bob Quinn 1987) and for the first time since the development of moving pictures, it provided Ireland with a body of work that could loosely be referred to as 'national cinema'. The defining thematics of this period centred on the notion of 'Irishness', particularly as a constructed form of identity, in features (*Anne Devlin*, Pat Murphy, 1984), short fiction films (*Our Boys*, Cathal Black, 1981), experimental works (*Waterbag*, Joe Comerford, 1984) and documentaries (*Atlantean*, Bob Quinn, 1983).

Most writers on Irish cinema agree that there is a marked difference between the cinematic material which emerged from the first Board (1981–1987) and that which is being produced since its re-activation in 1993, principally at the level of narrative form but also with regard to content (Barton, 2004; Ging, 2004; McLoone, 2000). Assessing the differences between these two periods in Irish film-making, how and why they emerged and hence establishing the more recent 'wave' as distinct and separate yet evolutionary and developmental, is an objective here. In achieving this goal, the methodology strives to establish a clear and practical nexus between theory and critical analysis as the dominant mode of interrogation of Irish film, and practical and specific script/storytelling strategies, the system developed here. This combined approach sets out a meeting point between theory and practice in the field of narrative studies. Some may argue that this need to relate theory and practice is a 'new millennium' urge on behalf of the *academy* for legitimacy beyond the enclosed world of the university; if so it points towards a widespread *praxis* concern among academics, from the work of media commentator and practitioner Des Bell (2004) to high-end cultural theorist Edward Said (Cleary, 2005). The work of this book emerges from my experience as both a practitioner and critic of Irish cinema and television drama, research work in the form of a doctoral thesis exploring narrative strategies in contemporary Irish film, alongside teaching experience at the Institute of Art, Design & Technology, Dún Laoghaire, home to the National Film School, an environment specializing in both theoretical and practical approaches to film narrative and the training of students in the practice and critique of film and television production.

Reflecting on the historical trajectory of film narration over a fifteen year period in Ireland, this chapter sheds light on the script development process supported by the Irish Film Board through an analysis of their structures and supports, and how they impact on the experiences of writers and directors. The central focus of the book is also what frames the discussion that follows – the examination of how contemporary Irish cinema adopts conventions and techniques of the cinematic apparatus and synthesizes them into narrative form, remaining a subsidiary of an international model yet exhibiting clear and distinctive local inflections. The basic techniques and conventions are understood universally while the meanings are modified locally. How contemporary Irish cinema variously accommodates the two within one design or construct is the key discursive objective of this book. In presenting a potted history of the Irish Film Board between 1993 and 2008, specifically on activity around script development, I am teasing out the central argument for a developmental and evolutionary approach to Irish cinema in this period, reflecting a struggle between trying to break away from the stranglehold of dominant traditions and attempting to establish fresh forms of expression reflecting the *new* Ireland.

Irish Film Board 1993–2008

Unlike most European countries, Ireland did not enjoy a sustained level of indigenous film-making until the 1980s and even then it was short-lived. Prior to this the official approach to Irish film was not constructed in cultural terms. Cinema was viewed with suspicion by the developing state, feared as an uncontrollable influence produced by outsiders, prompting censorship. At the same time, the economic value of foreign productions, 'off-shore', to the Irish state did not go unnoticed, impelling many active official supports to a wide range of requests by foreign film companies.[3] The period since 1993 offers the first sustained period of indigenous film activity, producing for the first time since the emergence of the medium, a critical mass of film material. Aside from sporadic activity in the 1970s and 1980s (first wave), this period comes closest to giving Ireland a semblance of an indigenous, national cinema through the production of well over one hundred and forty feature films, supported by the Irish Film Board. This support can take the form of development funding, production loan and completion finance or a combination therein. While many other films were produced in Ireland, by Irish or non-Irish production companies, the focus of this book is on those films receiving funding in some shape or form from the Irish Film Board. The centrality of the Film Board to the activities of film-makers cannot be overstated and the necessity for such state support is a given in most European countries. The fact that no such support existed in Ireland for most of the twentieth century is inevitably going to impact on the nature of film-making. Setting up a film infra-structure is a long, complex, often politically-charged process; reflecting this path in historical terms would involve another research project, shedding light on the 'behind the scenes' activity that undoubtedly influences but sometimes casts a shadow on the artistic and cultural process. Although the focus here is on the stories told, examined through a prism of narrative theory dealing with structural form and process without negating wider contextual factors, the nuances of policy development, undeniably important, are referred to.

While the Film Board's remit is specifically local/national and cultural, it is not immune and cannot remain isolated from international norms and standards. Its re-activation came about as a combination of diverse yet highly-linked episodes, sometimes specifically local, other times international phenomena. The difficult and often thankless task of political lobbying, particularly on behalf of film groups such as Film Base, a grass-roots organization set up in 1987 which lobbied continuously for the re-activation of the Irish Film Board, finally paid off in 1993, spurred on by the Oscar winnings of Irish films such as *My Left Foot* (Jim Sheridan, 1989) and *The Crying Game* (Neil Jordan, 1992), placing Irish film firmly on the international stage. The 'Celtic Tiger' economy was developing and establishing itself by 1993/94, giving Ireland a growing confidence in Irish cultural matter and an economic basis for re-establishing the Board. Finally, like all Irish political decisions which are based on clientelism, a practice intrinsic to the particular political system in Ireland, it took a minister with a vested interest to push forward and implement the decision. Michael D. Higgins, Minister for Arts, Culture and the Gaeltacht at the time and a member of the

Labour Party, a poet and academic serving the Galway constituency, had a commitment and passion for the arts and his local community. He is described as 'a public thinker, with his own ideas about media and the arts and passionate convictions about their role in a small nation exposed to major global trends and influences' (Corcoran, 2004: 47). Regarded as a reforming minister, he was not afraid to tackle the organizational structure of Irish public service broadcasting as well as introducing infrastructural changes to the Irish film industry. Hence, shortly after Neil Jordan's Oscar success, 'Best Original Screenplay' for (British-financed) *The Crying Game* in March 1993, Minister Higgins announced the re-activation of the Irish Film Board, to be located in his native Galway.

Reading the statements from the early days of the Board, one can detect a mixture of looking backwards (to the first wave) combined with an anticipation of new directions for the future. Given that there was such a rupture in 1987 when the first Board was terminated, the tone of Board statements links very much to the ideals of a national cinema. Writing in the 1994 Review and Annual Report of the Board, Lelia Doolan as Chair reflects on the first year of production, describing Irish film as 'postcards from the probings of our national psyche by passionate explorers … [who] plunge into the chaos of the unknown and draw out inner and coherent forms for our inspection, jolt our assumptions, fill us with wonder or anguish or laughter – and flesh out new identities and landmarks in the unfolding actions of fiction', echoing Zimmermann's emphasis on storytelling as a central human activity elementary to any traditional or modern society. In terms of culture, economics and aesthetics, the environment had changed quite significantly since 1987. At the same time, it is not surprising that the Board in 1993 would look back to the 1980s and attempt to form links between the two phases, if for no other reason than to fulfill a need for continuity. When Rod Stoneman, CEO of the Irish Film Board from 1993–2003, pays homage to the first wave in the Review of 1993 by writing that '*Eat the Peach*, *Reefer and the Model*, *Anne Devlin* [and] *Angel* were amongst the films, which in very different ways, initiated a rich period of film-making' in Ireland, he is recognizing and acknowledging the more avant-garde and modernist era and linking with the past as he advances forward. Indeed, the appointment of Lelia Doolan as Chair to the Board could be read as a formal continuity link with the first wave and in keeping with the minister Michael D. Higgins' position of cultural nationalism. She was producer of *Reefer and the Model* (Joe Comerford, 1988), the last film to receive financial support from the first Film Board, and active in film production as a practitioner and a lobbyist throughout the 1970s and 1980s. However, cognisant of a new era and in an attempt to strike political balance, Stoneman followed the previous statement by saying that

[the] second board sets off with the intention of achieving a judicious equilibrium between cultural and economic imperatives. To some extent even the short hand of this dichotomy is inaccurate as both factors are deeply entwined in a capital-intensive activity such as film-making: the largest budget movie produces a cultural artifact as an end result and the smallest amateur film has an economic life. (Review and Annual Report, Board Scannán na hÉireann, 1993)

While first wave practitioners tended to underplay the economic underpinning of film in favour of its art practice, Stoneman shifts the parameters in the direction of an economic model while clinging on to the notion of art cinema. He displays a fine balance between appeasing the former generation while introducing the new realities of the 'Celtic Tiger' era whereby the second Film Board will be under more economic scrutiny if it is to survive.

From the start the Board had a wide remit. Not only charged with issuing production loans, the Review and Annual Report for 1994/95 reveals that the Board undertook research into the distribution of Irish (and other European) films in the United States; analysed rural cinema exhibition and examined the facilities for production in Ireland and the state of the post-production base. Taking their role to encompass more than just production, as the decade progresses the Board became increasingly involved in a wider range of activities, including developing film companies and encouraging script development. While the Board's output has been criticized for being too 'mainstream' (Quinn, 2000: 27), its activities have not. Located in the west of Ireland city of Galway, the Board was conscious of its regional obligations, something that could easily have been overlooked if it was more centralized in the capital city, Dublin. Concerned with the non-metropolitan audience, the Board sought to develop regional exhibition centres, leading to the launch of a 100-seat mobile cinema, the *Cinémobile,* which tours local and regional centres that otherwise would not be exposed to Irish and other non-mainstream cinema. In 2003 the Cultural Cinema Consortium was established, a joint initiative with the Arts Council to promote the expansion of Irish arthouse exhibition. These are interesting developments in cinema exhibition, given the ever increasing centralization and domination of the multiplex cinema that has led to more screens often providing less choice. The Film Board's range of activities and responsibilities stretch from the various stages of pre-production, production and post-production and include exhibition and distribution. This menu of activity, while very broad, also has the potential to raise conflict in Board ethos. On the one hand, the organization is charged with funding film production that targets a mainstream audience, centrally placed within the cultural experience of the nation. On the other hand, it has the responsibility of promoting and facilitating a more varied cultural film experience for a sector of society located at the periphery. While the funding and support of all these activities inevitably dilutes the production budget, Ireland's isolation in relation to certain levels of film activity means that a non-interventionist approach is not an option if all society is to be considered.

Culture and economics

A state-sponsored subsidy-structured industry cannot, for economic and political reasons, compete with the Hollywood model. The approach adopted in this instance is not a radical departure from the activities of national cinemas elsewhere and ties in with developments since the 1970s between 'second' and 'third' cinema, responding to the dominance of the Hollywood model. In an interview in *Screen International*, referring to 'an exciting and dynamic range of

Irish cinema', Stoneman (1993) makes the point that the term 'industry' would not apply here or in most European contexts, despite many national cinemas defined more as 'industrial' than 'artisanal' – France, Britain, Italy and Denmark for example. According to Stoneman, 'what goes on in Ireland is a more cultural, more artisan level of production that plays to cultural strengths' (Stoneman, 1993). Further elaborating on his conception of artisanal cinema in an article published in the journal *Kinema* (2000), he suggests that the main difference between the artisanal and industrial approach is located at the level of budget and style. The artisanal budgets are inevitably low and the style is one that emphasizes diversity as opposed to Hollywood's repetition, featuring ways in which national cinemas can work together. Simon Perry, CEO since 2006, sees Europe as central to the funding of Irish film, citing *The Wind that Shakes the Barley* (Ken Loach, 2006) as the model for future directions – a five-way co-production between Ireland, Britain, Spain, Italy and Germany.

While the effects of this approach to funding could be seen as just another version of the euro-pudding phenomenon[4] that dilutes creative autonomy to the point of narrative construction by committee, it is a system familiar to most European countries as a way of counteracting Hollywood's dominance. On the other hand, negating the possibility of an industrial model in favour of an 'artisanal' approach surely limits the potential for commerciality and industry, raising questions about the career paths for film-makers. The question must be asked whether the Board spread itself too thinly, opting for quantity over quality, concentrating its budgeting policy in just one direction at the expense of a more diverse type of product. Yet, Rebecca O'Flanagan, Development Manager at the Irish Film Board (2000-04), suggests that the budgets did not pose a problem as the medium-scale facilitated the production of films similar to other national industries. She attributes the poor 'success' rate to the narrative and script techniques in this period, implying by default a developmental and evolutionary dimension to this phase.[5] The schemes put in place in areas of development and script editing were concerted efforts to address this.

One of the criticisms of the Board is that it took up to four years, on average, to make a medium budget feature (£3–5 million) in the early- to mid-1990s. This meant that while many directors got the opportunity to make their first film, relatively few progressed to a second or third feature, thus limiting the potential for nurturing and developing talent. This was addressed in 2002 through policy changes and the introduction of the low-budget fund, the 'Micro Budget Scheme', a film fund of €100,000 enabling the production of films along Stoneman's artisanal approach (more recently known as the Catalyst Project).[6] Ironically, smaller budgets can sometimes be a better option because they simplify the process, often allowing for creative autonomy and control to remain at producer and director level. While some notable films emerged from the support of this scheme (*Adam & Paul*, Lenny Abrahamson, 2004), it does not mean that the other funding mechanisms are redundant. The typical budget in 2009 for Irish films under Film Board schemes is between €1 million and €1.5 million, half what it was in the early days, part of which is funded by the Board. In order to maintain its eclecticism and because one size does not fit all, the Irish Film Board also has a policy to support films with big budgets (€8 million or more), possibly one or two

Adam and Paul (Tom Murphy and Mark O'Halloran), courtesy of Lenny Abrahamson.

a year (Orpen, 2008: 32-34). This means that the Board could fund up to €1 million in such large-scale budgets. For example, *Perrier's Bounty* (Ian Fitzgibbon, 2009) received €1 million from the Board for a budget of just under €5 million.

Rather than having a budget that will fund as many productions as it can, the consensus emerged to focus on the Board's objective output. In a *Film Ireland* interview in 1993 with Lelia Doolan, when asked where she would like to see the Board five years hence, she replied 'if we are successful and we manage to get maybe four or six films made a year, maybe a bit more, if we can keep the inputs going, then I would see the inroads we have already made in drawing attention to Ireland and its eloquence' (Doolan, 1993). Similarly, in an article around the same time in *The Sunday Independent,* Gene Kerrigan wrote that

> half a dozen solid proposals a year from people with track records could, with Film Board help, be developed to the point where private investment could be more easily attracted (almost certainly from abroad). If even one or two projects every one or two years worked out as well as such efforts as *My Left Foot* and *The Crying Game*, we'd be getting value for money. (Kerrigan, 1993)

Overtime, the view was reached to support a smaller range of films that would ensure more focused outcomes and success. One of the noteworthy characteristics of the Irish Film Board since its inception is its ability to respond to current economic climates, a constructive tendency not always evident in state boards. This means that funding schemes change, evolve and develop according to reflective policy and consistently encourage new talent. Even if they are not always getting it right, the decision-makers at the board are neither standing still nor resting on their laurels.

Production

The early years of the Board's re-instatement were generally regarded within the industry and the national press as successful, despite teething problems and the inevitable by-products of any learning curve. Writing in *The Sunday Business Post*, Marion McKeone states that in the previous year (1994) the Board backed eight features.

> All were produced by Irish production companies, and all were written or co-written by Irish screenwriters – and six of them featured first time directors. Given the number of inexperienced filmmakers who got projects off the ground as a result of Film Board backing and a s.35 investment, you would expect a fairly high dud ratio. But not so. (McKeone, 1995)[7]

Unsurprisingly, when the call for scripts was made in late 1993, there were numerous writer/director/producer teams waiting in the wings whose careers had been abruptly terminated with the axing of the first Irish Film Board.[8] Significantly, however, these directors were not to dominate the early output of the Board as many new directors and writers had graduated from the various film schools in Ireland, UK and North America and built careers in Ireland and abroad since 1987.[9] The first annual report of the re-constituted Irish Film Board shows that in the year 1993–94 the Board allocated £945,000 to film production, with a return on its investment of 25 per cent or £200,000. In this period nine features were produced at a cost of £6.7 million, the balance accumulating from a variety of other financial sources. Eight of these productions had Irish writers and directors and five were regarded as 'first-timers'. By the end of 1998 thirty-seven features had been produced with the support of the Board – a key year in the Board's development given that it now had five years behind it and a critical mass by which it could be judged. Around this time one can detect a shift in attitude towards the Board's output, from media commentators in particular. While a certain amount of goodwill could be expected for the early productions from film reviewers, critics and the wider film community, this appeared to be running out by 1998. The Chair at the time, documentary-maker Louis Marcus, saw funding as the primary issue, arguing that the capital grant of the time of £3.4 million was far too modest to meet the demands of the industry. All the same, having enjoyed a five-year running-in period with little criticism from the wider media, the lack of commercial or critical successes was now being highlighted. Marion McKeone in *The Sunday Business Post*, who previously had been less critical of Irish film, noted that 'a significant number of these films failed to attract any level of critical acclaim. Fewer still have been commercially successful' (McKeone, 1998).

While 1998 was a year of more critical commentary towards the Board, it was also a time to reflect. Accused by the British Press of being pro-Republican because of the apparent emphasis on 'nationalist' themes in the films they supported,[10] 1998 marked the year when there was a notable shift in thematic and subject matter. The 'holy trinity' of subject matter, referring to the dominant themes of 1950s' rural Ireland, the *Troubles* and the Catholic Church, had finally been cleared out of the 'national' system. Events in the 1950s and the *Troubles* provided many films with their central theme and subject-matter in the first few years (*Broken Harvest*, Maurice O'Callaghan, 1994; *Nothing Personal*, Thaddeus O'Sullivan, 1995; *Some Mother's Son*, Terry George, 1996; *A Further Gesture*, Robert Dorhelm, 1996; *Bogwoman*, Tom Collins, 1997; *The Boxer*, Jim Sheridan, 1997). Not surprisingly there is a preoccupation with these themes following the hiatus between 1987 and 1993. Repressed sexuality as a pre-occupation (*Circle of Friends*, Pat O'Connor, 1995; *Gold in the Streets*, Liz Gill, 1996; *Dancing at Lughnasa*, Pat O'Connor, 1998) and the 'coming of age' films (*Moondance*, Dagmar Hirtz, 1994; *The Last of the High Kings*, David Keating, 1996; *Spaghetti Slow*, Valerio Jalongo, 1996; *Drinking Crude*, Owen McPolin, 1997; *The Disappearance of Finbar*, Sue Clayton, 1996) begin to fade out around this time, particularly evident when compared with the types of films to emerge subsequently (*About Adam*, Gerry Stembridge, 2000; *When Brendan met Trudy*, Kieron J. Walsh 2000; *Goldfish Memory*, Liz Gill, 2003). These films reveal a shift, post-1998, in the direction of a more liberal, progressive and eclectic representation of sexuality in particular, situated mainly in an urban milieu, framed generically as romantic comedy (*About Adam*, Gerry Stembridge, 2000; *When Brendan met Trudy*, Kieron J. Walsh 2000; *The Most Fertile Man in Ireland*, Dudi Appleton 1999). The horror genre receives many re-imaginings in this phase (*Dead Bodies*, Robert Quinn 2003; *Dead Meat*, Conor McMahon 2004; *Boy Eats Girl*, Stephen Bradley 2005), presenting to and representing an urban and youth-oriented audience. Writing in a publication devoted to the discussion of John Ford's *The Quiet Man* (1952), Rod Stoneman states that

> the critical mass of the Board's funding went towards projects that engaged with modernity and change, tending towards forms of film that connected with the experience of modern-day Ireland. This took forms mostly situated outside of current representation of the rural … versions of paddywhackery were inevitably rejected with disdain as distorted and anachronistic manifestations of the past, intrusive and lacking integrity. (Crosson & Stoneman, 2009: 251)

These developments are precisely relevant when positioned alongside the change in direction detected from 1998 onwards. The following year saw the launch of the Film Industry Strategic Review Group's report: the deliberations of a Think Tank set up by the minister at the time, Síle de Valera, in the previous year. Reporting on the contents of the report Michael Dwyer in *The Irish Times* highlights the significance of the emphasis now being placed on script development.

> Calling for a radical increase of funding for script and project development, the report pinpoints a critical priority often underestimated by Irish filmmakers. This will be clear to anyone who has seen some of the Irish films which have been bypassed, or failed at Irish cinemas. The report notes how the Hollywood studios routinely spend as much as 10–15 per cent of a film's budget on development, and how their films are rarely put into production without being subjected to skilful editing, a series of re-writes and development team inputs. Typically the figure for Irish film projects is about 3%. In its recommendations for a strengthened and restructured BSE, the report commendably prioritises 'the provision, either directly or by access, of expertise in high quality script development that is strong on both artistic and commercial criteria'. (Dwyer, 1999)

Stoneman sees a wider context for this development, particularly in English-speaking Europe which witnessed the arrival of the Robert McKee 'road show' and the proliferation of scriptwriting and story manuals from Vogler, McKee et al., all of whom contributed to the growing and widespread interest in script development and the normalizing of the process within film pre-production.[11] While scriptwriting manuals had been available in Hollywood since the 1920s (about eighty craft manuals were circulating among script-writers during the studio system) and script development was an inherent part of the pre-production process under the studio system, the European tradition had been founded on improvisation of scriptwriting and non-studio based production to a significant degree (French New Wave,

Michael Gambon in *A Man of No Importance*, courtesy of Jonathan Hession, Photographer.

Italian Neorealism, British Social Realism). The use of the term 'development' is a more recent phenomenon and its emergence in Ireland reflects a wider European trend, including the support mechanisms put in place for script development. These include the MEDIA initiative funded by the EU, particularly through the *Arista* and *Sagas* programmes; Screen Training Ireland's (FÁS subsidiary) concentration on script development and editing and the growth in scriptwriting courses in Irish higher education.

At this time Ossie Kilkenny, accountant and media entrepreneur, was appointed to the position of Chair, reflecting the shift in perspective from cultural to economic. In the same article mentioned above, Michael Dwyer notes that Kilkenny's appointment comes with a commercial, corporate and non-protectionist approach to film, with a more apparent concentration towards international markets than before. The appointment of Lelia Doolan as first Chair (1993–96), followed by Louis Marcus (1997–99), 'film people' to be followed by Ossie Kilkenny (2000–05), reveals a key shift in direction, either by the Board responding to external factors or their political masters initiating or insisting on change. Balancing culture and economics for any arts organization is a challenge. Leaning too much in the direction of economics can set up false expectations, targets on which indigenous film cannot deliver, while also negating the central role culture has to play in any society.

2001 is documented as a record year for the Irish Film Board with the release of nine films in Irish cinemas. These films took in over £2.2 million at the Irish box office. Clarence Pictures, Buena Vista International and Abbey Films accounted for the release of eight of the films funded by the Board. While the shift towards script development may account partly for increased exhibition rates, the launch of Clarence Pictures and Abbey Films (Irish distribution companies) and the development of Buena Vista International focusing on Irish productions at this time meant increased opportunities for Irish films to progress towards box-office release and DVD/video distribution. The *Expenditure Review* of the Board (2008) details that during the period 1993–2003,

> the board received a total capital allocation of €76.1 million with a cumulative <u>average</u> recoupment rate of 13% on production feature loans during 1993–2000. While this has been suggested as a relatively low recoupment level, the Board argues that outside of the Hollywood studio system, few films return their budgets to the investors, let alone turn a profit. (Irish Film Board, 2008)

These recoupment levels when compared to other European territories fall in the middle (Swedish Film Industry has an estimated 3 per cent recoupment level whereas the UK Film Council New Cinema Fund claim a 35 per cent level), providing a strong argument for state supports and subsidies. 2004 was a bumper year, with the release of eleven Irish feature films at the box office. In this year, *Man About Dog* (Paddy Breathnach, 2004) reached the status of highest-grossing film since the Board's re-activation, a key success factor at this point when the continued existence of the Board was being examined.[12] The argument here is that while most films of this period were successful at a local level, few impacted abroad.

When successful locally, the box office returns are generally used to offset the cost of an international distribution, while international box-office success contributes to the return on investment. Thus the local successes go unaccounted when it comes to recoupment levels, yet their importance is indisputable in national and cultural terms, evident through the analysis of story and narrative strategies in the following chapters.

While Irish films produced over the past fifteen years have achieved relative successes with Irish audiences, through theatrical or DVD/video release or television exhibition, most films have failed to make an impact on foreign markets. According to Ruth Barton, 'none of the small films made in Ireland during the 1990s broke into the mainstream as *My Left Foot* and *The Crying Game* had done; nor has there been any equivalent of *Trainspotting* (Danny Boyle, GB, 1996), *The Full Monty* (Peter Cattaneo, GB, 1997) or *Billy Elliott* (Stephen Daldry, GB, 2000). By and large their core audience has been Irish, with few of the productions achieving notable success in overseas markets' (Barton, 2004: 179). As a film-supporting agency this must be a key concern as it attempts to consolidate and develop, and while the work of this book is not framed within a political – economic framework, a narrative study can illuminate the tensions and conflicts that contribute to this situation.

Impact of new policies on Irish Film

One of the early anecdotal criticisms about Irish film, within and outside the industry, was the poor standard of Irish scriptwriting, evident in screen stories. The role of writer and director in film production is an interesting one. Although both roles require quite different skills and talents, the early days of the Board had a notable concentration of directors writing their own scripts. It was argued that the absence of 'good scripts' meant that directors had to write scripts in order to direct films, even if they did not see themselves as writers. The implementation of the script-development process, it could be argued, sought to address this situation. A successful outcome, one might assume, is the shift from production teams where the writer and the director are mainly the same person to a situation where writer and director teams become more the norm. A quick overview survey of Irish films supported by the Board between 1993 and 2008 suggests that there is a leaning towards the writer/director model in Irish film, as opposed to the alternative, writer *and* director. The gap between the two approaches narrows as the decade advances. From 1993 to 2003, 49 films list the director and writer as the same person whereas 30 films credit at least two different people as director and scriptwriter. This gap narrows further between 2004 and 2008 with 29 films listing the writer and director as the same person and 22 crediting two different people in these roles. Taken together, the differential is 78 versus 52.

The shift, albeit slight, to a separating out of roles comes about possibly because writers are part of a wider infrastructure receiving more support through the development policies. In exploring the central theme, narrative strategies in contemporary Irish cinema, this book touches on the thorny issue in film production and narrative construction – who exactly is the storyteller? The unique aspect of the film process is that it is always a collaborative one. For a film to be made, a script must first be written, or at least imagined: sometimes a blueprint for the shooting schedule and post-production stages, other times simply a guide. In discussing storytelling and narrative strategies, both the writer and director are considered. The writer has the task of imagining the story in dramatic form and visual terms and committing this to a written document: the script. The director executes this imagined and written story, through filming and editing, to tell a visual story. The film, although often seen as the work of the director, is the result of much collaboration through three key stages: writing, filming and editing.

While it is relevant to look at these policies, particularly associated with the script-writing and development process, and why and when they were introduced from a purely institutional perspective, it is also useful as a prism through which to explore the Irish film landscape. If anything, these policy-shifts reveal the nature of Irish film and its dual relationship with European cinema and Hollywood film: the former historically an auteurist approach, while the latter's more industrial base promotes and fosters genre. In some respects, the age-old frameworks of film analysis involving the genre approach versus that of auteurism are coming to the fore again. Simon Perry, CEO of the Board since 2006, outlined his vision for the Irish film industry, which involved strengthening links with European partners and 'doing what European cinema does best … quality auteur work … the most exciting work in world cinema comes from directors with very small signatures, something to say and a powerful way of saying it' (Tracy, 2008). Like Rod Stoneman before him, he does not advocate the American industrial model but sees the future in co-production terms with European, Canadian, Australian and New Zealand partners.

Reading between the lines, the direction set down by Rod Stoneman during his tenure at the Board is being consolidated and developed with subsequent CEOs, Mark Woods (2005–06) and particularly Simon Perry (2006 to date). The low budget initiatives, which reflect the artisanal approach, exist alongside a significant emphasis on development. The approach of Stoneman and Perry is not that different, institutionalizing a certain type of film method, closely aligned to the auteur approach. However, aspirations towards a small, radical, auteurist, artisanal cinema inevitably clash with the economic imperative to produce films fitting a model of multiplex distribution modes: a tension facing most small indigenous cinemas, and echoed in the industry responses. The overall response from industry representatives indicated that, among other things, the Board should focus a greater proportion of their funds 'on a smaller number of productions rather than a "scatter gun" approach' and should 'be involved in more risky ventures; the approach being taken of late was more commercially orientated and business focused' (Irish Film Board, 26: 2008).

These policies and responses are useful to this study in so far as they contextualize the narrative activity of new Irish storytellers in the medium of film, revealing the tensions and conflicts which help energize the debates, showing an aspiration towards artistic stamp yet encouraging audience expectation of genre material. How these conflicts and contradictions surface in the narrative strategies of these films, revealing the developmental nature of Irish film over a fifteen year period, will be explored in the following chapters.

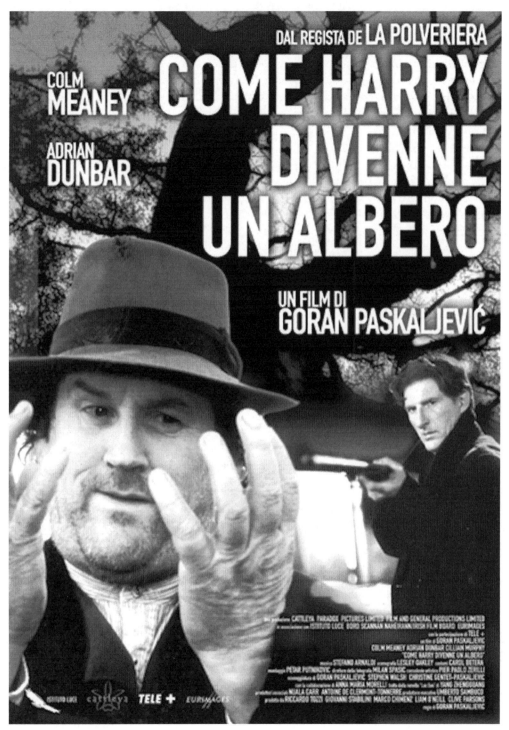

Courtesy of Liam O'Neill and Paradox Pictures.

Notes

1. See *Irish Film Censorship* by Kevin Rockett, 2004, Dublin: Four Courts Press for an in depth analysis and cultural history of film censorship in Ireland.
2. This was a period of economic recession for Ireland, high unemployment, high taxation and cuts in public spending. 1981 saw a change in government to a Fine Gael/Labour coalition, this changed again in 1982 when Fianna Fáil took power for a very short period with Fine Gael/Labour back in before the year was out. In 1987 Fianna Fáil was re-elected to government bringing an end to the short period of indigenous film production.
3. Hollywood directors like John Ford and John Huston received a lot of official support from the Irish government when they sought to make films here.
4. This 'euro-pudding' phenomenon refers to co-production deals which emerged in the 1980s whereby a number of EU member states' broadcasting institutions and/or film companies/agencies would contribute to the funding of a production. While it is a bemoaned phenomenon, particularly among film critics, it is an economic necessity in Irish film production. Bord Scannán na hÉireann does not offer 100% production finance and therefore any producer of an Irish feature film must seek funding outside of Ireland, from film investors or broadcasting institutions abroad. Inevitably, this leads to creative decisions being influenced by the combination of financiers and the dilution in creative autonomy for the writer/director/producer teams. Another negative of this phenomenon is that if a film budget is composed of a number of diverse financiers, if one pulls out suddenly the whole financial package can crumble, leading to delays in getting a film beyond the pre-production phase. This happened in the case of Pat Murphy's *Nora*. Furthermore, criticizing the Board for failing to nurture talent as very few directors get to make a second or third film may be mis-placed. Not totally the Board's fault, this could be as a result of the euro-pudding phenomenon which generally means that the timescale from pre-production through to post-production can span, on average, five years. Such a lengthy time on one production inevitably has consequences for people's ability to commit to a second or subsequent production along these timescales. While the euro-pudding phenomenon is an economic reality in the current production environment, its negative consequences for the fostering of creative talent and the establishment of career producers, writers and directors is rarely highlighted.
5. In an interview with Díóg O'Connell (unpublished) 13 Dec. 2004.
6. See www.filmboard.ie for details of all current funding schemes.
7. s.35 refers to Section 35, a state-supported tax incentive scheme for funding supports in the Irish film industry.
8. Some examples of films produced by those who were active in film in the 1980s include *High Boot Benny*, Joe Comerford 1994; *Korea*, Cathal Black 1995, *Snakes and Ladders*, Trish McAdam 1996; *The Sun, the Moon and the Stars*, Geraldine Creed 1996. Aside from Black's *Korea* these films had limited critical and commercial success and an analysis of their story strategies reveals tensions between old ways and new – it will be argued later that these films' narratives suffer from the vacuum created by the termination of the first Board. Had these films being produced when they were initially intended and written, they arguably would have had more relevance to an Irish audience. When not making films, 1st wave directors became involved in lobbying and agitating for an Irish film industry (Joe Comerford, Bob Quinn); in teaching (Cathal Black); emigrated to earn a living in commercials before returning to film-making (Thaddeus O'Sullivan) or were active in political organisations. Pat Murphy was closely identified with the Parade of Innocence, an event aimed at highlighting the 'miscarriages of justice', in particular the Birmingham Six and the Guildford Four.

9. It should be mentioned here that the growth and development of the 'short' film industry in Ireland, arguably, was a consequence of the axing of the first Irish Film Board. The vacuum created by this action gave rise to film organizations forming to lobby and agitate for an Irish film industry as well as providing low-cost facilities for the production of short films. Those who could not get involved in feature-film production opted for short-film production, a development that was to have its impact on the feature films to emerge subsequently. This proved to be an integral part of the Irish film industry, in some instances launching the feature film careers of some directors (Damien O'Donnell's *35 Aside,* for example, as well as being a widely acclaimed Short and winning numerous awards, acted as a 'calling card' for him in being selected to direct *East is East,* 1999).

10. See *The Sunday Business Post,* 18.1.1998, Marion McKeone.

11. O'Connell, Díóg, *Interview with Rod Stoneman, CEO – Bord Scannán na hÉireann 1993 – 2003,* (Unpublished), May. 2004.

12. It had grossed €2.4 million by the end of 2004 (htto://www.filmboard.ie/stop_press.php?press+286 (accessed 3 February 2005).

Chapter 2

Irish Road Movies – Narrative Strategies Re-imagined

In archetypal terms, road movies commonly entail the undertaking of a journey by one or more protagonists as they seek out adventure, redemption or escape from the constricting norms of society and its laws ... The road movie frequently begins with the expression of a search for self by an individual or individuals disenfranchised from society ... but the journey's end rarely brings peace or contentment, but most likely further suffering or even death at the hands of everyday life. (Wood, 2007: xv)

In the world of film, the double-edged sword of genre studies is impossible to ignore, both for practitioners and theoreticians alike. Although genre has been viewed as prescriptive and limiting, some arguing that its only application is an industrial scenario like the Hollywood studio system, it has an undeniable guiding hand at many levels of the production process right through to distribution and exhibition. This applies not just to the main industrial centres of movie-making but equally to the periphery of small national cinemas. David Herman's (2007) genre definition for film sees it as directing the way in which film narratives are imagined, constructed and received; at the same time it '*prescribes* artistic practice'. For ease of appraisal at many levels, genre facilitates the grouping of films together on the basis of shared features and helps evaluate artistic works (Herman, 2007: 109). Narrative theory and genre studies are linked theoretically through evaluating the aesthetic and structural form of an artistic work. Tzvetan Todorov (1982), for example, argued that to transgress a genre does not mean to negate it and, although his discussion applies directly to the field of literature, the basic tenet of his point which states that artistic forms require laws, to work with or work against, is equally relevant to film. Genre is widely accepted as the bedrock of the successful and dominant output of the Hollywood studio system and, even though the economic infra-structure had changed by the 1960s, genre is still important in the post-classical period, when the economic model alters and the approach to narrative shifts in a more fluid and less structured direction. According to Herman, for Todorov, referring to literature, readers and writers alike cannot do without genres, 'for they not only ensure intelligibility but also enable us to perceive innovation' (Herman, 2007: 112), a position Hollywood thrived on. Genre functions as an enabling device and fosters 'generic competence, that is, an ability ... to recognise and interpret the codes typical of a given genre; and ... to perceive departures from it' (Herman, 2007: 113).

Genre studies, therefore, lends itself in an interesting way to the analysis of narrative on two levels. Firstly, subscription to a genre entails a balance between constructing similarity and difference across narrative structure and aesthetic form. Not only does this guide original practice at the level of creativity, it ensures the audience has something new yet familiar to enjoy. Within the art form itself, understanding, interpreting, challenging and deviating from the codes is what guides the artistic expression and the pleasure in reception. Beyond the specific text-based approach to genre lies a wider relationship the film-maker has to the generic art form and industry. No national cinema can escape the influence of genre from the dominant mode of Hollywood. While it guides at a very basic textual level, it also reveals the distinction between how local or peripheral cinemas engage with the centre. The principle concern here is this dual balance as explored through the relationship of recent Irish cinema and mainstream narrative film; how, at the level of film text, writers and directors work with and against genre. Through this examination of narrative strategies at a textual level, the dynamic between a small nation's cinema like Ireland and that of the central player, Hollywood, can be revealed.

Thus, in this chapter I explore how certain films appropriate the American road movie by transferring it to the Irish landscape, combining a genre analysis with scrutiny of formal elements. By examining structural features of narrative and story construction, this approach compares the multiple interpretations of the road movie genre at the levels of form and content to reveal the 'Irishness' of these films, within an internationally-understood form. Revealing how the Irish movie fits the genre and how local film-makers may act against the genre, the points of appropriation and rejection combine to distinguish the narrative in terms of authorship but, equally, cultural determination. Identifying tensions and fissures in these constructions might suggest reasons why many of these films, while meeting local critical and commercial success, often fail to travel beyond national borders. These films re-imagine a conventional genre in a variety of original ways, particularly through the approach to humour, the portrayal of landscape and the rite-of-passage trope, in the formal approach as well as thematic exploration. While these are not unusual devices of the genre, nor unfamiliar to Irish film, the treatment and re-imagining meted out in these films signals a shift in style and structure in contemporary Irish film that this discussion will bring to light. What an examination of narrative strategies might reveal is whether the deviations are part of the process of genre production and/or reception at a specific but also general level. According to David Herman, generic definitions extend in two directions: 'they not only define what a given genre is but also define what it is not' (Herman, 2007: 114). Whether these films and their relationship to genre extend beyond the art form to reflect on the wider cultural or industrial setting is equally a concern of this discussion.

Generic forms

Even though at face value the iconographic, narrative and ideological milieu of the American road movie is a far remove from the verisimilitude of contemporary Irish society, some of the more interesting and topical recent Irish films have situated their storyworlds within this context, appropriating, framing, referencing and re-imagining the imagined visual space for

Irish audiences. The road movie as a genre has infiltrated the consciousness of many writers and directors working outside the studio system, leaving its mark historically on European film-makers and their work, in diverse institutional set-ups. Although an iconic American symbol, the road movie is testament to the complex relationship European film has with the American industry. Not only have European directors contributed to the iconic status, they have institutionalized it in European culture also (*La Strada,* Federico Fellini, 1954; *Wild Strawberries,* Ingmar Bergman, 1957; *Paris, Texas,* Wim Wenders, 1984; *Ariel,* Aki Kaurismaki 1988).

Given the dominance of US film on Irish cinema in terms of scale and volume, it is not surprising that this quintessential of Hollywood films has influenced new Irish writers and directors in recent times. It is well documented that Irish cinema has sought to invoke various Hollywood genres rather than alternative forms of cinema, with the number of Irish films displaying and resembling a European aesthetic being marginal. Looking west rather than east, Irish cinema references American popular culture in a much more frequent way: a cultural practice not just confined to cinema. Not a recent trend simply coinciding with the emergence of the improved economic standing of Ireland during the 1990s and early 2000s, Irish cinema practice, aesthetics and narratives, have always operated in an international arena. Cinema, by its nature, ensures that.

More recently, and in this context, films such as *Drinking Crude* (Owen McPolin, 1997), *Spaghetti Slow* (Valerio Jalongo, 1996), *I Went Down* (Paddy Breathnach, 1997), *Accelerator* (Vinny Murphy, 1999) and *Disco Pigs* (Kirsten Sheridan, 2001), in their own right exhibit characteristics and traits of the road movie genre. By and large mainstream expressions of generic formula, each of these films manages to display individual inflections of the road movie, both at the level of visual style and narrative expression, while deviating significantly from each other in terms of content and form. While genre productions rely on the combination of similarity and difference to satisfy the dual expectation of familiarity, recognition but also surprise and anticipation, when the narrative goes beyond this template, either in terms of counter- or anti-generic strategies, the more interesting local inflections are found. Conventionally, these films incorporate the familiar generic traits: narrative conventions of journey and travel; the iconographic details of the road and landscape; the recurrent patterns of wandering agents; and story elements that coincide with audience expectations. However, while simultaneously realized and challenged in a recognizable way, it is the overarching typology of mode of address and subject matter, and its relationship to similarity and difference in these films, that suggests something specific about new Irish cinema.

In academic discourse, Genre studies and Irish film have received closer attention in recent years (McIlroy, 2007), arising out of the production of a more concentrated critical mass. Between 1994 and 2008 over one hundred and forty Irish films have received Irish Film Board support while many other Irish productions have emerged without this institutional backing. Many of these films can be arranged generically with a handful of genres appearing more frequently: thriller; gangster; horror; romantic comedy, for example. Dervila Layden observes that 'the intersection of both commerciality and globalization mean that a new generation of film-makers (who grew up with genre film and were very much influenced by the new Hollywood advances in form) felt that they could produce films about Ireland that spoke to a global audience' (McIlroy, 2007: 27–44). While it may appear that this shift to genre film is a recent practice, facilitating the film-makers to operate within a structure they are both familiar with as practitioners but also immersed in as spectators, genre production is not necessarily a new phenomenon. However, the scale and critical mass of genre production in recent years provides a number of points of reference that may shed light on the nature of contemporary Irish film and generic production. While these productions, as Layden points out, have often been criticized for 'global blandness and commodified Irishness', they beg the question why, if the film-makers are so familiar with generic trends and traits, are these films awkward fits for these global forms. It is this two-tiered level of narrative difference, within the generic formula and the industrial set-up that this discussion will explore and elucidate.

Genre application, by its nature, is loose and flexible. These Irish films can variously be described as car-chase movies, urban thrillers, gangster films and/or tragic romance, often centred on the 'couple/buddy on the run' formula. For the purpose of narrative analysis these films are bunched together, although they can be categorized and boxed in many other ways and can be read generically, anti-generically or counter-generically. The loosely-defined road movie genre embodying a typically established iconography, visual style and narrative exposition is applied to reveal, in equal measure, what is present and absent. These films, while lending themselves to this generic analysis, also echo and reflect other Irish films made at the time, not necessarily of this genre. *Accelerator* and *Disco Pigs*, for example, parallel such productions concerned with 'youth issues' – *How to Cheat in the Leaving Cert* (Graham Jones, 1997), 'the disaffected Irish male youth' – *Crushproof* (Paul Tickell, 1998), 'the social problem' – *Flick* (Fintan Connolly, 2000), 'Northern Ireland' – *Nothing Personal* (Thaddeus O'Sullivan 1995), as well as reflecting what was happening in British cinema at the time described in terms of New Laddism. *I Went Down* is not alone in exploring Ireland's underworld and criminal fraternity – *The General* (John Boorman, 1998), *Ordinary Decent Criminal* (Thaddeus O'Sullivan, 1999) and *Night Train* (John Lynch, 1999). In films such as *Garage* (Lenny Abrahamson, 2007), *Small Engine Repair* (Niall Heery, 2006) and *Wide Open Spaces* (Tom Hall, 2009) the aesthetic construction and imaging of the Irish countryside suggests parallels with the American road movie, although at a narrative level these films cannot be described as such. This narrative labyrinth of multi-generic story matter reveals the difficulty of assessing Irish films in isolation from each other and other world cinemas, and the contentiousness of exploring the concept of Irish film as a 'unified whole'. Genre acts as a structural, formal and aesthetic umbrella to reveal the nuances, idiosyncrasies and parallels across a range of new Irish cinema, without negating its wider context of European, independent and/or Hollywood film.

Why this particular genre has captured the imagination of contemporary Irish writers and directors can be explained in a number of ways. The typology offers the film-maker a canonical story format and defined structure – most often a journey, search or quest, metaphorically or realistically executed – as a means to explore such human themes as rebellion, insecurity, alienation and angst, bringing together character and plot in narrative form. In this genre, travelling becomes the means of freeing the protagonist from the roots of social, political and cultural life and allows the human exploration of broader universal traits. The journey removes the character from their everyday environment and allows them the pursuit of something new and different. Often the characters seek insight, need change, are called to reflect and aspire to renewal. In its various mutations and guises within cinema, the road movie shifts from the straightforward Western imagining of the frontier to the more recent constructions that present an ironic twist in the tale, sometimes revealing nihilistic tendencies, as times change and writers and directors fulfil a different purpose. The road movie offers a recognizable iconography, narrative structure and visual style, both for the writer and director in their craft, but also for the audience as points of recognition and identification. Open spaces, the road, landscape, absence of the claustrophobic city as well as more iconographic symbols of imagined American life on the road – diners and snack bars, neon lights and highway signs, gas stations and motels and most importantly the car – are all identifiable indicators of the road-movie genre, easily appropriated and applied to most modern Western cultural and social landscapes.

The narrative trajectory of escape from some sort of threat, unwanted lifestyle or just the norm, to the embarkation on an existential journey in the pursuit of knowledge or a new lifestyle, as a means of challenging the status quo and re-imagining an alternative (often unsuccessfully), is a central tenet of the story arc in this genre. Steeped in a story structure rooted in ancient classical drama, Hollywood formats present a user-friendly approach for producer and consumer alike. There is a view that the creative potential for striking out individualistically is arguably more feasible in a pre-defined structure. Within the basic story format of escape, search, renewal, the possibilities are endless. Genre, when not rigidly applied, facilitates a conventional display on one level (similarity) with complex subtleties sprinkled throughout (difference), providing possibilities for national as well as global or universal address. This structure facilitates a reading which can reveal to what level a specific film, or body of work, resonates culturally and cross-culturally.

Although the road movie is 'quintessentially American', its embrace by cinema cultures around the world ensures its elasticity and relevance outside of America. Ireland, as evident through the examples mentioned, is no exception. What is curious about the road movie is not how national cultures seek to appropriate the genre for their own cinematic landscape but how they re-imagine, adapt and change the format to a local milieu, thus creating a new aesthetic. In such an examination, the framework of genre analysis has its limitations. Its most useful application, it could be said, is in assessing similarity and differences according to the 'blueprint', if this can be established, adding a typographical approach to the task in hand. However, what remains after this assessment, in many instances consideration of the bulk of the filmic text, is where the light needs to shine. The nuances of artistic style and specific resonance are revealed in the shadows and on the sidelines.

The Irish road movie

To what extent are the Irish examples surveyed here simply examples of an imitation *or* original imaginings of form? In the case of the examples cited, *Drinking Crude* and *Spaghetti Slow* use the 'road' to re-imagine the family, a common trope in Irish film over thirty years (*Reefer and the Model*, Joe Comerford 1988). While the journey and theme of travel is central to the story being told, these more recent films more comfortably slot into 'coming of age' films – a familiar genre in nascent 'national' cinemas. While the basic elements of the genre have appeared in some manner or form in these various examples of new Irish cinema, by distancing contemporary Irish cinema from the less-conventional predecessors, *I Went Down*, *Accelerator* and *Disco Pigs* present a range of relevant films that mark out the significance of new Irish cinema. All three films use the visual iconographical markers of American road movies, such as the expansive highway, the journey, the car and the buddies, and transplant them to the Irish landscape, mostly re-codified. These films are significant in their own right because of the mark they left on recent Irish cinema.

While *Drinking Crude* and *Spaghetti Slow* failed to receive a theatrical release, *I Went Down*, *Accelerator* and *Disco Pigs* carved out some significant space in the distribution and exhibition circuit of Irish film. In terms of what David Bordwell calls *Historical Poetics*, these films exist in the mind set of the audience before, during and after the production phases. In pre-compositional terms, for example, *Disco Pigs* is based on the popular stage play by writer Enda Walsh[1] while *I Went Down* and *Accelerator* link culturally to the modern state's preoccupation with two underworld phenomena, organized crime and joyriding, retold across a range of storytelling media. In archetypal terms, the characters in these films embark on a journey seeking out adventure, redemption and/or escape from their familiar environment, facilitating the construction and reading of these films with the familiarity of a globally-recognizable genre, while the local inflection of each narrative makes their address culturally relevant. These films enjoyed a certain level of commercial success at the Irish box office, evident through box-office takings and viewing figures (Barton, 2004: 191–92), yet, when they travel abroad on the festival circuit and through foreign distribution, the response, both critically and commercially, was much more muted. This combination of success and failure, characterizing recent Irish film, remains a conundrum. A close genre analysis may shed some light on this situation.

Accelerator, written and directed by Vinny Murphy, opens in the wasteland of an urban ghetto where 'joyriding' is considered a way of life. Johnny T (Stuart Sinclair Blyth), the main protagonist, is on the run from paramilitary vigilantes because of his 'anti-social behaviour'. From the outset Johnny T is introduced as a character on the cusp of change. Having stood up before his community admitting he was a joyrider before going on yet another spree, he needs to escape from his community, heading to Barcelona, stopping off in Dublin en route. It is here that he meets Whacker (Gavin Kelty), his antagonist, who challenges him to a race from Belfast to the Papal Cross in the Phoenix Park, Dublin – a distance of about one hundred miles. The prize of the 'girl', in the form of Louise (Aisling O'Neill), Whacker's girlfriend, and the £1,200 prize money convinces him, after his initial reluctance, to rise to this challenge before finally hanging up his 'hot-wires' for the last time. The structure of *Accelerator,* which uses a multi-protagonist, episodic approach, was unusual in Irish film when this film was produced but it anticipates a trend that becomes more pronounced later on (*About Adam,* Gerry Stembridge, 2000; *Intermission,* John Crowley, 2003; *Goldfish Memory,* Liz Gill, 2003). The episodic nature of the narrative (a trend established in independent American cinema with the launch of *Slacker* (Richard Linklater, 1991), and continuing throughout the 1990s) is what permits a whole range of characters to be introduced, established and explored at an *objective or exterior* level, simply by taking the focus and emphasis off the central main characters, resulting in a plot-driven narrative. Consequently, what *Accelerator* combines is a generic road movie structure with a 'social-commentary' that speaks specifically of a time and place through its plot, characterization and *mise-en-scène*. The race is not a two-hander between Johnny T and Whacker but involves six cars (six couples) in total, providing an eclectic representation of contemporary Irish urban youth.

Another film structured around a journey between north and south, *Man About Dog* (Paddy Breathnach, 2004), is an Irish comedy-caper-road-movie about three Northern wide-boys who manage to get their hands on a prize-winning greyhound. They travel from North to South in pursuit of their fortune, chased by a big-shot greyhound breeder and a group of Irish travellers, who are intent on claiming their winnings. *Man About Dog* can be categorized as a 'post cease-fire' film, whereby the North of Ireland is used as a location backdrop with little exploration of politics in the storyline and almost no reference to the 'Troubles'. In a similar way to *Accelerator, Sunset Heights* (Colm Villa, 1998) and *The Most Fertile Man in Ireland* (Dudi Appleton, 1999), the backdrop of Northern Ireland is used to launch the narrative and locate the story. While the premise of the plot may be linked to the 'Troubles' or remnants of the conflict since the cease-fire, the central dramatic theme is more universal, less locally-specific and rarely political: a characteristic of contemporary Irish writing that, on a surface level, could take place 'anywhere'. In this film the viewer must sieve through the overt 'Americanness' of the film, through its referencing popular culture spanning a whole range of mainstream films from *Mad Max* (George Miller, 1979) to *Pulp Fiction* (Quentin Tarantino, 1994), either through deliberate appropriation or straightforward self-reflexivity. While the iconography of the 'Troubles' has not been left behind – murals, west Belfast, isolated farms – the American road movie dominates with its symbols of isolated diners and gas stations against a 'sublime' landscape.

Disco Pigs opens at the moment of birth, when Pig and Runt are born on the same day and in the same hospital. They are placed side by side in the nursery and reach out, moments old, to hold hands: a literary motif that will recur in the narrative. The events advance forward to age sixteen – Pig and Runt are inseparable, living next door to each other, excluding the outside world from their imaginary one. They envisage themselves as king and queen and co-exist in their imaginations. The narrative displays the unique friendship that these two characters have with each other, which is at odds with the conventions of their outside world, dysfunctional from early on. The scene in the off-licence, when Pig and Runt bully and attack the boy behind the counter, and the scene in the disco, where Pig and Runt play out a game of seduction and attack, are examples of this disturbing world they have created and inhabit. Rather than embarking on a journey to this world, Pig and Runt are there from the start. However, this is set to change with Pig's growing sexual awakening towards Runt, first signalled through point of view cinematography in the key scene in Shandon church tower and further reinforced when he tries to kiss her.

A straightforward if flawed plot, with a fragile premise, *I Went Down* tells the story of Git (Peter McDonald) when he is released from prison only to find his girlfriend has left him for someone else. Git carries out a favour for his ex-girlfriend's new boyfriend only to find himself having to repay a debt for the privilege. The debt he has to pay is the narrative event that sets in motion the characteristic journey of the road movie. Sent to retrieve cash from the gangster Tom French and find a missing conman, he is teamed up with unlikely 'buddy', Bunny Kelly (Brendan Gleeson). Through a busily-plotted narrative, Git and Buddy travel from Dublin to Cork and back again with task in hand, and, presumably, on a generic journey that will reveal their characters to each other, to themselves and to the audience. Executed through a series of sketches and episodes, the narrative unfolds as the 'buddies' get acquainted on their journey, performing a specific mission, forced to rely on each other despite divergent personalities. Already, through the basic narrative structure, the deviations as well as allegiances to the genre are revealed.

I Went Down met with the most critical and commercial success of the three films examined here, apparent through higher domestic returns and viewing figures alongside wider foreign distribution. However, when broken down along narrative lines, it is most resistant to canonic story-format lines and yet it might be described as the closest 'generic' example. The primary story premise raises basic narrative questions. What motivated Git, on immediate release from prison to get himself into a situation with obviously nothing to gain? By the end of the film, he has not achieved anything in story terms – insight, material gain, the girl! His narrative destiny is the anti-climactic, anti-cathartic solution of emigration: an escape, but from what? In story terms this film is less satisfactory than *Accelerator* and *Disco Pigs*, failing to deliver enigma either at the level of plot or character. While it does combine generic elements satisfying the need for familiarity and recognition, it signals a dominant trend in recent Irish cinema that continues for fifteen years: active deviance from the genre. *I Went Down* embodies the idiosyncratic elements of localized humour, recognizable actors and the quintessential 'Irish' *mise-en-scène*, clearly popular with the audience. It connects through multi-referencing within a shared and understood popular culture for a highly ciné-literate audience. Genre analysis along formal lines illuminates the function this film plays alongside its generic counterparts within the overall 'oeuvre' of recent Irish film, and therefore suggests why it strikes a chord with a localized audience while leaving those beyond Irish cultural borders indifferent and unenthused.

Peter McDonald in *I Went Down*, courtesy of Jonathan Hession, Photographer and Treasure Films.

The generic fit

The basic application of genre analysis requires the identification of similarity and difference across a range of films. According to David Herman, 'generic definitions extend in two directions, for they not only define what a given genre is but also define what it is not' (Herman, 2007: 14). The three films discussed here, *I Went Down*, *Accelerator* and *Disco Pigs*, embody some or all of the multiple aspects of the road movie genre in the form of iconography, narrative strategy, visual style and *mise-en-scène*. These films run the full gamut of road movie from the existential (*Disco Pigs*) to the absurd (*I Went Down*) and echo some of the multiple meanings the genre displays through its evolution. While all films can act as a metaphor for life and function as metamorphosis, either morally or socially, the road movie most often articulates a notion of freedom from the constraints of conventional life. In sending the character on a personal quest, it portrays a sense of rootlessness and aimlessness, often critiques society and gives voice to the concept of male existential angst. The narrative device of journey allows the character to be taken out of the 'normal' environment to pursue *himself* or *something* as different, as well as providing a finite structure of beginning, middle and end. Through the loosely-appropriated genre of road movie, some or all of these meanings and structures surface in an Irish context through the narratives of *I Went Down*, *Accelerator* and *Disco Pigs*.

In terms of narrative trajectory, each of the films in their own individual and diverse way evokes the road movie genre of journey, quest and search by structuring the story around a physical objective of getting from one point to another, posing questions requiring answers. Through a plot-driven approach in *I Went Down*, that develops awkwardly and sometimes unclearly, the main character, Git, is an unconvincing small-time Dublin criminal just released from prison. Along with his narrative 'buddy' Bunny Kelly, he is forced to find a missing conman and retrieve a wad of cash for crime boss Tom French, as a way of buying his freedom. The journey embarked on is closely aligned to a very specific plot task, freeing up narrative space to concentrate on the evolving 'buddy' relationship. *Accelerator*, in a more clearly defined and simple plot-line, sees a multi-protagonist cast embark on a joyride race from Belfast to the Phoenix Park in Dublin. In both films, the journey is the driving action, sustaining the plot and story through ninety minutes, with little metaphorical thrust. While *Accelerator*, by rooting its story to a class-defined milieu through visual iconography, presents a degree of social comment, *I Went Down* is a simple, straightforward, plot-driven criminal caper in comic mode. On the other hand, with an absence of the various road-movie devices dominating the *mise-en-scène* of *Disco Pigs*, the metamorphosis and metaphor goes deeper and lingers longer through the escapades of Pig and Runt. Here, the plot intent is about separation after growth, as each character has an alternative path to furrow. The journey, therefore, requires separating before coming together again, structurally dividing the *mise-en-scène*, in contrast to the other two films.

One of the most identifiable visual signs of the road movie and a way of explicating the narrative purpose, the iconography of landscape and the road, materializes in all three films

Brendan Gleeson in *I Went Down*, courtesy of Jonathan Hession, Photographer and Treasure Films.

by degrees of similarity and difference. Not so much in the recently-constructed motorway routes of Ireland, clearly a symbol of progress, modernization and the 'Celtic Tiger' and therefore what might be expected in new Irish cinema at the time, the 'road' is visualized through the byways, rather than highways of contemporary Ireland, as a means of executing the journey. Visually this allows for more activity outside of the interaction between characters (*I Went Down* in particular) but narratively it slows down the development, allowing for more local and culturally-resonant sub-plots (*Accelerator* specifically). The journey, therefore, takes on a physical plot dimension in *I Went Down* and *Accelerator*: the need to get from Dublin to Cork in pursuit of a package (*I Went Down*), and the race from Belfast to Dublin chasing the prize money (*Accelerator*). In contrast, while not occupying as much in terms of narrative diegetic space, the road and the journey in *Disco Pigs* is more metaphorical and existential as Pig and Runt travel on a journey that will inevitably lead them apart. Structuring the story and plot within this identifiable genre, from the outset these films deviate from the template and from each other. The significance of the road is not simply a matter of iconography, allowing the task of film classification, but is intrinsic to how the story and plot develop.

I Went Down, through its visual style, lends itself more readily to this genre, albeit in a comic, possibly ironic, mode. Through numerous car changes (stolen bangers) and stops along the 'highway' at isolated 'gas stations', the narrative pace of the road movie is suggested. In a peripheral and local construction, the bog-road is to the highway what bog-land is to the vast openness of the American landscape. The dingy pubs and threatening, smoky back-room spaces, suggesting popular American icons, evoke the gangster movie in cross-generic referencing. Yet, while there are attempts to suggest a monotony only broken by isolated pubs, derelict buildings and neon signs in the distance, it is difficult to make the psychological leap that the topography of Ireland can sustain the type of metaphorical journey required by the road-movie narrative. Thus, possibly as an ironic twist, Git and Bunny reach their journey's end quite early on in the diegesis, only to turn around and head back, still on the quest of their mission. Just as the gas station or liquor store is the locus for robbery in the American road movie, it is the sweet shop where the buddies carry out their theft. Although Ireland has been, for some time now, a place of twenty-four-hour petrol stations and convenience stores, it is the quaint, if rather rustic, garage/sweet-shop of childhood memories that is evoked, even eulogized, through contemporary screen images. Just as recent Irish film casts itself in the vein of American generic material, it does so on its own terms. Taking the characteristic tendencies of genre production for similarity and difference, it is at the level of difference that the potential for local inflection and identification is best realized. In the Irish road movie the opportunity is often seized on through visual style and *mise-en-scène*. Although the visual imagining of location is similar across the three films, the iconographic detail, the robbery, is executed very differently: in the style of comic-book in *I Went Down*; cops and robbers in *Accelerator;* and nihilistic and disturbing violence in *Disco Pigs*.

In the road movie the car is central to the developing relationship of the main characters, appropriated in an Irish context through the narratives of *Accelerator* and *I Went Down*. Unlike the role it serves as ironic visual device in *I Went Down*, the car takes on a central function within the narrative of *Accelerator*. Starting with the scene in the multi-storey car park where, like 'mall rats', the gang of characters choose and select the car to reflect their personae and match their quest, the car defines and punctuates key narrative moments. The 'wide open landscape' in generic terms suggests the possibilities as the characters embark on their quest, whereas the interior space of the car structures and defines the characters, the relationships and, ultimately, the limitations in what the quest or journey can achieve: a narrative knitting together of plot and character. Presenting the binary opposites of possibility (open road) and limitation (car interior), these films make use of the generic narrative strategy, even if the icons are highly localized. Through the conversation between Git and Bunny in their shared claustrophobic space, we are fed crumbs of personal detail, and experience the highly localized humour. The range of misfits that pepper the narrative in *Accelerator* is revealed through intimacy or claustrophobia as they journey in their stolen cars. The narrative device of contrasting interior and exterior space is similar in both films, whereas the narrative function served is quite different. Rather than the car, it is the national bus network that facilitates Pig's physical journey – the claustrophobia metaphysically in his head instead of between the characters. Rather than embarking on a journey together, like Git and Bunny and Whacker and Johnny T, Pig and Runt have reached the end; the narrative purpose is how to go it alone, how to separate. The conventional approach to friendship and love is easily digestible in the narratives of *I Went Down* and *Accelerator*, facilitating the appropriation of the car icon readily and seamlessly. *Disco Pigs,* however, has a much more destabilizing and unsettling effect. Ordinarily, the road movie would provide the narrative impetus for escape from normality, but Pig and Runt have existed for sixteen years in a parallel world to wider society. Thus, it is the need to negotiate re-entry (Runt) or permanent exit (Pig) from the conventional world that shapes the narrative path of this film. In this context, therefore, it is not so much the visual icons that categorize this particular film as road movie but, rather, the narrative thrust.

While the similarities in these films allow the taxonomy approach of genre analysis, the differences reveal the style and substance of the individual films, canonicity and breach in narrative terms. The car, journey and buddy aspect are what audience expects of the road movie; how these are configured individually at the level of film text is what keeps the genre alive. Genre analysis within the context of the Irish film industry is tenuous enough, given the absence of a highly-developed and evolved economic infrastructure. Thus it is appropriated not in an industrial context but rather as a point of reference, for producer and consumer alike, in framing popular culture, revealing this dual purpose of audience and film-maker functioning within a global network of shared visual and narrative reference. In the case of recent Irish film, that network nods much more in the direction of American film than European cinema. Simply applying a genre analysis to a range of Irish films is the first step. There is no doubt that these films are part of the mainstream that dominates contemporary European cinema. However, the moments of tension within this mainstream reveal at what level the narrative is working, either as a homage, an endorsement or a critique of the dominant cultural forms.

Going against the grain

The principle definable trait of the road movie genre is the journey; travelling with no particular place in mind allows for the internal quest or exploration to take place. This device is well documented as a mythic structure stemming back to Homer's *Odyssey* and analysed through formalist and narrative schema (Vladimir Propp, 1929; Joseph Campbell, 1979; Christopher Vogler, 1999; Kristin Thompson, 1999) across a range of narrative forms. The journey is structurally suited to set in train the narrative path of equilibrium and disequilibrium and is intrinsic to the concept of classical narrative systems. In this context Jean Baudrillard's contention, that in the course of travelling, time and motion become a form of amnesia or 'extermination of meaning' (Baudrillard, 1988: 9–10), suggests that the potential for multiple meanings is much greater within mainstream generic productions such as the road movie. This type of story can create the metaphysical, metaphorical or symbolic journey just as much as high-concept, plot-driven and action-based scenarios, depending on the formal narrative tools employed, satisfying a range of audience needs and tastes. The genre evolved in the popular medium to explore such complex human tales involving change, development and growth, or destruction, demise and downfall at a deeper level, in a palatable and popular format. The narrative possibilities of the highly-popular format facilitate a range of responses, including plunging to emotional depth way beyond what characters simply 'say and do', to seeing, hearing, feeling, thinking, etc. In the popular American versions such as *Easy Rider* (Dennis Hopper, 1969), *Bonnie and Clyde* (Arthur Penn, 1967) and *Thelma and Louise* (Ridley Scott, 1991), the narratives resonate far beyond the notion of 'couples on the run', commenting in wider cultural and human terms.

In the examples examined here, while the journey takes on a meaning in *Accelerator* and *I Went Down*, it is largely externally *focalized*. The characters employ a narrow if focused range of narrative tools. Embarking on an outward journey from A to B, the causal agents proceed through various stages of narrative development, overcoming obstacles and solving problems as they strive for their goal. Because the narrative information is disseminated through the interaction on screen by characters 'saying and doing' rather than 'seeing and hearing', what emerges narratively is a goal-oriented physical and material journey. Rarely do we get an insight into the interior motives of the characters in these films, instead the audience is held at arm's length through comic devices and car chases. While this brought a level of satisfaction to the Irish audience, if support at the box office and television viewing figures are an indication of endorsement, it may account for the failure in accessing a wider (non-Irish) audience. Much of the humour, one of the principle narrative devices, is highly localized. The phrase 'in the bath fella' resounds locally and through the enunciation of internationally-recognized actor Brendan Gleeson, but is this enough to appeal further afield? The Irish police force (An Gardaí Síochana) have long endured their role at the butt end of Irish ridicule and send-up within popular culture and, while cops are not necessarily an unusual target, it is the specific nature of poking fun that Irish audiences are privileged in 'getting'. Thus, in narrative terms, the appropriation of the road movie genre in *I Went*

Down functions well as a tenuous structure for a localised, self-conscious exposition of comic characters.

With the comic element largely absent, the narrative in *Accelerator* reverberates sociologically. Johnny T as the main protagonist is positioned objectively in relation to the narrative. The opening sequence, visually locating the urban milieu at the heart of social deprivation, structures the main protagonist around what he 'says and does'. Through the phone call he makes to his cousin Crunchy (Mark Dunne) in Dublin (objective point of view), the audience learns of his desire to go to Barcelona to escape his fate. His encounter with Whacker, his antagonist, is direct and head-on. The spectator sees what the character sees, but not from the character's position in the narrative. This form of expression, external focalization, allows for the spectator to share the understanding or attention of the character but not their experience. In terms of 'plunging into the psychological state of the character', external focalization or objective narrative is confined largely to the surface, thus structuring the narrative of *Accelerator*. This situates the film more in the realm of social-realism drama whereby the main characters sometimes perform the role of ciphers with a message to impart, rather than causal agents with a dramatically-structured role.

As a consequence of the restricted points of view given to the viewer, insight into how Johnny T is feeling and thinking is largely absent. Whacker's character is affirmed by what others say about him rather than revealed through his own agency: his mother is absent and his father is in prison, details the audience learns from others. The other characters are central to the narrative but because of the episodic nature of the plot the audience learns little about their motivational factors as they embark on the joyride race. What is suggested early on in the film is that the characters are united through the absence of any parental guidance. 'Whacker's ma kicked him out of his gaff', which is why he has nowhere to stay, while Sharon's parents are always in the pub: it does not matter if she gets in trouble. As she says of her father, 'sure he's always killing me anyway, what's the difference?' This approach to narrative is interesting in suggesting an 'other' contrasting world to that displayed directly on screen, lending it more to a sociological reading.[2] Not an uncommon trope in youth-oriented films, the gang steps into the breach where the family fails and is therefore central to the narrative's action. However, in the absence of deeper story-penetration, the gang members' main function is limited to that of ciphers, standing for something outside of the narrative. Ripley (Mary Ellen McCartan) and Spock's (Philip Richie) sole narrative purpose, it could be argued, is as cultural reference and stylistic device.

Accelerator, through characterization, gives access primarily to plot events (restricted narration) and is therefore mainly action-driven. The distinction between internal and external focalization is useful in representing the different levels of character experience and engagement. External focalization is what distinguishes the approach in *Accelerator* and *I Went Down* and is common to the industry-defined 'high concept' film. While character motivation can be generated by external factors, such as race, gender, nationality or socio-economic position, when combined with internal character motivation, agency, a more complex representation of humanity is constructed. In this film, the narrative presents the events to the audience through what the characters 'say and do' – externally focalized. The interiority of character and deeper thoughts are largely absent from the story and plot, with the pleasure in watching derived from another source.

A key scene in this film is when the two cars (occupied by Johnny T and Whacker) encounter the British army border checkpoint. Analysing this scene along the lines of subjective and objective narrative reveals core narrative tensions. The audience is presented with two subjective positions: firstly when the checkpoint is revealed from Johnny T's point of view and secondly when the soldiers are seen from Whacker's point of view. When Whacker shoots at the soldiers, the camera shots are presented in an objective way as Whacker utters the words 'Shoot to Kill Mother Fuckers': a localized reference to events during the 'Troubles' in Northern Ireland.[3] Continuing the trend of fatalism attached to characters in films about Northern Ireland, the explanation for Whacker's actions appear to remain outside of the story. It does not fit the narrative set-up either as a sociological statement or a way of progressing character and plot. On the other hand, the fatalism attached to male characters in road movies is a commonly-occurring generic trait. Whacker has no political or social motivation as displayed through narrative devices: the function, therefore, is generically defined. Furthermore, the road movie often functions as a simplification of all life. Developed through the travelling trope that defines the genre, it generally has a restive and recuperative function. Travelling frees the character from the social and puts him/her on a different plane, often propelling them in a spiritual direction. In the absence of this generic marker, character motivation and reason go unexplained.

Beyond the limits of genre

Within this context *Disco Pigs*, while visually and iconographically least like the American genre of road movie, presents the most metaphysical journey-experience for characters and audience alike. From the outset, Pig and Runt embark on a journey together that will inevitably lead them apart. The narrative typically starts in a state of equilibrium, plotting the formative years of Pig and Runt. Things change to upset this state when Runt begins to move away, age sixteen, as her attraction for Markey grows. The narrative embarks on a stage of disequilibrium, plotted along the action line of Pig's simmering violent tendency in contrast to Runt's sexual awakening. According to film narratologist David Bordwell, at any moment in a film the spectator can ask 'how deeply do I know the characters' perceptions, feelings, and thoughts?' In narratological terms, the answer will point directly to how the narration is presenting or withholding story information in order to achieve a formal function or a specific effect on the viewer (Bordwell & Thompson, 1990). *Disco Pigs* uses a wide range of narratological devices in contrast to the restricted focus of *Accelerator*, creating narrative layers that demand more processing by the audience. *Disco Pigs* achieves this through point of view shots.

A key illustrative scene occurs as Pig surveys Cork city from the top of Shandon church. Runt calls Pig to come and look at the skirt she made. From the top of the church, the camera

Cillian Murphy and Elaine Cassidy in *Disco Pigs*, courtesy of Patrick Redmond, Photographer and Element Films.

cuts to a long shot of Runt: 'what do you think?', as she holds out her skirt. In an externally-focalized shot, the camera cuts to Pig and zooms in; the spectator shares the character's attention, rather than his experience. The camera then cuts to Runt from Pig's point of view (internally focalized). A series of soft-focused, close-up shots follow as Pig describes how Runt looks: 'like some model you see off the telly'. The audience now shares the character's experience, rather than attention. Runt breaks this internal focalization and the two head off. The internal focalization or subjective narrative is repeated throughout the film. After Pig kisses Runt, through his voiceover, he verbalizes his fantasy. In story-design terms, once he starts on this trajectory he is heading in one direction: towards his downfall. When Runt goes to Donegal the presence of Pig is felt throughout, even though he is not with her on screen. Adopting a catatonic state, spatially the two are held together in the narrative. Runt senses his approach when she says, 'he's close', while Pig jumps off the bus as it passes the big austere building that is the reform school.

From the opening sequence the audience is plunged to the 'subjective levels' of characterization in narrative terms. The device central to this approach in *Disco Pigs* is the use of voice-over providing an entry point to the world of Pig and Runt, where they reign as King and Queen in their imagined kingdom. In the opening sequence, the homodiegetic voiceover of Runt is internally focalized: 'Once upon a time before there was blue', over visuals of the baby Runt just before and during the moment of birth. Conveying her inner thoughts and feelings from the moment of birth, she says in voiceover: 'I want for something different and that's when I hear him … at that moment we become one and we need no one else. Nobody.' This sequence, establishing the subjective narrative style which explores 'simple perception' and 'deeper thoughts' as it works through the inner turmoil of its characters, is articulated through image and voice. From the outset, the poetic, allegorical style is in contrast to the socio-realistic style adopted by *Accelerator*. *Disco Pigs* hinges on many themes that are seen as characteristically 'road movie' or 'buddy movie', as the visual style deviates. The rebellion, insecurity, alienation and general angst of the typical road-movie character is reflected in *Disco Pigs,* and the road movie as a rite of passage for Oedipally-driven young males could explain what is happening to Pig.

Central to defining the American road movie is the visual iconography of the wide-open space: a dimension of *mise-en-scène* allowing the journey to take on its wider, existential thrust and the potential for change. It does this by physically removing the characters from their normal social, cultural and political milieux, projecting them on a journey unbounded by the structures of their 'normal' life as a means of narrative purpose. Contrastingly, the interiority of the car, for very practical purposes of storytelling, allows the relationship between the 'buddies' to develop. For ease of classical framing, the interior of the car frames the space between the characters, containing them at one level, while the struggle for freedom and escape takes place outside, in the wide-open spaces. In these Irish examples, almost in a counter-generic way, the visual iconography does not always coincide with the narrative tendencies. Negating the opportunity to create in the audience's minds-eye the sense of wide, infinite, open space, the characters in *I Went Down* are on no greater mission

Cillian Murphy and Elaine Cassidy in *Disco Pigs*, courtesy of Patrick Redmond, Photographer and Element Films.

than the one indicated through dialogue in the early scenes. Simply put, Git and Bunny are running an errand for bigger crime-boss Tom French. Without any deeper narrative purpose in terms of character development, the narrative presents a circular, return journey, defined and contained both physically and imaginatively.

While *Accelerator* has a counter-generically defined physical journey to undertake, a race among joyriders from Belfast to Dublin's Phoenix Park, like *I Went Down*, its visual style is contained by the narrative attempts to cross the border, with only the two main characters managing to escape. Using the road-movie genre to comment sociologically on the lack of opportunity in economically-deprived communities of modern Ireland, and how the cycle gets repeated with little opportunity for escape, this message is endorsed visually in a way similar to *I Went Down*: through the absence of the wide-open road. Instead, the back roads of the border region of Northern Ireland resemble a maze dotted with traps, preventing escape, a theme surfacing in Johnny Gogan's 'imaginative thriller' *Mapmaker* (2001). Where escape happens, it was already sanctioned diegetically at the start of the film with Johnny T's indication of his desire and intention to depart for Barcelona. This high degree of closure is anathema to the road movie. The end of the journey in *I Went Down* and *Accelerator* corresponds to the outcome for the characters. This does not involve an internal change, a realization or character growth, instead it is an escape abroad from the material and physical constraints of home. The traditional ending of the road movie is variously uncomfortable, unsettling and tragic (*Thelma and Louise*, Ridley Scott 1991; *Badlands,* Terence Malick 1973; *Bonnie & Clyde*, Arthur Penn 1967) and true to the generic narrative tendency. In the absence of a more existential or metaphysical thrust for the narrative journey, emigration wraps up and closes off the plot in an anti- rather than counter-generic way. The road movie presents a story format that negates, by-passes or simply ignores the 'outside' world so that the internal journey and relationship between the buddies can take on more significance – a central tenet omitted from *I Went Down* and *Accelerator*.

On the other hand, *Disco Pigs*, which least resembles the American road movie in terms of iconography, does not turn its back on this narrative potential. Far from presenting the audience with a safe, high degree of closure in this film, the narrative both ends and starts at the same time. The journey embarked on by Pig and Runt at the start of the film reaches finality without closure, echoing the opening voice-over and Runt's dreams and desires for her life. Before the moment of birth, through the use of voice-over, Runt says 'the noisy world outside … that was the time when silence was some sort of friend. A time before he arrived … before I hear the Pig', indicating Runt's existence prior to meeting Pig. After Pig's suffocation Runt returns to the theme of silence, which is delivered once again in voice-over, from Runt's point of view:

> And so it's all over then, Pig and Runt they leave and Runt all alone it seems. It's like I do really want for something else. Something different. That silence again and though I know that he too is silent and safe … the sun, it really is a big beautiful shining thing. Where to? Eh pal, where to?

The road movie is particularly important and culturally significant in the misplaced and lost characters – a description more befitting Pig than Git or Joh. is never a sense that Git is lost, as such. And Johnny T has already been found, before the plot is firmly established. On the other hand, in keeping with the generic trait of the road movie, and its potential in narrative terms, centring on characters whose ultimate destiny is to be always on the move, *Disco Pigs* ends, like many road movies, with the main character dead but doomed always to wander. Thus, in aesthetic and storytelling terms, *Disco Pigs* presents a narrative world that lingers long after the credits have rolled.

Conclusion

Distrustful of the hippy past, dismayed by the yuppie present, disillusioned with a bumpy future, so the narrative goes, a bitter Gen-X retreated into ironic disengagement as a means of non-participatory coexistence with boomers and their domination of cultural and political landscape. (Sconce, 2002: 355)

Applying a formalist analysis to these films is useful in revealing stories that resonate at many levels, appropriating, negotiating and reflecting international trends. Genre studies framed along formalist lines facilitates the reading of Irish film, not in terms of conforming and aping an American genre but rather revealing the idiosyncratic nature of narrative strategies in contemporary Irish film. It is how Irish writers and directors establish similarity and difference before seeking to deviate from the type that throws up the most interesting observations and discussions. While cause and effect play a dominant role in structuring the story and plot events in *Disco Pigs* and *I Went Down*, chance is *Accelerator's* underpinning structural motivation. Similarly, *Dead Bodies* (Robert Quinn, 2003), *Goldfish Memory* (Liz Gill, 2003) and *Intermission* (John Crowley, 2003) rely on a series of chance encounters to motivate the action and justify the consequences in these narratives. When Geoffrey Sconce talks about American independent movies in ironic terms, with 'characters trapped by annihilating fate and narrational strategies that seem without empathy' (Sconce, 2002: 364), he could be variously referring to new Irish cinema.

Far from constructing heroic icons, many Irish films are vehicles for the exposition of the anti-hero, and the road movie has presented a ready-made structure for such construction. Living on the fringes of society, occupying space beyond and separate from normality, wondering where they fit in and deciding to remain apart, are common preoccupations of recent Irish male cinematic characters. Git, Pig and Johnny T are codified versions of contemporary Irish men as represented in recent Irish cinema. In representational terms, these characters present the Irish male as marginal and confused: a theme much explored in the discourse of cultural identity and issues of male identity (Ging, 2002). While these films may well be tapping into a wider postfeminist malaise in Irish and Western male identity (Ging, 2002; 2004), in the context of this study, what these stories reveal is the attachment Irish writers and directors have to American popular culture and, more interestingly, their desire not simply to model on or imitate, rather, to reject and inflect, however subtly, in an original way. The Irish road movie has taken the road-movie hero, generally constructed him as 'anti', but played with him in various imaginings from existential to ironic. The existential Pig questions his whole reason for being while Git and Bunny exist 'in quotes'. At this formal level the idiosyncratic nature of narrative construction is revealed. Parallels between *Disco Pigs*, *Accelerator* and *I Went Down* with the American 'smart' films are evident in the nihilistic approach to characterization, yet these Irish films reveal strong, clear, local resonance as outlined above. The foregrounding of urban, male, often working-class, youth culture echoes the trends in recent independent American and British film. Yet the omniscient narrative devices, such as soliloquy as a form of exposition in *Disco Pigs* and the reflective dramatic form of inter-titles in *I Went Down*, suggest that contemporary Irish writers and directors, while very rooted to the Hollywood system, are not simply creating derivative versions of established, tried-and-tested formulae.

If the road movie is about a personal quest in the form of a search for something or someone or as a process for coming to terms with something, then *Disco Pigs* is most true to the genre. In this film, Enda Walsh and Kirsten Sheridan use the format as a classic story-telling device to unearth the complex human experience of coming-of-age, friendship and lost love. These Irish films can be appraised as an evolution in new Irish cinema, from *I Went Down* to *Disco Pigs*, from the telling of straightforward comic caper to more reflective tales centred on the 'awesomeness of life', all displaying a high degree of local inflection. However, it may be that these local inflections are what simultaneously align the local audience while alienating the global spectator as these films hit cinema screens. Although these films achieve a level of authenticity through local, well-known actors (Brendan Gleeson, Peter McDonald, Cillian Murphy, Aisling O'Neill), speaking in familiar accents, dialects and with idiosyncratic humour, it is at a cost. While measuring the success of a small nation's film industry in box-office terms alone is contentious, it is worth noting that these three films received a cinema release and met with a high degree of support, both critically and commercially, remaining in the consciousness of the Irish audience. But, like many other recent Irish films made at this level, they failed to impact abroad. Striking that balance between global audiences and local identity is arguably the greatest challenge of all local cinemas in this age.

Notes

1. There is a tradition in recent Irish cinema of playwrights also writing for screen including Conor McPherson (*I Went* Down, 1997; *Saltwater,* 2000; *The Actors,* 2003; *The Eclipse,* 2009), Billy Roche (*Trojan Eddie,* 1996) and Mark O'Rowe (*Intermission,* 2003; *Boy A,* 2007; *Perrier's Bounty,* 2009).
2. In contrast, *Adam & Paul,* which is analysed in Chapter 4, negates the opportunity to contrast by way of another world and therefore constructs a very different narrative at the level of character.
3. This refers to an alleged 'Shoot to Kill' policy of members of the IRA by British soldiers and the RUC during the Northern Ireland 'Troubles'. For a detailed account see *Stalker* by John Stalker (1988).

Chapter 3

Irish Romantic Comedy - Strategies of Characterization

I would say that politics, topicality and prosaic realism have generally been over-valued in Irish cinema, and they threaten to keep that cinema from making its next creative leap. To put that another way, works of genre or imagination (ghost stories, romances, action films, say) here tend to be viewed as *inherently* commercial, i.e. frivolous, while realistic depictions are seen as *inherently* serious, worthy, artistic. That 'inherently' … points straight into a cul de sac, for several reasons: It obliges artists to obey arbitrary limits; it sets up barriers against various kinds or experimentation. (Cheshire, 2001)[1]

Choosing four recent Irish films categorized within the genre of romantic comedy, cast within a mainstream narrative and aesthetic, with a popular local appeal, gives some insight into contemporary Irish film at the turn of the millennium. *A Man of No Importance* (Suri Krishnamma, 1994), *The Most Fertile Man in Ireland* (Dudi Appleton, 1999), *About Adam* (Gerry Stembridge, 2000) and *When Brendan met Trudy* (Kieron J. Walsh, 2000), when grouped together, facilitate a reading of character construction within narrative form, with a specific emphasis on themes and issues *masculine* and *feminine*. Using the dramatic device of conflicting opposites, the way these films structure the main characters in relation to masculine and feminine identities reveals patterns and styles at work within contemporary Irish film. *About Adam* and *When Brendan met Trudy* have, in general, been welcomed as a positive development within Irish cinema in terms of style and representation. Debbie Ging regards *When Brendan met Trudy* as 'a far more self-conscious attempt to break into a modern narrative tradition' (2002: 177–95), while Gerry Stembridge describes *About Adam* as 'guilt-free sex, about young people who are fairly happy in their lives and are free of certain moral imperatives' (McCarthy, 1999: 6). The writer/director of *About Adam* says 'I'd like to think the film is political in that sense, like films by some of the younger directors coming up now, free of constant introspection of what a terrible country this is. Free of introspection about Irishness.'[2] A similar position was espoused by Vinny Murphy after the release of his film *Accelerator*. Receiving almost totally positive reviews, *About Adam* is described as 'the first movie to celebrate an evolving metropolitan culture that believes in itself and couldn't care less what the neighbours think anymore' (Carty, 2000: 19). This echoes the words of Stembridge when he says 'it is celebrating a city that I have lived in for over twenty years and love living in and I have often wondered why it is not depicted in the way that I see it. I wanted it to be full of freshness and charm and affection and make people feel good about living here' (Tierney, 2001: 14–17). These statements, while part of the publicity machine of the film production and distribution process, provide a useful barometer measuring the prevailing mood at the time: a specific cultural moment of celebration during 'Celtic Tiger' Ireland. They reveal the shared perceptions of an imagined Dublin, between audience and producer, subscribing to the imagined construction of Dublin in the film, more utopian than reality, as Ireland was aggressively distancing itself from its past.[3] With the benefit of hindsight, it is suggested that these films represent a fleeting moment in Ireland's recent boom-time.

In contrast, *The Most Fertile Man in Ireland* and *A Man of No Importance* have received a combination of lukewarm reviews or simply negative comment from film critics writing in Irish and British newspapers and film magazines. Dudi Appleton, director of *The Most Fertile Man in Ireland*, points out that the criticism waged against his film is primarily concerned with the portrayal of the July 12 bonfire. The Orange parade, in contrast to the dominant media images circulating at this time which highlighted the sectarian divide, is portrayed as modern, celebratory and good-humoured, satirical and fantastical, in post-*Riverdance* Ireland. Appleton is bemused when he places this criticism in the context of the film itself. He points out that nobody seems to view the basic premise of the film as stretching credibility (a man who has the power to impregnate even the most infertile woman with one sexual encounter) yet commentators are troubled with how the July 12 celebrations are depicted. While the critics variously describe the film as 'a send up of the proverbial Irish bachelor' (Carty, 2001: 5) or criticize it for not 'treating the issue of infertility with more seriousness' (McMahon, 2001: 8), it gets overlooked as a multi-layered narrative. In a way similar to *About Adam*, this film taps into a specific moment of optimism in Ireland and distances itself from the dominant representations of Northern Ireland. For Appleton (who grew up in the Jewish community in Belfast of Irish and Israeli parents), the film is about challenging preconceptions and perceptions. He embraced the opportunity to tell a universal story in a generic format, yet firmly rooted it to a local setting in post-ceasefire Ireland.

Like *The Most Fertile Man in Ireland*, *A Man of No Importance,* while generating a positive response, failed to arouse any level of debate. Geoffrey Macnab, in *Sight & Sound*, describes the film as 'portraying its little corner of 60s Dublin as a picture postcard community, full of loveable eccentrics' (Macnab, 1994) while Paul Power in *Film Ireland* sees it as a film that is 'not given enough justice in its direction … the overall impression is of a film with the writer far more apparent' (Power, 1994: 40). Michael Dwyer, in *The Irish Times*, sees more in the film through his observation:

> … but this was a time when 'the love that dare not speak its name' was still considered unspeakable, and while the movie displays an affectionate and jovially nostalgic feel for the period, it eschews any predictable 'rare auld times' trappings and further sets about exposing the bigotry and hypocrisy that lurked beneath the superficial bonhomie. (Dwyer, 1995: 15)

Analysing form within a corpus of films loosely fitting an over-arching generic framework reveals insights into the storyworlds created but also uncovers the nature of what is culturally

Albert Finney and Rufus Sewell in *A Man of No Importance*, courtesy of Jonathan Hession, Photographer.

specific. Genre analysis is useful here, not as a blueprint for measurement or as a gauge of difference but as confirmation that new Irish film-makers, while sometimes working within international norms, are never immune from them. Obviously influenced through their own experience of popular culture, both as spectators and practitioners, these film-makers display a nod in both directions, Janus-like, towards the Hollywood genre of romantic comedy and a preoccupation with local themes and issues.

Evolving narrative forms

> It's good, as the Stoics tell us, to have tools that are simple to understand and of a very limited number – so that we may locate and employ them on a moment's notice. I think the essential tools in any worthwhile endeavor are incredibly simple. And very difficult to master. The task of any artist is not to learn many, many techniques but to learn the simplest technique perfectly. In doing so, Stanislavsky told us, the difficult will become easy and the easy habitual, so that the habitual may become beautiful. (Mamet, 1994: 411)

Narrative theory is a useful tool for exploring the different levels within the constructed narrative and in the case of characterization it can reveal two levels of action and engagement – what is termed interiority and exteriority. While characters function on a range of levels, for the purpose of this discussion two levels are identified. Appropriating from the writings of narratologist Edward Branigan in particular, the basic analytical device is what the character says and does (exterior action) and what the character sees and hears (interior actions) of this narrative task. Tipping in either direction to varying degrees implicates the nature of the story told. At its most basic narrative level, this device reveals how a character and plot relate to the storyworld in terms of the emotional experience, both on screen among characters and within the auditorium for the audience. In terms of narrative, characters act at a number of levels, by 'telling' the story in a broad sense, through living in their world and relating to other characters (Branigan, 1998: 100). A character therefore is a causal agent, who reveals events in the narrative through action and dialogue or suggests story resonance and nuance through their point of view. In this discussion, the narratological concept of focalization is useful as a way of revealing how the character functions in the storyworld. For Branigan, as explored in the Introduction to his book, focalization refers to the character neither speaking nor acting but experiencing through seeing and hearing, extending to internal activity such as thinking, remembering, and wondering (Branigan, 1998: 101).

The films discussed here have a central comic thread, can be categorized as 'romance films' and play with the tropes of love, sex, masculinity, femininity and the public and private

Opposite: Kris Marshall in *The Most Fertile Man in Ireland*, courtesy of Samson Films.

spheres. *A Man of No Importance* tells the story of Alfie Byrne (Albert Finney) who conceals his homosexuality in the sexually-conservative Ireland of the 1960s. A bus conductor in Dublin's inner-city, he is a devoted Wildean who proposes to stage a play involving the local people on his bus route and in his community. *The Most Fertile Man in Ireland* is a romantic-comedy about Eamonn Manly (Kris Marshall), a Catholic who, once he has accidentally discovered his 'hyper-potency', offers an insemination service that guarantees pregnancy after his carnal attentions. Initially just helping infertile couples, he soon becomes central to the race between Catholics and Protestants to out-breed each other: a comic trope with serious resonance in the power struggle of Northern Ireland. *About Adam* and *When Brendan met Trudy* concern the more general themes of romantic love and relationships. While these films are similar in a number of ways, their main point of contrast is at the level of characterization. Adam (Stuart Townsend) is confident and assured in his purpose, whereas Brendan (Peter McDonald) is awkward and shy. Like Alfie, Brendan's character changes along the narrative trajectory, while Adam's purpose is to bring change to those he encounters. These films, while products of Irish cinema, reflect and comment on the universal themes of love and sexuality central to the genre of romantic comedy.

While some would argue that love is a socially-constructed phenomenon invented by a 'group of Provençal poets at the end of the eleventh century' (Deleyto, 2003: 167), it is a concept and experience sufficiently widespread to be taken as an expression of the human condition, although its understanding and application has changed over time. Cognitive theorists (Currie, 1995; Grodal, 2008; Tan, 1996) argue that there is a clear link between biology and culture and that popular storytelling genres like romantic comedies serve a very clear human role in cognitive development and experience. Torben Grodal's theoretical assertion is that stories activate brain patterns, particularly central emotions and action patterns, when they are constructed in popular established forms. According to bioculturalism, originality in stories should only be a surface novelty; deeper structure goes back thousands of years. Concurring with the formalist position, the same story is retold in new ways. Referring to what is termed the 'novelty-habituation mechanism', familiarity and novelty are linked to aesthetic attention and liking (Grodal, 2008). Contrasting with the position adopted by cultural studies, cognitive theorists draw on anthropological evidence to suggest that romantic love is universal and not a cultural invention, suggesting that genre serves a clear biocultural role for human development. This theoretical position, while contentious, is useful in terms of popular film and the profusion of genre, not just in mainstream Hollywood but across most local and world cinemas.

In genre studies, Evans and Deleyto track the changes in the representations of love and romance, different now from 'the kind of madness that it was in classical literature, the devouring passion of the Middle Ages or the frivolous game of late medieval romances' (Evans & Deleyto, 1998: 5). In Hollywood, romance and love formed the thematic basis of the screwball comedies of the 1930s and 1940s, was complicated in the melodrama genre of the 1950s, changed in the 1970s to reflect a liberal approach to sex and shifted once again in the 1980s and 1990s to link positive sexual encounters with romantic love, but tied to an inevitable outcome – marriage. While the deeper structure, a Bakhtinian narrative device of boy meets girl, remains the same, historical moments are reflected in the surface variations. While the emotion identified with love, according to sociologists, is a universal phenomenon, romantic love is often taken as culturally specific (Evans & Deleyto, 1998: 4), with its representation 'a complex and spiritual and emotional force which guarantees the stability of the social structure into which it has been incorporated' (Evans & Deleyto, 1998: 5). This may account for the generic shifts over time and place and, read in these terms, suggests that the gap between cognitive theory and cultural studies need not be so vast.

The emotion associated with love and romance is not only a generic theme for film-makers but also a narrative and formal device. How the narrative works to evoke an emotional response is a concern of film studies dating back to Russian formalism (Eisenstein, Propp) and equally relevant now through the cognitive sciences. As David Herman points out, while Aristotle subordinated character to plot, 'Propp's approach constituted the basis for structuralist theories of characters as "actants", or general roles fulfilled by certain characters' (Herman, 2007: 13). The writings of Propp and Eisenstein, alongside narratologists such as Bordwell and Branigan, are useful in developing this approach. Combined with genre analysis, it is illuminating and revealing about both the global (universal) and local (cultural) extent of these stories.

Sex, love, romance

> Romantic comedy is devotedly urban. Its milieu is the city. It loves the night-life, the high-rise, the dance floor. Its fated couples rent designer apartments, wear high fashion, flick through lifestyle magazines, and bump into each other at nightspots. The city buzz is background noise for romantic comedy's rapid-fire conversation on the dialectic of sex. (Collins, 2004)

Central to this analysis is an examination of the storyworld formally created in each film within the mythic structure of romantic comedy, what purpose the narrative thematically serves and how this is achieved. In applying a formal examination of narrative structure and storyworld, the multi-layered narrative of *The Most Fertile Man in Ireland* and *A Man of No Importance* is revealed. According to Aristotle's *Poetics*, the fundamental building blocks of drama are tension and conflict, which evoke pity and fear leading to *catharsis*. One way this process is realized is through the playing out of opposites – pitting oppositional characters against each other or playing out opposite themes until one supplants the other: traditionally the opposites of good and evil. An examination of each film looks at how the form and content play out oppositional states as a means to realizing conflict. What are the outcomes for the storyworld based on these conflicts of opposites? How does this formal approach tally with recent generic trends in the romantic comedy coming from Hollywood? What does it reveal about narrative strategies in new Irish cinema?

The thematic and structural conflict between the search for love and sexual gratification manifests itself at some level in each of these films. The internal struggle of Eamonn in *The Most Fertile Man in Ireland* is his attraction for Rosie (Kathy Keira Clarke) who works in the nearby funeral parlour. His search for love is contrasted with the world around him, which is superficially concerned with sexual gratification as expressed through the visual iconography (dating agency, the love-themed posters, graffiti and wall murals), a common generic device of 1990s' romantic comedy. The dramatic tension of this theme is brought to the narrative surface through a locally-resonant device: the complication arising from his Catholicism and her Protestantism. Eamonn, the central protagonist, is portrayed as *different* from the 'standard male': he is still a virgin, in contrast to his macho brother, and his mother is concerned that he does not have a girlfriend. As he says himself, 'just because I'm not chasing skirt does not mean I'm a homosexual. I'm looking for love'. This theme is echoed in *A Man of No Importance*, where sex and love are clearly distinguished as separate and not necessarily linked. After Alfie discovers Ms. Rice (Tara Fitzgerald) having sex with a stranger, he is visibly distressed. In keeping with contemporary genre coding, Adele points out that sometimes sex and love have nothing to do with each other. The central conflict in *A Man of No Importance* is Alfie's awakening sexuality, in which he is required to recognize his homosexuality, allowing its expression and enabling him to proceed from the private to the public domain. In narrative terms, his progression from a conservative and naive disposition is realized through his relationship with his sexuality, accepting sex and love as not necessarily entwined.

The inevitable surfacing of local themes and issues is what simultaneously defines and sets apart these films from the genre framework. The depiction and exploration of sex and love as tropes expressed in these films and in *Intermission, Goldfish Memory, Separation Anxiety* (Mark Staunton, 1997) among others, displays a shift in second wave films from the fixed meta-narratives that connect the portrayal of sex to guilt, religion and moral ethics (*Hush-a-bye Baby*, Margo Harkin 1990; *December Bride*, Thaddeus O'Sullivan 1991; *The Playboys*, Gillies MacKinnon 1992). Recent Irish film has been less concerned with the links between the individual and religious/national norms and instead focuses on exploring the broader universal themes of sex and love. Whether achieved through a visual style that is upbeat, vivid and vibrant (*About Adam; The Most Fertile Man in Ireland*) or through a distinctly modern theme situated diegetically in a nostalgic past (*A Man of No Importance*), these narratives are different from their cinematic predecessors. *About Adam* centres the plot action around the Temple Bar area and the leafy suburbs of Edwardian Dublin while *When Brendan met Trudy* portrays an angst-ridden suburbia (of which Brendan is a product) in contrast to the easy-going life of the city. The characters in *About Adam* frequent ultra-chic cocktail bars and live in sophisticated, modern apartments or beautifully-restored period residences. In *When Brendan met Trudy*, taking symbols of the Catholic Church (music) and locating them in a non-religious setting (the pub) echoes this device that clearly marks out this cinematic phase in Irish film. These depictions, in particular Temple Bar, capture the excitement of the 1990s when the 'Celtic Tiger' was peaking and the city façade was changing in line with a more affluent, modern society, and echoes the style of the romantic-comedy genre in US and Australian films in the 1990s (*Sleepless in Seattle*, Nora Ephron 1993; *Clerks,* Kevin Smith 1994; *Love and Other Catastrophes*, Emma-Kate Croghan 1996). Possibly reflecting a fleeting moment in Ireland's boom years, these storytellers are carving out new territory and distinguishing from past cinematic representations.

Yet these films are clearly separate from each other, particularly at the level of narrative layering. Through their exploration of the tensions between sex and love, these films move from one position to another – where sex is acknowledged as having dual functions. In the case of *The Most Fertile Man in Ireland*, it is seen as a means to procreate but is also an expression of love that has nothing to do with sexual reproduction. The narrative trajectory of this theme culminates in the final scene, whereby the only future for Eamonn and Rosie is for him to have a vasectomy which will secure their love by ending Eamonn's 'service to the community'. More significantly, it ensures an end to procreation but not sexual activity. In its own way, this film signals a clear move away from the traditional, nativist position of Catholic Ireland, whereby sexual gratification is linked to guilt and the portrayal of sexual intercourse outside of wedlock is tied up with risky, unwanted pregnancy.

Similarly, in *A Man of No Importance* (see Figure 1), the narrative moves forward at two levels. At the level of *exterior* struggle, Alfie attempts to stage a production of Oscar Wilde's play *Salomé* in a society that is closed, inward looking and censorious. This is matched by the *interior* struggle of his awakening sexuality. Figure 1 illustrates the two lines of narrative action – interior and exterior character engagement – displaying the complexity of character function within this film. Exterior action positions the character as a causal agent within the narrative: the role they perform as the story unfolds. It is shown through camera set-ups and eye-line matches, not from the unique spatial positioning of the character, but from a non-specific locale requiring the audience to infer the character's experience and point of view (Branigan, 1998: 103). The interior action is where the character, through internal focalization (such as point of view or voice-over), reveals an inner thought or feeling. These lines of action are determined by the *mise-en-scène* and how the character engages within the narrative, whether they share looks on screen or with the camera (interior action) or whether their point of view emanates from an undefined space within the frame (exterior action). Unlike *About Adam* and *When Brendan met Trudy,* these interior and exterior struggles progress in tandem to present a storyworld that is structured around dual conflict. Consequently, this presents more narrative space to explore the story from the individual's perspective (universal) and the community or society with which they are attached (the local), commenting at two levels, through individual voice and narrator.

On the other hand, *About Adam* and *When Brendan met Trudy* operate principally at one level, that of exterior action (see Figures 3 & 4). In contrast to *The Most Fertile Man in Ireland* and *A Man of No Importance*, Figures 3 and 4 reveal two narratives that are predominantly externally focalized. Because there is little revelation of the interior aspect of the characters (limits placed on the number of point of view shots), the narrative trajectory, as depicted in Figures 3 and 4, reveals stories that rely on what the characters 'say and do'

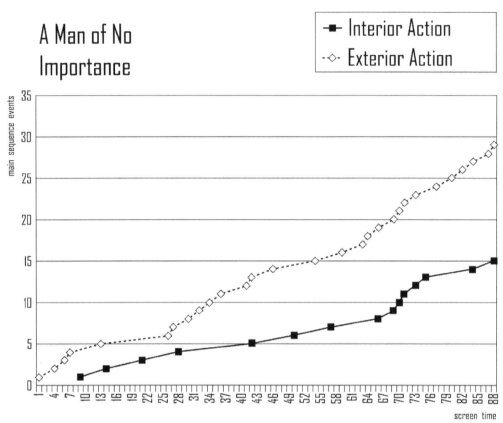

Figure 1: Interior and Exterior lines of action in *A Man of No Importance*.

rather than demonstrating them as 'seeing and hearing', manifesting in a dominance of exterior action and little interweaving between internal and external characterization. One of the consequences for the narrative experience is the absence of psychologically-complex characters, revealed through focalization.

From these figures, the volume of shots from a character's point of view is revealed (interior) alongside the level of action performed but not revealed from an identifiable diegetic position. While the characters become familiar through their action and performance, how they are thinking and feeling remains elusive. These figures reveal the diverse approach to narrative strategy among the films, as well as similar and common ground across the range. On the surface, *About Adam* is refreshing in its theme and visual style by presenting an imaginary world that is fun-filled and pleasurable. The narrative, in its self-conscious effort to represent an Ireland free of sexual guilt, presents a world where sex is the key to happiness, personal development and liberation, and Adam is charged with bringing that

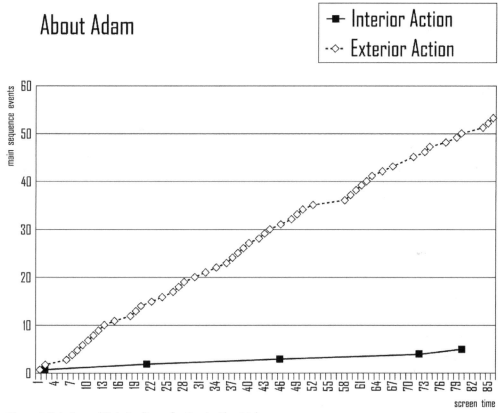

Figure 2: Interior and Exterior lines of action in *About Adam*.

gift to those who need it. In *About Adam*, most of the action is external or plot-driven and therefore externally focalized, as illustrated in Figure 2. The themes of sex and love, which are central to the narrative and the storyworld, are uncomplicated. This is evident primarily because of the absence of a narrative layer dealing with internal conflict. While the narrative is complicated in an interesting way along structural lines by the use of the episodic device, the absence of dual focalization negates the tension created by the playing out of opposites.

The narrative in *About Adam* is divided episodically into four sub-narratives: Lucy (Kate Hudson), Laura (Frances O'Connor), David (Alan Maher) and Alice (Charlotte Bradley). Adam's narrative function emerges within each of the four other narratives, in which he plays a central part. However, the only level of internal focalization in the four episodes is when each of these characters introduces their own narrative. What each character presents is Adam from their individual experience (not necessarily their point of view). The absence of an 'Adam' narrative, while clearly a structural device to pose questions, instead simply

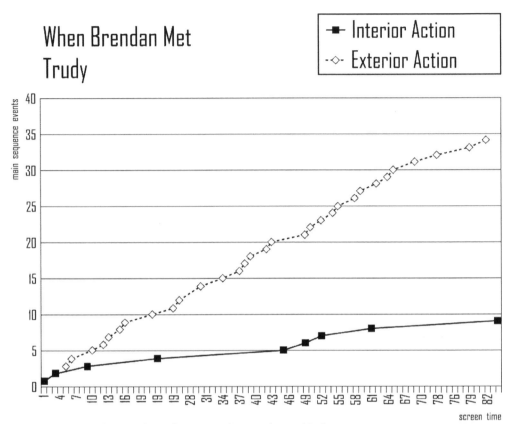

Figure 3: Interior and Exterior lines of action in _When Brendan met Trudy_.

functions to construct Adam as elusive, puzzling and superficial. According to Phil Parker in 'Reconstructing Narratives' (Parker, 2000: 66–74), for romance stories to be recognized, certain events need to be included in the narrative: a character that is emotionally lacking is introduced; a solution is presented; barriers to reaching this are erected; and the character ultimately overcomes these by rising to the challenge. For Northrop Frye,[4] the 'complete form of romance is clearly the successful quest, and such a completed form has three main stages: the stage of perilous journey and the preliminary minor adventures; the crucial struggle, usually some kind of battle in which either the hero or his foe, or both, must die; and the exaltation of the hero' (Frye, 1957: 187). Although cast within the genre of romantic comedy, which often conforms to these schema, the narrative in _About Adam_ negates such structural devices, principally because of the way Adam's character is constructed, presenting a greater challenge in figuring out what is at work. Is this narrative reacting against, deliberately challenging or simply negating the formal characteristics developed over time?

In story terms, Adam can be viewed as a prince-like character or 'fair', bringing each person he encounters his or her wish. An analysis of character, acc Vladimir Propp, suggests development in stages through the narrative, by performing functions 'which are an act of character, defined from the point of view of its significance for the course of action' (Berger, 1992: 14). Probing Adam's action and performance reveals character. After an encounter with Adam, each character is diegetically enriched and better-off, personally or professionally. Laura finally writes her thesis (by rejecting all her original ideas) and David gets to have sex with his girlfriend (after Adam has seduced her, transforming her from virgin to vamp). Even Alice finds her husband appealing after an encounter with Adam. Adam lends weight to this theory when he says to Alice 'would you believe me if I told you that when I am with people, I notice that they always want something from me and it does not annoy me, I really like it, I like to give people what they want if I can, whatever makes them happy it is a very easy thing for me to do'. In traditional fairy tales the prince emerges at the end to save the princess, while the fairy-godmother appears at key moments when she is needed. Adam's actions of seduction lead to a specific outcome for the other characters, one that enriches their lives, thus suggesting more fairy-godmother than prince.

Masculinity/ femininity

According to Jungian theory, each human embodies the masculine and feminine, the animus and anima, but society, or culture, prevents co-existence irrespective of gender. Post-Jungians regard patriarchy as the expression of the suppressed anima, which explains why the anima is aligned with the shadow in the psyche of contemporary males. Each of the four films discussed here, in their own way, is concerned with these issues, not so much in a representational way but through affirming a position on the subject. Along these lines, it is argued that these films present a universal theme (concerning the complex nature of masculinity and femininity) in a local setting, revealing the tensions therein when humans attempt to articulate outside the perceived norms. Unlike earlier Irish films which were concerned with issues of masculine and feminine identity in a political way (*Maeve*, Pat Murphy 1981; *Anne Devlin*, Pat Murphy 1984; *Poitín*, Bob Quinn 1978; *Reefer and the Model*, Joe Comerford 1988), the approach here is not to reveal the national or political dimension but rather the human or universal approach to this subject matter, as cognitive theorists would have it. At a thematic level, feminine and masculine identity is indeed political, but at a structural level the exploration serves the purpose of creating conflict and tension in the drama as it relates in a human way.

Arguably the most interesting exploration is in *The Most Fertile Man in Ireland* (see Figure 4) where, from the outset, Eamonn's 'feminine' side is presented in a progressive and appealing light. Figure 4 reveals the complexities and intricacies of the narrative when the interior and exterior levels of narration constantly entwine. Living in a society

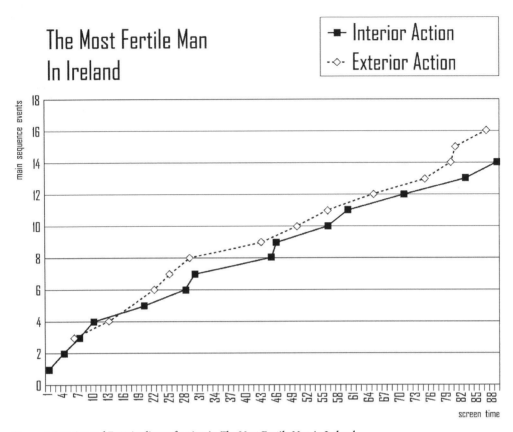

Figure 4: Interior and Exterior lines of action in *The Most Fertile Man in Ireland*.

of machismo values, Eamonn chooses to surround himself with the 'feminine' (the dating agency, buying flowers every day, being a confidant to his mother). When Mary seduces him he openly discusses his virginal status with anybody who will listen as he prepares for his first sexual experience. The barman presents him with a pint of Guinness: 'that'll sort you out, it's an aphrodisiac'. The taxi-driver advises him, 'It's like a ride on a bicycle. Take hold of the handlebars and keep peddling'. Like Alfie in *A Man of No Importance*, Eamonn is not averse to doing a spot of ironing. When he finally secures a first date with Rosie, he is keen to know what 'her Ma was like'. In both films, the main male character is complicated at the level of the masculine and the feminine. Alfie cooks 'exotic' meals, such as spaghetti bolognaise, for his sister Lily (Brenda Fricker) and he likes to dress up and put on make-up. This clearly contrasts with the portrayal of masculinity and femininity in *About Adam* and *When Brendan met Trudy*. Adam's masculinity is what defines him as 'predator' while Brendan's choir practice, his feminine pursuit, is plainly a source of fun and ridicule

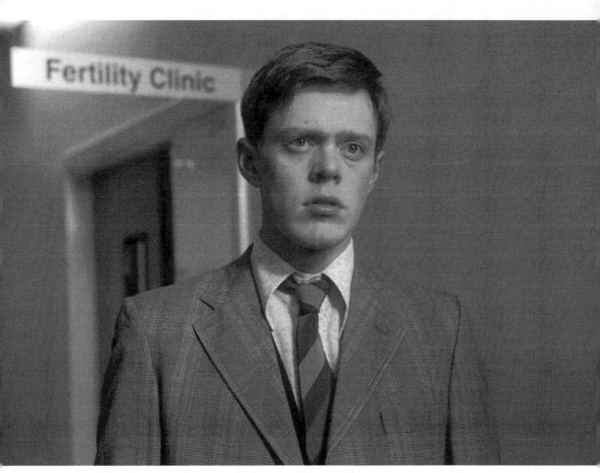

Kris Marshall in *The Most Fertile Man in Ireland*, courtesy of Samson Films.

within and outside the film – or, in Jungian terms, his shadow. It could be argued that the gendered roles are being subverted, particularly in *When Brendan met Trudy*, depending on whether the audience is invited to laugh with or at the character. However, the incongruity of the relationship and the dominant role Trudy occupies suggests that, far from being undermined, the roles are simply being reversed.

On the other hand, the portrayal of masculinity and femininity is challenged in their traditional sense in *The Most Fertile Man in Ireland*. Now that he is with Rosie, Eamonn faces losing her when she finds out about his 'virility'. According to Northrop Frye, 'comedy often includes a scapegoat ritual of expulsion which gets rid of some irreconcilable character' (Frye, 1957: 165); in film this often refers to negative aspects of characterization. Rather than being a bonus, Eamonn's hyper-potency is clearly his nemesis. Unlike Adam, whose virility is his most positive attribute and valued possession, Eamonn's extreme sexual powers threaten to ruin his relationship with Rosie. It also brings the wrath of the loyalist ringleader Mad Dog Billy Wilson down on him when the latter wants Eamonn to help increase the Protestant population by impregnating childless Protestant women. 'But your women are fat and ugly', Eamonn says. Billy Wilson replies, 'You are fucking for us now, boy!' As life gets more difficult and Eamonn is being presented with the challenge of 'using his gift to help others', he does not see it this way. 'Cut it off', Eamonn says, 'it's a monster and I don't want it anymore'. In keeping with Northrop Frye's *mythos* of romance whereby 'the enemy is associated with winter, darkness, confusion, sterility, moribund life and old age and the hero with spring, dawn, order, fertility, vigour and youth' (Frye, 1957: 187–8), *The Most Fertile Man in Ireland* taps into generic forms of character that transcend cultural determinations.

The tension between his masculine aspect and feminine side comes to a climax when Eamonn meets his father (old man versus new man). His father says to him, 'c'mon son, be a man about it', to which Eamonn replies, 'what the fuck does that mean?' While Eamonn's father clearly sees himself as 'a real man' and Eamonn's mother has enshrined his memory in this way by pretending that he is dead rather than acknowledging that he has betrayed her, the film presents 'contemporary' man through the character of Eamonn as far more complex, one that can allow the masculine and feminine, anima and animus to co-exist. Complicating the notion of 'manhood', *The Most Fertile Man in Ireland* seeks to position the traditional father figure as an anachronism. Furthermore, in post-ceasefire Ireland it could be argued that the traditional man has no future. Not only are the paramilitaries, who hang around telling everybody how fierce they are, now redundant, they are impotent and unable to keep the tribe going. The demands for narrative closure are met when Eamonn has a vasectomy after Rosie gives birth to twins. Knowing that 'other women will want him and that Eamonn will want to help', Rosie tells him that she cannot take him back. The only way he can be reunited with her is to undergo a vasectomy, much to the chagrin of Mad Dog Billy Wilson. The operation over, Rosie takes him back and the film ends on an image of Rosie, Eamonn, his father and the twins lounging in the hospital bed; traditional and modern Irish expressions of masculinity having found a space to co-exist. This film offers a counter-force to the new-lad influences (Ging, 2002) that dominate other recent Irish films, such as *I Went Down*, *Flick* and *Accelerator*.

Public versus private

Continuing the exploration of opposites as a primary device used in drama, these films play the public and private personae off each other in order to work through their separate narrative threads. A central narrative theme that activates the tensions between public and private is the need to keep secrets. In these four films, the heuristic aspect of the plots is fundamental to the unfolding stories. Not only is the notion of 'secrets' pivotal to universal narrative structure as a device for creating tension and conflict, it has played a key role in many aspects of Irish cultural history.[5] Significantly, each film scrutinized here uses secrecy not only as a narrative device (universal) but in a culturally-specific way to resonate locally. Despite the frivolity of films such as *About Adam* and *When Brendan met Trudy*, the underlying meaning within the wider body politic of the local and the global cannot be hidden.

In *A Man of No Importance*, the dual world that Alfie occupies is symbolized through the juxtaposition of the fictional world of reality (public) versus his world of theatre (private). The narrative device that interweaves the public and private manifests itself in his staging of *Salomé*, using the passengers on his bus as his cast. The narrative is complicated at the level of *mise-en-scène* by interweaving the public and private, interior and exterior action. The 'secret' in this film does not function as an enigmatic device that is simply concealed in order to be uncovered at a particular dramatic point in the narrative. Its role is much more central to the dramatic architecture. Not only is Alfie's concealed sexuality a dramatic theme, it functions also as a structural device. In the opening sequence of this film, it is clear (to the audience) that Alfie is in love with Robbie, his bus-driver – 'a love that dare not speak its name' – affectionately referring to Robbie as Bosie. As Alfie recites poetry, Robbie replies: 'You're at it again, big words, poetry. I'm going to find out who this Bosie is, better be a bloke, regular young fella, you know what I mean.' Robbie knows that Alfie is gay, thus representing the unofficial acceptance (private and secret), which contrasts with the official suppression (public) of homosexuality. The fictional structure necessitates the bringing together of the public and private narrative dimensions for effective narrative coherence. The only place that Alfie can be himself is in private – in his room that he keeps locked and concealed from public access. When the public and private converge, the secret is out. As Alfie encounters expressions of sex/love (Adele having sex with a stranger; Robbie kissing his girlfriend) in the public domain, he is motivated to finally 'come out'. As he quotes 'all that remains is the recollection of a pleasure or a regret', it becomes clear that, having brought his secret out into the public, he now faces the consequences.

In a society that seeks to repress at many levels, the consequences of breaking the spell of secrecy is often a positive and liberating outcome – used as a narrative device in this film. When Alfie cooks Lily's favourite dish, sweetbread, she responds, 'I couldn't touch a thing, when I think of where your hands have been.' 'That's the point, they've never been anywhere, I've never been close enough to anybody to rub up against them let alone lay my hands on them ... the one person I like, well love damn it ... yes Lily, it's a fella.' He finally brings his secret out into the public. 'So eat up, my arms are innocent of affection', he concludes poetically. The strength of this narrative, like that of *The Most Fertile Man in Ireland*, is in its interweaving of interior and exterior lines of action and the playing out of opposites. Bringing the theme of homosexuality from the private to the public, and thus breaking the spell of secrecy, corresponds to Alfie's awakening sexuality. By integrating the character development and exploration (universal) with the plot exposition of theme (local), the writer and director create a storyworld that resonates on two levels. This film indeed is reminiscent of films from the 1950s' and 1960s' British Social Realism (Hill, 1986) at the level of narrative and visual style, which may account for its perception as overtly sentimental and innocent. Geoffrey Macnab in *Sight & Sound* says that 'rather than acknowledge that Alfie is a victim of a prejudiced, repressive society, it persists in portraying its little corner of 60s' Dublin as a picture postcard community, full of loveable eccentrics' (Macnab, 1994: 50). However, far from looking back with nostalgia, this film has an edge to it, particularly in the 'coming out' scene, which is carefully crafted to eschew any definite positions. Not only is conventional society hostile to Alfie's sexuality, the gay community is not yet ready to embrace femininity alongside homosexuality and hence greets Alfie's 'outing' with a violent and brutal response.

This contrasts with the films *About Adam* and *When Brendan met Trudy*, where the interior line of action and thought is sparse, almost non-existent, and submerged in the shadow of the external line of action. *About Adam*'s story is structured around a secret but, in this case, Adam is reliant on the sisters (and possibly their mother) keeping a secret from each other – that they all had sex with Adam. The episodic narrative style is interesting in suggesting an Adam of many different personae. However, when examined more closely, it is a narrative of Adam: a chameleon that produces a persona to suit every occasion. While the proposal scene is used in each narrative to present different perspectives, it reveals Adam's ability to switch. Adam plays the role that other characters want him to play rather than presenting different character layers. In the absence of internal focalization, the 'Adam' character is never revealed, which has the effect of creating an enigma, but to what narrative end is unclear.

When Laura asks if he is going to tell Lucy about them, Adam replies, 'God no, your whole family would disown you, you would be denounced as a jezebel, Laura, I couldn't bear to see you treated that way, I'm crazy about you, what I feel, it's like you said, it's not about settling down and planning our whole lives together, it's a different kind of passion.' Rather than pleading with her to keep their secret, he turns the tables and persuades her that it is in her best interests. Laura's voice-over replies, 'Oh Laura, just go with it.' Adam's powers of persuasion mean that Laura will keep a secret from her sister and finally write her thesis, but first she must revoke her original ideas: 'Those women, those stupid women, my Victorian women putting all that mad passion into their novels and their poems instead of just doing it.' Secrecy is a central theme and strategy of this narrative. Adam is reliant on all the characters subscribing to his world of secrets, unbeknownst to each other. Far from being a progressive, modern take on contemporary Ireland, by rejecting the device of opposites, this narrative sanctions 'secrecy' as being good for everyone. When Lucy wants to tell Adam that she slept with Simon before going through with the wedding, he silences her: 'We all need to have secrets Lucy. I'm not going to tell you mine.' Rather than sustaining the air of mystery or enigma attached to Adam's persona, he simply silences her so as to survive: a survival technique used by many public figures in recent Irish history (clerics, politicians, bankers *et al*).

Ironically, if read along certain lines, it could be argued that this film presents a more conservative and nativist portrayal of sex than the other films. While most of the film reviewers appear to have taken their lead from the pre-publicity of the film and therefore failed to see its inherent contradiction, one reviewer questioned its sexual politics. Ciara Dwyer in *The Sunday Independent* says 'screwing around I can cope with. Infidelities are fine. But sisters betraying each other without a smidgin of guilt? Not an ounce of moral conscience? This I cannot swallow' (Dwyer, 2001: 2L). After interviewing the main actor, Stuart Townsend, who persuaded her to give the film a second chance, she concluded by saying 'and in the end I [didn't] believe the film'. The film, in its efforts to be modern and sophisticated, negates the use of multiple formal features of drama to explore conflict. Sex is presented in a unidimensional way as a gift from Adam. In the absence of a counter force, while gratification is achieved in terms of entertainment or pleasure rather than bliss, the narrative fails to resonate or linger at a deeper level.

Far from presenting a narrative symbolic of the perceived 'new' Ireland of openness and pluralism, this film relies on the negative characteristics of deception and secrecy as central to its narrative coherence. And yet, if one does 'lighten up' and look for meaning in this film through its generic counterparts, what emerges? Celestino Deleyto notes the resilience of romantic comedy, which may be due to 'the powerful need in human beings to believe in the utopian possibilities condensed in the image of the couple, or … to the irresistible attraction of the notion of love' (Deleyto, 2003: 167). While audiences may no longer believe in the traditional values attached to love, the genre of romantic comedy provides an outlet for entertainment and emotion, with more recent genre examples confirming the 'presence of a postmodern aesthetic of ironic vampirization of tradition rituals' (Deleyto, 2003: 170). While *About Adam* scoffs at the traditional expectations of romance, its ending is not so much ironic as sinister. While an analogy has been drawn with Pasolini's *Theorem* (1968), it could be argued that, like *Intermission*, this film displays the unease Irish film has with its Hollywood influences without embracing the intentions of European art cinema. Pasolini's film is about destroying the bourgeois family and hence functions politically, whereas *About Adam* appears to celebrate it, secrets and all.

Critics and audience alike responded very positively to this film because it marked a break with what has come to be accepted as 'Irish film'.[6] Desmond Traynor in *Film Ireland* referred to it as 'a defining moment in the growth to emotional maturity (if that's not too boring a concept to introduce in this context) of indigenous Irish Cinema' (Traynor, 2001: 43) and, at the level of visual style, it does mark a break with the past. However, the potential offered from the episodic, multi-layered narrative style is largely negated by the absence of an interweaving exterior and interior line of action. On first viewing it presents a fun-filled experience, principally of visual pleasure and excess. However, unease lingers when the sexual politics are mulled over and subsequent viewings induce a level of suspicion, particularly around Adam's character and motivation. When Jake Wilson (2003) says, talking about *Love and Other Catastrophes,* that 'at the time, [it] felt silly and delightful; seen again today, it's all too obvious that just about everything in the preceding ninety minutes is driven by a related, faintly irritating narcissism', he could easily be referring to *About Adam.* If a mark of narrative coherence and complexity is one that reveals layers and demands re-visits, when the froth is blown away from the surface of this film subsequent viewings unveil an endorsement of old ways rather than new, where the public and private function to keep people in a controlled place.

Conclusion

The Most Fertile Man in Ireland and *A Man of No Importance,* by creating an internal and external dimension to their main characters, present a subversive discourse that has been overlooked heretofore. The conflict played out between Eamonn's internal and external struggle, his masculinity and femininity, his desire for love and sexual gratification is what complicates this narrative, and contributes to a structure of 'discovery and reconciliation'. By creating these layers through using the full range of story devices, this film presents a storyworld that acts simultaneously as an expression of the universal with some sharp local commentary. *A Man of No Importance* shows the journey towards the sexual awakening of Alfie as he explores his internal struggle. This is mirrored through the exterior line of action, which is his attempt to bring his community together through the staging of *Salomé,* in a closed, conservative society. Alfie's interior and exterior struggles constantly intertwine, as does his masculinity and femininity, until one becomes dominant. In the scene when Alfie bravely goes out dressed in his Wildean garb, the feminine dominates by giving expression to his hidden secret. At this moment Alfie has reached the point of sexual awakening. However, with it comes the trauma of rejection and assault. Far from presenting a sentimental, nostalgic picture of 'coming out', it is the gay community who reject Alfie foremost and most aggressively as he appears to transgress the acceptable norms of 'deviancy'. It is narratively challenging and interesting that Alfie's attackers come from within the gay community and unusual in representational terms that it is among his own domestic community where he receives acceptance and support. The complicated and complex multi-layered narrative (that allows the interior and exterior struggles to weave and coil) gives rise to a storyworld addressing both the universal and the local. When Alfie is found beaten and bruised he encounters the obvious discriminatory comments, but the people who matter (Lily, Robbie, Adele) acknowledge and endorse who he is, tapping into a level of contradiction in the local environment.

This more complex address is clearly absent from *About Adam* and *When Brendan met Trudy,* not just at the level of content but, arguably more importantly, at the level of form. While

sticking stylistically and visually to the genre of romantic comedy, it is at the level of different
that local inflections emerge. Although there are attempts to mark off this film from earlier
portrayals of Ireland, and Dublin city in particular, lurking beneath the surface are remnants
of a traditional past. In *About Adam*, the old Ireland is very much alive and kicking: the Ireland
where a woman's place is clearly with her man, where family relationships are shrouded in
secrecy, where sex is hidden and not discussed. In its attempts to be modern and progressive,
it could be argued that, ironically, this film is more traditional and nativist. By rejecting
structural complexity, Adam's character simply performs functions within the narrative that
are devoid of challenge, conquest or resonance. The interior layer of *When Brendan met Trudy*,
while present diegetically, is often unclear in terms of purpose. The internally-focalized shots
of Brendan the teacher gazing out of the window fail to present an explanation – what is his
interior struggle about? Unlike Eamonn or Alfie, Brendan's purpose or function within the
storyworld is cloudy and, as a result, the narrative is compelled to rely on self-conscious, self-
reflexive signifiers (inter-textual references to the Nouvelle Vague being the most dominant)
that simply jar the story in a postmodern way. This approach to structure and focalization may
also account for the confusion around Adam's character. While his role and function is more
obvious than that of Brendan, the deliberate rejection of any internal focalization leaves him
elusive. While there is an argument to be made that these films present shallow characters for
a shallow postmodern world, maybe these films present new pleasures for this new age.

The self-reflexive references in *When Brendan met Trudy* are clearly deliberate in narrative
terms, echoing a recurring tradition in cinema revived by *Pulp Fiction* (Quentin Tarantino
1994). However, when used elsewhere (*À Bout de Souffle*, Jean-Luc Godard, 1959), they
function as quotes or comic notes in addition to the story and have an important extra-textual
function, rather than dominating the narrative flow. Although *When Brendan met Trudy*
has a cinematic message to impart, unlike *À Bout de Souffle*, which was Godard's attempt at
simultaneously challenging the dominance of Hollywood and paying homage to its auteurs,
the function here is unclear. Inter-textual references are often embedded in the narrative in
order to be effective. However, these references in *When Brendan met Trudy* serve no inter- or
intra-textual function because they do not relate in a focalized way to Brendan's character.
They are separate and distinct from his function as an agent within the narrative.

Godfrey Cheshire identifies an inherent problem with Irish film narratives in that they
place 'commercial' in opposition to 'worthy': commercial attracts negative connotations
while 'worthy' has been celebrated (Cheshire, 2001). In broad terms there has been a
tendency to perceive the first wave of Irish film as realistic, artistic and challenging whereas
the more recent second wave is regarded as superficial and commercial. The analysis offered
here of *The Most Fertile Man in Ireland* and *A Man of No Importance* suggests that genre or
imaginative films can be 'worthy' *and* 'commercial' by offering entertaining material that
has an inter-textual commentary to impart. It could be argued that the satirical approach in
The Most Fertile Man in Ireland has been overlooked while the ironic dimension in *About
Adam* has been over-celebrated. *About Adam* and *When Brendan met Trudy* display an urge
not 'to be shackled to the initial paradigm' (Cheshire, 2001), a feature of film in Ireland since

ờ

97) which sought to put distance between new Irish cinema and what is
film' – a preoccupation with the 'Troubles', the Catholic Church and rural
)s.

_rgued here that the films generating least comment (*The Most Fertile
Man in Ireland* and *A Man of No Importance*) are the films that reveal more depth about
contemporary Ireland by using the full range of narrative devices of interior and exterior
space. Ironically, these films situate their storyworlds within the representative space of
Northern Ireland and 1960s' Ireland. While giving expression to the universal, they also echo
local preoccupations. According to Dudi Appleton, like Pat Murphy twenty years before
him, he was responding to media images of his environment that failed to correspond to
the reality he lived in, hence he was driven to portray Northern Ireland differently. While it
could be said that his motivation was not all that different from Gerry Stembridge's response
to 'his Dublin', the use of narrative layers create a resonance absent in the other film.

Notes

1. The US film critic Godfrey Cheshire delivered a paper at the Galway Film Fleadh (13 July 2001)
   entitled 'The State of Irish Cinema in the Light of Changing World Cinema'. An edited version of
   the paper was published in *The Irish Times* (16 July 2001: 9). At the time Godfery Cheshire was the
   film editor and senior film critic for the *New York Press* and a contributing film critic to *Variety*.
   His visit to the Galway Film Fleadh was part of the Arts Council's *Critical Voices* programme,
   in partnership with *The Irish Times* and *Lyric fm*. The purpose of the programme was to bring
   international writers, critics and artists to observe the cultural scene in Ireland and to participate
   in public debate.
2. Stembridge's earlier film, *Guiltrip* (1995), is political in a different way. Released just before the
   Divorce Referendum in 1995, it tells the story of psychological abuse within marriage.
3. Interestingly, in a recent interview Gerry Stembridge stated that he would not make the film *About
   Adam* in this way now, suggesting that the developing Ireland (or Dublin) of the late 1990s did not
   mature into the expected advanced, progressive society of Stembridge's imagination.
4. It was with the publication of *Anatomy of Criticism* in 1957, exploring literary symbolism and
   structure, that Frye became internationally regarded as a literary theorist. He subsequently wrote
   over twenty books on Western literature, culture, myth and archetypal theory. While his work now
   is sometimes regarded as having a 'distinguished obsolescence', it is still useful and important to
   formal analysis, and easily adaptable to film discourse.
5. As a colonized nation that rebelled against its colonial power, the place of secret societies was
   essential to aspects of Irish life at particular historical moments. More recently, the revelations over
   the past ten years of endemic child abuse at almost every level of Irish life (the family, religious
   orders, educational and reform institutions), have uncovered another layer of secrecy that was
   woven into the very fabric of Irish life and thus protected the abuser for many decades by keeping
   their secrets.
6. It took IR£158,000 from 42 screens in its first seven days on release. This made it at the time the
   highest-grossing Irish film released by Buena Vista, whose previous biggest success was *I Went
   Down* which took IR£137,000 on its opening week. Source: *The Irish Times*, 31 Jan. 2001.

Chapter 4

Immersed in Two Traditions - *Adam & Paul*, *Garage* and *Prosperity*

The request is universal: we like to hear stories, known to be fictive or believed to be true, and the impulse to shape our experiences or desires in narrative form and thereby to control and share them is a fundamental human trait. Both teller and listener must have a command of the basic rules according to which narrative utterances can be generated and understood. (Zimmermann, 2001: 9)

This chapter examines the various links between contemporary screen stories and other narrative traditions in Ireland. While it is fair to assume a connection between Ireland's international recognition and success in literature and drama during the twentieth century and the path developed in contemporary dramatic writing for screen, it has led to a certain expectation not often realized. Much of the criticism of contemporary Irish film targets the scriptwriting and storytelling processes more so than direction and visual style. In this context, the work of director Lenny Abrahamson and writer Mark O'Halloran presents an interesting case study, principally because of the critical and commercial success of *Adam & Paul* (2004) and *Garage* (2007). These films, alongside the four-part television drama series *Prosperity* (2007), reveal much about the links between Ireland's dramatic heritage and contemporary screen productions. In terms of pre-compositional factors, the set-up behind these films is worth mentioning. Mark O'Halloran, a professional actor, has performed in many productions in Galway's Druid Theatre, the Lyric in Belfast and the Gate in Dublin and has written and directed for the stage. He plays the role of Adam in the film *Adam & Paul*. Lenny Abrahamson worked in television commercials before he directed feature films – his best known is the popular and successful 'flatmates' *Carlsberg* advertisement. This creative trajectory is significant at two levels. The films they collaborate on, as will be illustrated, create a link to Ireland's cultural heritage through visual and narrative reference, yet the experience of the writer/director team is more rooted to contemporary media and art forms, revealed through the deeper narrative structure.

Most reviewers and critics, responding to the work of Lenny Abrahamson and Mark O'Halloran, identify the debt owed to Irish writers such as Samuel Beckett and James Joyce as well as early narrators of the silent era of cinema, Charlie Chaplin, Laurel and Hardy and Buster Keaton (Gillespie, 2008; Monahan, 2006). In interviews, Abrahamson himself highlights his own Jewish background and the influence vaudeville has had on his work. These connections are more playful in their ease of recognition rather than taxing in terms of symbolism. Scenes constructing the hapless approach to the characterization of Paul (Tom Murphy) evoke the mood and tone of *Waiting for Godot* (Beckett, 1948/49). Early in the film

Paul stumbles into the path of a passing moped, causing him to limp for the rest of the film. Later on, while minding his own business, he gets struck across the head by a passing football in St. Stephen's Green. The irritating stone in his shoe is more than simply a literary and visual coincidence, clearly evoking, even re-imagining Estragon, for a contemporary audience. A description of *Waiting for Godot* with words such as poignancy, oppression, camaraderie, hope and bewilderment could easily be mistaken for a summary of *Adam & Paul*. The existential nature of Beckett's *Godot*, the search for meaning in the human experience on earth and the minimalist style and aesthetic are paralleled in these works.

Michael Patrick Gillespie (2006) also identifies literary parallels by suggesting that '*Adam & Paul* attempts nothing less than a cinematic treatment of early twenty-first century Dublin that matches Joyce's literary portrait of one hundred years earlier', not an unusual imagining in new Irish cinema. Evoking the 'city' in a range of guises is an identifiable trope of cinema representation of the past fifteen years and, such is the prolific nature of Joyce's leitmotif of the city and the *flâneur* in the consciousness of Irish cultural and literary life, that to see it reinvented and re-imagined many times over is relevant to discussions of contemporary film. For example *Bachelors Walk* (2000/1, John Carney & Tom Hall) imagines the city in a state of flux. Far from the 'reality' of car-clamping, commuting and almost full employment during the boom years, this drama suggests a more traditional Ireland, evoking Joyce's *Ulysses*, whereby bumping into friends and dropping everything to go for a pint in Mulligan's on Poolbeg Street is the order of the day. Themes such as community and group identity are articulated at one level, particularly in the protected world created inside the house on Bachelors Walk where the 'kitchen table', another visual device of Irish screen stories (*Tolka Row*, 1964–69; *The Riordans*, 1965–79; *Glenroe*, 1983–2001), is resurrected and centrally placed. On the outside, experiences of alienation and confusion dominate: the three main characters can neither secure employment nor are successful romantically, either aimlessly wandering the city streets or chasing opportunities, only to end in a cul-de-sac.

Barry Monahan (2006), commenting on *Adam & Paul*, points out that because these similarities (between Joyce and Beckett for example) in terms of characterization and mood 'were so evident … few of the journalistic critics ventured to assess the extent of the resemblances'. Although Monahan suggests that the way the various appropriations from Beckett are used to explore and develop themes relevant to contemporary Ireland, it is suggested here that looking for formal parallels in this way might be a distraction. Certainly recognizing the links between these contemporary narratives and their literary and film antecedents is important but probing why such references are both apt, for the text itself and also relevant and recognizable to the viewer/critic, is arguably more culturally significant. While the visual representation is widespread across a range of limited narratives, the function and purpose is diverse and complex. These connections are easy to make at a textual level but, when a closer narrative examination takes place, the links between this literary tradition and contemporary Irish screenwriting is less definite. Although contemporary writers and directors owe a lot to the literary traditions of Ireland, they are not bound by them. By making references to them, they are acknowledging the legacy. Yet these productions are not necessarily important for these links but because of the way they carve and cast cinema in Ireland in a contemporary way.

Irish social realism

The visual and narrative references to Ireland's great literary tradition, therefore, are obvious. However, looking closely at the work of Abrahamson and O'Halloran might suggest that the legacy left for contemporary Irish screenwriters and directors lies not, as one might think, in the writings of Joyce, Beckett, Shaw, Synge *et al*, but, rather, much more recently – in the field of television and recent dramatic forms. O'Halloran, as an actor, brings with him the dramatic traditions of the stage while Abrahamson, with experience in the advertising world, has a very keen narrative sense. Skills of theatrical dramatic form meet the discipline of telling sharp, succinct stories, shaping this body of work in a particular way. If we look towards popular culture in the technological age as an area of influence for contemporary Irish screenwriters and directors, more light might be shed on the nuances of dramatic form over the past fifteen years.

These writers and directors grew up in the televisual age and, for many of them living outside Dublin in the 1970s and 1980s, the experience of television was restricted to just one channel (RTÉ 1), a situation familiar to Mark O'Halloran who grew up in Ennis, Co. Clare. The east coast of Ireland received television signals from Britain, with BBC and ITV beamed into many Irish homes – Lenny Abrahamson's experience of television as a child and teenager growing up in Dublin in the 1970s and 1980s. This meant that east-coast audiences, and those working within RTÉ, were exposed to high-quality BBC drama from early on. RTÉ, therefore, because of its proximity to Britain, came under the influence of the BBC on a number of levels. In the early years many personnel were BBC-trained, returning to Ireland in the 1960s and 1970s with experience of public service broadcasting, filtering that back into the creative process through programme-making, not just in news and current affairs but also in television drama. Because the east-coast audience was exposed to the tradition of BBC drama, which was generally regarded as having 'a level of prestige and autonomy ... exceptional in terms of the marketing outlooks and vertical power structures that characterize broadcasting organizations' (Gibbons, 1996: 45), the bar was set quite high for Irish television drama. In the 1970s, therefore, Irish audiences were exposed to a diet of single plays and serial dramas of a quality and volume unparalleled for a country of its size. In the case of Abrahamson and O'Halloran, this tradition of television drama is reflected throughout their collaborations 30 years on and re-invented for a contemporary audience. Taking this point further, while influences of popular culture through the movies have been noted in the work of many Irish screenwriters and directors, the impact of television drama in both narrative theme and narrative scale is equally significant for this generation.

This tradition is clearly evident in stories concerned with social themes and issues. While the portrayal of social exclusion and social deprivation reveals the legacy of social realism in many contemporary Irish films, these films are not hindered by the potentially 'dead hand' approach. Social realism evolved from realism, a term with multiple definitions but most associated in television drama with 'kitchen sink' drama, soap opera, etc. Its affiliation to film is historically more complex, surfacing in many European movements – from the 1930s in France and 1950s, 1960s and 1970s in Britain – while also having a complex and topical relationship with Hollywood. Realism is linked to verisimilitude, differing from naturalism by drawing attention to 'truth'. As a concept, realism has a powerful philosophical thrust, relying on an ideological commitment to an objective, external reality (whether of timeless universal abstract notions like 'human nature', or of historical but objective facts like class struggle) (Cook, 1992). The status of external reality is privileged over its representation, i.e. we look through the representation for a 'truth' beyond, or else some kind of cultural resonance, significance or explanation. Realism can then be understood as an aesthetic construct dependent upon a set of artistic conventions and forms.

Social Realism developed in British cinema in the 1960s, in particular, and like other political movements in the field of cinema (French New Wave, Italian Neorealism for example) emerged as a result of critical writings in film journals. Lindsay Anderson and Karel Reisz argued in the seminal film publication *Sight & Sound* for a new type of film 'which would discard out-moded artifice in favour of the simplicity and freshness of personal observation of every day reality' (Cook, 1992: 147). As socialists, these critics/writers pitted themselves against the artificiality of Hollywood and requested a personal poetic observation of reality, giving rise to the documentary forerunner of British Social Realism known as Free Cinema. Like all movements, it lasted just as long as it was commercially viable and its formation policy remained intact – in this case its adherence to realism. The films directed by Lindsay Anderson (*If....*, 1968), Tony Richardson (*A Taste of Honey*, 1961) and Karel Reisz (*Saturday Night and Sunday Morning*, 1960) were generally centred on themes that embodied issues of class, sex and youth, exploring what became known as the social-problem film, demonstrating a committed left-wing view of British films and an interest in artistic form. This aesthetic and narrative form was appropriated into television drama in the 1960s, notably in such groundbreaking productions as Ken Loach's *Cathy Come Home* (1966) and *Kes* (1970), continuing the tradition of observational style, long takes and improvisation. These productions brought a political edge to the realism approach by combining the specific subject matter with a distinctive aesthetic approach.

As Helena Sheehan has meticulously documented (Sheehan, 1988) and Luke Gibbons argues (Gibbons, 1996), Ireland's output of television drama in the 1960s and 1970s was remarkable for a country of its size and the infancy of its broadcasting service. While the 1960s was characterized by a predominance of Abbey Theatre stage play adaptations, the 1970s was the most innovative decade for the eclectic range of dramatic productions. Ireland's close proximity to Britain and its nearest competitor, the BBC, meant the standards of production values were set very high. A strong tradition of social realism drama filtered through and surfaced in the work of writers and directors of television drama in Ireland in the 1970s, in such notable productions as *A Week in the Life of Martin Cluxton* (Brian McLoughlin, 1971).

Telling the story of a male youth just released from a reform school in the West of Ireland and how he tries to re-integrate into society in the absence of any state support or efforts at rehabilitation, this drama can be seen as a political drama in a similar vein to *Cathy Come Home*. McLoughlin mixes documentary-style approaches such as the voice-over and direct address to the camera with fictional drama, portraying urban Dublin through an aesthetic of social realism. While not having the same political impact as *Cathy Come Home*, *A Week in the Life of Martin Cluxton* is an important historical document in revealing the close relations between British traditions and the nascent television station in Ireland of the 1970s. Irish writers, producers and directors were exposed to and familiar with weekly BBC television drama, consequently their work was both innovative and experimental.

How this is relevant now is in the work of Lenny Abrahamson and Mark O'Halloran, who tell stories about those living on the edge of society who may be perceived as marginalized and socially excluded. While aesthetically suggesting a debt to social realism and embodying a philosophical thrust towards a perceived reality, these films deviate by leaning towards a 'global vernacular', to borrow Miriam Hansen's phrase. The stories are located in an Irish milieu and the characterization is identifiably local; at the same time they speak about a modern experience the world over. A close reading of these narratives suggests that, rather than pointing to a 'reality' defined politically, socially or economically, these films establish a link to the experience of what it means to be 'emotionally human' in all its complexity, influenced but not wholly defined by external experience. These films link to the tradition of drama evolving in Ireland over a thirty-year period, small scale and televisual, yet the address reaches out beyond the periphery, reflecting the literary traditions referenced in the texts. Taken as a whole, these productions suggest that the shared experience is one of 'modernity', crossing a range of cultural groups. In doing so, rather than representing these characters as 'other' or 'them', the narrative implicates the audience on an emotional level through empathy and imagination, an argument that will be explored in detail later.

Narrative address – action line

What makes the narrative address of Abrahamson and O'Halloran across a range of productions, from film to television drama, particularly pertinent at this critical juncture in Irish cinema? A common thread in all three productions is a unique approach to dialogue and action in particular, which focuses on the ordinary. While the coming of sound in film afforded a greater realism and led to dialogue-laden narratives, O'Halloran and Abrahamson choose sparseness over verbal articulation, yet these are not silent films. The link between dialogue and action is significant in revealing the legacy left by literary and film traditions already mentioned, internalized through the artistic expression of these stories but also the story function of these films. It could be argued that the central narrative purpose of these productions is an attempt to narrate internal human emotions, even when they appear illusive. The acting styles adopted here are intrinsically linked to the narrative theme, mood and tone. According to Paul McDonald, writing on film acting, 'the role played by the actor can be divided between the "agent", or narrative function, and the "character" formed from a set of individuating traits and peculiarities' (Hill & Church-Gibson, 1998: 31–2).

It is this combination articulated through voice and body, with an emphasis on 'physicality' and performance of the everyday, that distinguishes these films – an approach first executed by Abrahamson in his earlier half-hour drama *3 Joes* (1991). In this film, the three flat-mates go about their daily tasks: eating breakfast, hanging out laundry and smoking cigarettes, in a beautifully-shot and carefully-crafted depiction of the ordinary. The mundanity of the everyday becomes dramatic as Adam and Paul aimlessly wander the streets of Dublin; while Josie in *Garage* gives the attention demanded of much more complex behaviour to very ordinary everyday actions. The presence of these characters in almost every scene of the film allows for a closely-engaged study of their human emotional states through the action, motion and mood depicted, albeit in the absence of an over-reliance of the close-up shot. The camera remains at a distance, filming in long and medium shots, to observe and reveal the character or their situation on a gradual basis. Far from exposing Stacey's interior state in *Prosperity* through internally-focalized point of view close-up shots, the audience becomes acquainted through observation of daily, routine, and ordinary activity, performed through voice, gesture and movement.

Telling the story of two junkies trying to score a heroin fix, the narrative of *Adam & Paul* follows them on their journey over one day. Reading like a fly-on-the-wall documentary, this film contrasts with *Disco Pigs*, explored earlier in the book, a film also dealing with social exclusion and male existential angst. Told through the prism of 'a day in the life', *Adam & Paul* portrays the hapless, aimless life of the drug addict where they never know where they will wake up but, when they do, their driving force is centred around achieving release from withdrawal and getting a heroin fix. The film opens on coastal wasteland where Adam and Paul have spent the night, evoking a similar yet less-romanticized landscape to *Disco Pigs*. The musical score by Stephen Rennicks sets the mood and tone of the film, which combines comedy with tragedy as it follows the two protagonists on their quest. Close-up shots of wild flowers and plants negate the potentially-gritty urban realism often associated with drug-addiction films, the concrete jungle being the conventional signifier, yet neither detracts from the tragic effect nor romanticizes this existence through visualization of nature. The combined music and visuals in this opening sequence prime the audience more for Laurel and Hardy films (1920s–50s) than *Trainspotting* (Danny Boyle, 1996), with a distinctive Eastern European aural aesthetic – the first indication that this narrative challenges expectations and deviates from the social-realism norm.

Eschewing the potential of character identification, the audience does not learn who is Adam and who is Paul until the credits roll at the end of the film. Instead, what is presented through the storyworld is the portrayal of a problem through the agency of two characters rather than two individual characters pursuing some goal: identification takes place at the level of Adam (Mark O'Halloran) and Paul (Tom Murphy) *as one*. Its similarities to *Disco Pigs* principally lie within the construction of characterization. In one respect, these characters

Adam and Paul (Tom Murphy and Mark O'Halloran), courtesy of Lenny Abrahamson.

ιown as 'victims' of an unjust society. While Adam and Paul's social environment is
, the absence of a contrasting depiction eludes the sociological statement that these
are society's 'fall guys'. While they are shown in the context of their own social grouping,
they remain outside of this and on the edge, in the pub and in the park. In dramatic terms
the characterization of Adam and Paul suggests that their lot in life is a combination of free
will and fate. Neither fated through social or economic circumstances, nor immune to wider
forces, it is suggested that they are in this situation as a result of a combination of factors.
On the one hand, just like the characters in *Disco Pigs,* there is a fatalistic element to their
story but, as a result of choices they make, that fatalism is their own doing. This is suggested
in other narrative layers. As the narrative progresses, characters are encountered who chose
an alternative route (Janine) or met an alternative end (Matthew), counteracting a simplistic
encapsulation of the drug-addict theme.

The narrational motivation is at the level of a complex and unusual characterization
throughout the film, yet the audience rarely gets a glimpse of the world from the characters'
point of view. The characters are articulated through their actions and dialogue: what they
'say and do' rather than 'see and hear'. Potentially hindering in terms of narrative resonance
because the focus is on external activity, this approach manages to articulate at a level beneath
the surface. In this instance, the effect is to facilitate emotional involvement without voyeuristic
gratification. The earliest piece of action evokes the absurdity of the tale when Adam wakes to
find himself glued to the mattress he has just spent the night sleeping on. Like a devoted yet
fussy spouse, Paul, in his hapless way, attempts to disengage Adam. Helping him to take off his
clothes and retrieve his glued jacket from the mattress as Adam shivers in the cold morning air
half naked, Paul comments on the jacket's source of origin, Bulgaria, starting a dialogue that
will continue throughout the film – irrelevant but deeply revealing.

In a scene visually evocative of the Irish short *He Shoots, He Scores* (John Moore, 1995)
(also a *Godot* re-imagining), Adam and Paul wait for a bus against the backdrop of the old
Ballymun, before regeneration. In contrast to the romanticizing of urban deprivation by
Hollywood and British films (*Into the West*, Mike Newell 1992; *The Commitments*, Alan
Parker 1991), there are no shots of children swinging out of lamp posts or horses in the
tower blocks. Instead, shot with a tungsten tinge of blue, this film continues the evocation
of Dublin city and suburbs as 'anywhere', grey and desolate, set up in the opening sequence.
This place could be any modern Western European city dogged by the ubiquitous problems
of social deprivation, drug abuse and alienation. At the same time, the two characters
suggest a misplaced pride in a city that clearly has not served them well. While many films
of this period sought to invoke a new 'hip', trendy city that had come of age (*About Adam*,
Gerry Stembridge 2001; *Snakes and Ladders,* Trish McAdam 1996; *Goldfish Memory*, Liz
Gill 2003), *Adam & Paul* negate the pleasure of familiarity and identification by showing
a series of Spar shops, anonymous office blocks and commercial areas dominated by glass
facades. Continuing the *Godot* theme, this film evokes the alienating, fragmented space
of modernity, eschewing the romanticized portrayal of Dublin city. Yet in a contradictory
parallel narrative the film suggests the 'village' approach of Joyce's Dublin, re-imagined and

romantically invoked in many recent films as a city modern yet friendly. In their search for heroin, and in an attempt to while away the day, Adam and Paul embark on their journey into town to see what is going on and who is around. They head for the city-centre park, St. Stephen's Green, where they meet a gang they know who are both friendly and hostile. As the action continuously confounds the dialogue, it is revealed that little or nothing is going on beyond tossing a football and drinking beer: hanging around is the order of the day.

Garage similarly places an externally-focalized emphasis on action while sparsely distributing the dialogue in the narrative: when characters speak, it is generally idle and platitudinous. In the opening sequences of Abrahamson and O'Halloran's second feature, the audience is introduced to the main character Josie (Pat Shortt) as he goes about his daily chores in the garage where he is employed. Putting distance between traditional representations of Ireland through landscape (either the romanticizing of the landscape as in British and American constructions of Ireland (*Ryan's Daughter*, David Lean, 1970; *The Quiet Man*, John Ford, 1952) or the harsh realism of Joe Comerfored (*High Boot Benny*, 1994) and Bob Quinn (*Poitín*, 1978)), this film, like *Adam & Paul* and *Prosperity*, portrays the characters firmly within the landscape but neither contained nor constructed by it. The opening shot tracks Josie on his way to work across the desolate featureless landscape of the bog, evoking the natural countryside that surrounds him but does not define him. The beauty is visualized but in an understated way, with a visual style more aligned to European cinema than mainstream Hollywood. Josie, like Adam and Paul, is surrounded by beauty but, equally, desolation.

As Josie arrives at his place of work, with the boss already there, he launches into the apologetic mode that is his trademark. Trading in platitudes, the brief exchange, which has the owner announcing that the garage will open late and sees Josie pitching his idea about the oils, reveals an atmosphere similar to *Adam & Paul* and *Prosperity*: the pace of life is slow; not much goes on; the characters passively exist almost as extras or bystanders in their own lives. They go about their daily routine with an attention to mundane detail; when engaged in dialogue they do not say much. In the absence of a deeper emotional articulation, the emphasis on corporeal activity defines the characterization of these films whereby action is central to their existence.

Yet in an ironic contrast to many European films, this existential approach that suggests 'doing' rather than 'saying' might be an appropriation direct from Hollywood. That great Hollywood maxim, 'show, don't tell', guides at the most basic level in terms of scriptwriting by getting over the most fundamental hurdle of writing for screen: how to get into the mind of the character. While there have been many imaginings of how to internally focalize, external focalization is the dominant mode of expression in mainstream cinema – an approach adopted here. Hence Josie is portrayed going about his daily toil, organizing the oil cans, serving the 'passing trade' and then ritualistically locking up at the end of the day. While the narrative pace is inevitably slow with the emphasis on basic, mundane and routine tasks, it evokes the character of Josie who, in a similar construction to other characters in the Abrahamson/O'Halloran repertoire, is isolated, lonely and lives on the fringes. What sets these films aside from similarly-themed narratives is that these characters, while not centrally placed in society, the community or the family, at the same time are not marginalized in the sense of being out on their own. Josie is no more segregated or separate than the other characters he encounters as he moves through his day: the bar-flies in the pub who attempt to belittle him, or Carmel, the woman he fancies, who works in the shop. While the other characters attempt to maintain Josie as peripheral, on the fringes, there is little in story detail suggesting or stating that they are any more central or part of 'something' than Josie.

Similarly, *Prosperity* follows the lives of four people living on the fringes of 'Celtic Tiger' Ireland over one day. Each episode is devoted to one character, with their lives overlapping tenuously. Characterized by a low-key approach to narrative development, little in the way of plot points and dramatic moments are knitted into these stories. These dramatic scenarios unfold as observationally constructed, with the significance of their stories not realized until the closing sequence, and on reflection when the subtleties of approach have sunk in. Episode One, for example, focuses on Stacey (Siobhan Shanahan), a 17-year-old single mother who whiles away her time on the streets of Dublin with her small baby, hanging out in the new 'Mecca of Ireland', the shopping centre, looking for appropriate places to feed and change her baby, while waiting to return to her welfare Bed-and-Breakfast accommodation each evening. In keeping with the style of *Adam & Paul* and *Garage*, Stacey's attention to the action detail of her life, meticulously and methodically feeding, changing and settling her baby, devoid of the traditional creature comforts of a home-life, is what articulates the narrative level of action and plot. She pleads with her landlady for more time to make up the bottles and let the baby sleep before facing a day of wandering the city's streets. The performance is more about physical gesture than vocal projection, articulated in a minimalist rather than melodramatic way.

Like Josie and Adam and Paul, Stacey lives an isolated lonely existence but is not portrayed as marginal or victim-like. Stacey's world is privileged in the narrative, as are Adam, Paul and Josie's, through their central diegetic positioning. In these films, these characters occupy most of the storyworld space and time and act as the principle narrators. In the absence of conflicting or alternative levels of narration, the primacy of these characters is ensured. This approach defines these narratives as both separate from traditional Irish representations of social problems (*Accelerator*, Vinny Murphy 1999; *Crushproof*, Paul Tickell 1998) but also places them in a more universal construction of humanity. By eschewing the sociological explanation of events, these characters are articulated through a 'global vernacular'. The particular condition of modernity which encapsulates alienation, disorientation, absence of coherence and fragmented experience, identifiable across a range of life experiences, is what is being articulated here.

Narrative address – dialogue track

Yet, through the construction of individual characters, each figure has a distinctive and unique voice. The prosaic, meaningless conversations that Stacey has with strangers echoes

Paul and Adam (Mark O'Halloran and Tom Murphy), courtesy of Lenny Abrahamson.

the verbal exchanges between Adam and Paul as they go about planning their day, discussing the task in hand, scoring heroin. This approach is more finely developed and continues as a defining narrative device in the later narratives. In *Garage*, through the character Josie, the action line and dialogue track are placed in entwined diegetic space, both equally fundamental to these characters' existence. Adam and Paul straddle a fine line between 'lovable rogues', who fall into a trap impossible to extricate themselves from, to ruthless thugs without empathy who will stop at nothing to get money for their fix. On the one hand they are gentle in suggesting to each other ways of attracting money, at times mildly bickering as they stumble from place to place. On the other hand, they display a ruthlessness in purpose when they do not think twice about luring a boy with Down's syndrome down an alley to mug him.

The narrative style and structure of *Garage*, while echoing the action of silent movies, evokes one European propensity towards slow, stilted dialogue. It is through Josie's idle chit chat that we get to know him within the context of his community, either through the range of inanities he constantly utters as he encounters people in his day-to-day life. 'You're always going some place, or coming back' he says to the truck-driver as he is filling the tank before embarking on another journey. 'Are you having a party Josie?' Carmel sniggers as she tots up his few paltry purchases, half a sliced pan and a tin of tuna, in the local shop. Alone at night, Josie starts up a dialogue with himself just as he has completed his ritual of tasks. 'Will we go out? … we will, c'mon Josie … switch off … do we have keys … we're all set' – conversing with himself as he contemplates, decides and then gets organized to go out. The banality of his action is reflected in his idle conversations with himself and others, the dialogue directly mirrored in tone and mood through the action on screen. While he does not say much, it is these banal encounters that link him to the outside world. Although alone, he is neither completely solitary nor fully marginalized in the community characterized by detachment. Josie inhabits almost every frame in the film, either by himself or with others in the community. What the sparse dialogue, long silences and daily toil suggest is that Josie, while clearly different in many ways, when viewed up close he is no more detached, isolated or marginalized than the other characters he encounters. When this marginalization takes place at the end of the film, Josie is doomed.

Yet, these humdrum encounters evoke deeply-revealing conversations at the most unlikely turn. While out walking the country lanes, Mr. Skerrit stops and offers Josie a lift. 'I've been looking for you Josie', he says, 'I'm heading out to the lake … we can have a chat, hop in … have to put the blankets on the back seat, the dogs are shedding.' Josie takes up the offer and gets into the back seat of the car as a child might. When they reach the lake, Josie and Mr. Skerrit, framed in a characteristic frontal two-shot sitting on a bench against the backdrop of a scenic yet undramatic landscape, discuss the fishing potential of the lake. While united visually within one static frame, the gap between Mr. Skerrit and Josie grows as Mr. Skerrit slowly breaks down and Josie continues his idle chit chat about 'pike and eel'. Focusing the scene within the thematic device of 'emotional inarticulation', Josie displays an inability to empathize and engage. 'You're keeping well anyways' is more a statement to plug a silence

Pat Shortt in *Garage*, courtesy of Lenny Abrahamson.

that a heartfelt enquiry after his well-being. This display of emotional impediment highlights a lack evident in many characters created by Lenny Abrahamson and Mark O'Halloran. The dialogue and action are mundane and ordinary for a reason: they keep the characters engaged bodily when they cannot engage emotionally.

While it could be argued that the recurring Bulgarian theme running through *Adam & Paul* is an awkward aspect of diegesis, not so much seamless to the plot as self-consciously jarring with the mood and tone, it could equally serve a narrative function and plot detail that further paints the characterization of Adam and Paul. Paul arrives at the 'bench on the canal' with the broken baguette and carton of milk he procured from the nearby Spar shop, to find Adam seated right beside the Bulgarian character, leaning on his battered suitcase tied with string. Paul asks him to move up so that he can sit beside his friend. 'I'm sitting here first, I've got my bag here, it's public property', he says aggressively. This sequence, while potentially functioning simply to refer to the racist responses of some Irish to the recent influx of migrants during Ireland's economic boom, instead reveals the limited engagement Adam and Paul have with their society. The Bulgarian eventually moves up to let Paul sit down, having conceded part of the bench. Clearing up the misunderstanding that he is from Romania by declaring 'I am from Bulgaria', Paul replies, 'so is his jacket', recalling the opening sequence of the film. The scene plays out a dialogue whereby Paul suggests it must be a relief to be in Dublin: 'Bulgaria is a shit-hole', and when the Bulgarian says he had to leave Sofia, Paul asks 'was she pregnant?' Echoing the tone and theme of *Waiting for Godot* and the burlesque comedy of Laurel and Hardy, the Bulgarian roars in response to Paul's question about why he is here. 'Why am I here? Did you ever ask yourself the same question, why are you here? Why the fuck are you here?' and, before waiting for an answer, he gets up from the bench and storms off. Adam and Paul, unmoved by the Bulgarian's departure one way or another, stumble on their way. Adam says 'Fuck this, let's go', 'Where?' Paul wonders, 'Just move' responds Adam. This sequence displays many of the influences already noted in Lenny Abrahamson's approach to narrative construction: visual and thematic references to Ireland's literary heritage – Beckett's *Godot*, Joyce's Dublin, Kavanagh's connections; revealing an affinity with the culture of Eastern Europe; and nodding towards vaudeville and burlesque theatre as well as the narrative style of minimalist yet oblique encounter. He gives this directorial treatment to O'Halloran's script, a closely observed study of an ambivalence and ignorance towards the unfamiliar.

However, it is the darker side of slapstick comedy suggested here that is more enlightening, highlighting the central narrative thrust of characters disembodied from their emotional connections and experiences. In the previous scene, Paul gets caught trying to shoplift and thus comes away empty-handed only to be given the broken baguette that he was attempting to steal, rescued from the bin by another homeless character. Seated on the bench, Adam tries to open the small carton of milk after Paul's failed attempt but manages to spray half of it over himself and the Bulgarian, starting a caricatured outburst in slapstick fashion. The action and dialogue of this scene, while potentially self-conscious in an otherwise seamless narrative, reveal the distanced nature of Adam and Paul's characters. Utterly unreflective, they see their awful lot in terms far superior to that of the migrant. When challenged to reflect, they neither react nor respond, such is the intellectual and emotional shut down of the characters. Clearly functioning at some human level, particularly as they relate to each other like a bickering married couple, somewhere along the way the emotional switch has been turned off. This narrative conveys an image suggesting the real ravages of heroin addiction and how it impacts at a deep emotional level to effectively cut off the individual from feelings, experience, and reflection. The theme is suggested in many parts of the film through encounters with Janine, Georgie, Wayne and the boy with Down's syndrome whereby Adam and Paul are simply not engaged: 'the lights are on but there's no-one home'. It is only through the dream-like, internally-focalized sequences in Janine's flat that the characters function beyond detachment.

Articulating emotions through narrative devices

[I]t is a mistake to suppose that fictions, cinematic and other, create an illusion of reality. Fictions … appeal not to belief, but to the faculty of imagination. (Currie, 1995: 141)

In *The Poetics*, Aristotle argues that the pleasure we take in mimetic works is a pleasure that comes from learning. The pronouncement that our pleasure in Tragedy is derived from the arousal and subsequent catharsis of pity and fear, links pleasure in Tragedy to learning and to emotional response (Neill, 1996: 179). More recently, the branch of film studies concerned with philosophical questions of art has turned its attention to how film gives aesthetic expression to human experience and how the audience deals with aspects of the human experience in an emotional and cognitive way, through the medium of film. The aesthetic experience can be content-oriented and/or affect-oriented, the former being the experience of the aesthetic properties of a work; the latter is concerned with 'attention and contemplation' (Carroll, 1999) of any object. Alex Neill notes that '[a]ncient questions as to how and why it is that we respond emotionally to characters and events which we know to be fictional, and whether it is rational to do so, have in recent years resurfaced and been at the heart of a debate as lively as any in contemporary aesthetics' (Neill, 1996: 175).

The discourse has developed along the lines of empathy and imagination. For Neill, one of the key ways of achieving new emotional experience is through empathetic responses. He argues that responding to others whose outlook and experience differs from our own may teach us something new in emotional terms. One way of experiencing and achieving this new state is through works of fiction. Neill distinguishes between empathy and sympathy, stating that 'with sympathetic response, in feeling *for* another, one's response need not reflect what the other is feeling … [whereas] … in responding empathetically to another I come to *share* his feelings, to feel with him …' (Neill, 1996: 175, original italics). Writing on philosophy and cognitive science, Gregory Currie argues that it 'is when we are able, in imagination, to feel as the character feels that fictions of characters take hold of us', this process of empathetic re-enactment of the character's situation is what he calls secondary imaginings (Currie, 1995: 153), a position similar to the one Susan Feagin (1988) adopts while writing on this theme. She suggests that feeling empathy with a character also involves imagination:

> Having imaginal and emotional responses is part of appreciating an artwork, and an important part of what we appreciate about art in general is that it breaks us out of ordinary patterns of thoughts and feelings. Fiction trades on what we already know and how we can usually be expected to respond, but it shouldn't do only that. Art can expand experience by leading us to engage in imaginings whose overall patterns are identified after the fact, but not where beliefs and desires can be appealed to in order to explain why we engaged in the particular (set of) imaginings we did. (Feagin, 1988: 500)

Empathy attached to imagination is a useful explanation for the emotional connection between character and spectator in works of fiction. When Noel Carroll states that 'the emotional state of the audience does not replicate the state of the characters' (Neill, 1996: 176), he is suggesting the audience does not experience the emotion but feels the effect of the emotional state, which involves some activity of imagination. But what sort of imaginative activity is involved in empathy? For Noel Carroll, imagination is about assimilating the characters' situation which he suggests involves having a sense of the characters' internal understanding of the situation, understanding how the character sees their situation or having access to what makes the characters' 'assessment intelligible' (Neill,1996: 185). For Carroll this is about having 'internal understanding', which for Neill requires imagining the world or the situation that the character is in, from his or her point of view. The character becomes 'the "protagonist" of an imaginative project, a project in which I represent to myself her thoughts, beliefs, desires, feelings, and so on *as though they were my own*' (Neill, 1996, original italics). How this is achieved is through complex narrative layering, meaning that the audience can *share* Adam, Paul, Josie and Stacey's feelings – a more involved state than simply feeling *for* Adam, Paul, Josie and Stacey. The audience feels because they can empathize and imagine the emotional state being conveyed or suggested: in Plato's words 'poetry waters the passions, to the detriment of reason' (Neill, 1996: 178).

How this works at a narrative level is illustrated through the careful deconstruction of a pivotal and illuminating scene in *Adam & Paul*. The exterior of Janine's flat complex, grey and vandalized through graffiti with no personal or individual stamp, is in direct contrast to the interior, which is ordered, tidy and clean to the point of obsession. Adam and Paul knock on the door to find it ajar and no-one apparently home. They enter, survey and comment on the ordered and tidy home they find – 'it's crazy spending all your money on your flat' – revealing the gulf between them and their friends and suggesting the certainty, however misplaced, they hold about their world. As they casually plan in detail how they might steal the television, a step removed from any emotional guilt about the crime they are about to commit on a friend, something gets knocked over and wakes the baby. Forgetting the task in hand, they approach and enter the baby's bedroom and, while Paul picks up the baby, Adam searches the cot, where 'auld-ones and aunties' leave money for the 'baba'. Unexpectedly consumed by what he has encountered, Paul coos at the baby, affectionately reciting 'who's the baba, you're the best baba, who's the baba then' until, infectiously, Adam takes the baby and, like doting parents, Adam and Paul sit on the edge of the bed captivated. The intimacy of the scene is quietly interrupted by a cut to a shot of Janine in the bedroom doorway looking on. When spotted by Paul, the narrative seam shifts to an internally-focalized shot of the three adults embracing as they hold and share the baby, soft-focused and silent. Unsure as to what is going on in diegetic terms, the scene's mood is broken by a cut to an over-the-shoulder shot of Paul from Janine's perspective, revealing the previous shot to be illusionary and imaginary, a fantasy.

> Internal focalization is more fully private and subjective than external focalization. No character can witness these experiences in another character. Internal focalization ranges from simple perception (e.g. the point-of-view shot), to impressions (e.g. the out-of-focus point-of-view shot depicting a character who is drunk, dizzy or drugged, to "deeper thoughts" (e.g. drams, hallucinations, and memories). (Branigan, 1998: 103)

Adam & Paul, it could be argued, is a triumph of focalization, by revealing through a very brief sequence the wish fulfilment and emotional need of somebody who has been ravaged by his drug addiction. As they lounge on the couch smoking, Janine comments that 'it's good to have yiz around'. Paul, looking at Adam, smiles like a little boy receiving positive emotional reinforcement. Although unclear as to who is the baby's father, through empathy and imagination the tragic nature of Adam and Paul's life is realized. In functioning at this level, the narrative addresses not the sociological context of drug addiction but the human drive and craving for emotional connection, expressed in the 'global vernacular' and articulated in emotional terms. Where Carroll, Feagin and Neill concur is by centring the imagination as playing a part in empathetic responses towards fiction, which allows for the audience to become involved in the emotional life of the character without having held the specific emotions themselves. As Neill states, the less substantial the knowledge the audience holds about the character, the more difficult it will be to imagine things from his or her point of view, suggesting why the audience achieves greater emotional involvement with some films and less with others, and linking to the cultural specificity of films as they connect with local audiences.

> So in engaging with the characters of film fiction we are in a position much closer to the position we are in when we engage with actual persons than we are when we read about characters of literary fiction ... And it is partly this ... that gives film fiction its value: it gives us practice, so to speak, in a mode of engagement and response that is often crucial in our attempts to engage with and understand our fellow human beings. (Neill, 1996: 188–9)

This suggests the cultural importance and universal significance of cinema that allows us to 'see *our* world and *our* possibilities anew' (Neill, 1996: 192, original italics). Part of the value of fiction, therefore, is the broadening of our perspectives through empathy and imagination, achieved in Irish cinema through the narrative address of these productions. Because most of the narrative action and dialogue in these films verges on the banal and vacuous, certain sequences stand out as illuminatory, revealing what is at the heart of the specific film. As explored and argued in Chapter 3, it is at the level of internal focalization that the deeper emotional experience is rendered for the audience. In *Adam & Paul*, the sequence in Janine's flat combines the emotional articulation of each of the characters and goes beyond a superficial interpretation of the hope a new baby may represent. Instead, what this scene with Janine's baby suggests is the human need for emotional experience, engagement and attachment. A by-product of the modern experience can sometimes be a deep void in emotional articulation for people living at the edge – unspoken and unheard experience reaching the centre.

Stacey's character resonates at a deeper level through the absence of verbal expression. Failed somewhere along the way (by her family, her education, her society – we can only surmise) she has been rendered inarticulate about her own situation. This is not to say she does not experience or feel emotionally, she just cannot find the means to express it. This inability, or disability, is brought into sharp relief through her relationship with her baby's father and other people around her. The absence of control over her own life is in stark contrast to the perceived nature of modern Ireland, evoking a bygone era whereby Stacey moves through her days, ghost-like. In fact, the main characters in this range of films, it could be suggested, function as ghosts within contemporary Ireland, not in the shadows or in the margins but centrally positioned in Irish towns and cities. These films tell familiar stories from Irish society, stories that are whispered through characters present but ghost-like. Because these narratives reject the tendency of positioning such characters as 'other' or removing them from their centrally located space, taken as a whole, this body of work suggests that the experience of what has been known as the 'marginalized, the dispossessed and the isolated' is more normal than exceptional, evincing a discourse of modernity.

Conclusion

In active defiance of the Hollywood classical ending, which is redemptive, upbeat and reliant on a high degree of closure, a number of notable recent Irish films have ended with death: *Adam & Paul*, *Garage*, *Disco Pigs* and *Accelerator*. The characterization in these films is significant, not so much as an exploration of how the characters see the world but rather how the world accommodates them. The bleak ending could indeed leave the audience with a negative, downbeat sense to closure if not read in keeping with the exploration of the emotional states being developed and exposed within the dramatic structure. The poignancy of Josie's life in *Garage* – according to Abrahamson, 'small and unremarkable' – is what

Pat Shortt in *Garage*, courtesy of Lenny Abrahamson.

gives the narrative its dramatic focus, while Adam and Paul, two inconspicuous junkies who ordinarily fade into the crowd, are given prominence and resonance through the dramatic exposition. The stark, brutal ending for these characters, while in keeping with the narrative function and dramatic development, is what distinguishes these films in the broader context of recent Irish film.

According to Luke Gibbons, 'landscape has tended to play a leading role in Irish cinema, often upstaging both the main characters and narrative themes in the construction of Ireland on screen' (Gibbons et al., 1988: 203). Kerstin Ketteman observes that the 'Irish landscape is significantly used to facilitate violence, particularly in the use of cliffs and deep wells, as signs of abyss' (Ketteman, 1999). In *Garage*, the tranquillity of the lake contrasts with the brutality of the act of suicide. The bleak, nondescript landscape is in keeping with the absence of expression by Josie, his inability to articulate his feelings and emotions coming to a head after he has had a visit from the police. In *Adam & Paul*, like *Garage*, the landscape is appropriated as Gibbons and Ketteman describe, but in its less dramatic aesthetic. The evocation of the coastal location where Adam meets his end, in an understated way, echoes the stillness of the lake that Josie walks into. Unlike the earlier films which portray the Irish landscape, mainly of the west in all its sublimity, the aesthetic here simply reflects and expresses the understated nature of the preceding narrative.

Narrative closure linked to death is not an unusual trope in recent Irish cinema. *Accelerator* and *Disco Pigs* both hinge on the dual approach of hope and despair in their conclusions. *Accelerator*, arguably the more mainstream approach to narrative closure, simultaneously evokes redemption (Johnny T) and futility (Whacker), presenting the audience with a neatly-coded classical finish, whereas with *Disco Pigs*, while also presenting the audience with hope, the despair serves a purpose. *Disco Pigs* and *Adam & Paul* are narratively linked through the visual iconography adopted. Where *Disco Pigs* and *Adam & Paul* diverge, however, is at the level of style. While *Disco Pigs* uses violence to display the hopelessness of Pig's situation, *Adam & Paul* adopts a visually more subtle approach. For example, the robbery in the off-licence at the start of *Disco Pigs* is in stark contrast to Adam and Paul leading a boy with Down's syndrome down a lane in order to rob him: the latter more under-stated and subtle yet displaying the desperation and detachment more forcefully. The subtlety here is in stark contrast to the overt violence of similar scenes in *Disco Pigs* and *Intermission*. As Michael Patrick Gillespie states, 'through the anarchy of its discourse, the film invites us to experience, without endorsing, the world that Adam and Paul inhabit' (Gillespie, 2008). In this way, while these endings are counter-intuitive in terms of classical expectation they are in keeping with the aesthetic of modernity framing these narratives.

In *Disco Pigs* the reason for Pig dying is metaphorical: to allow Runt to separate, grow and continue to live, thus serving the purpose of narrative closure, albeit in a fatalistic way. The fatalism of *Adam & Paul* functions at a level of social-realism, and therefore resonates in a less redemptive manner. Adam dies of a heroin overdose and Paul, not able to care for him or about him, leaves him at a similar coastal location to Pig. However, whereas *Disco Pigs* evokes a peaceful, almost serene aesthetic, in *Adam & Paul* it is wind-swept and desolate, suggesting *scenic* wasteland. Whereas there is hope for Runt in subsequent events, there is little hope for Paul. The convoluted nature of characterization in *Adam & Paul*, whereby both characters are intertwined, suggests that the same fate awaits Paul. In *Disco Pigs* and *Adam & Paul* the choice of location serves different aesthetic purposes. While ironically very similar locations, the narratives contrastingly articulate a discourse of hope and fatalism, an oppositional romantic and tragic end.

Viewing cinema as a 'metaphor of global sensory vernacular' rather than a 'universal narrative idiom' (Hansen, 2000), we can make sense of these films within the context of contemporary Irish cinema. At this level, Lenny Abrahamson and Mark O'Halloran, through writing, acting and directing, work film for an Irish audience 'as a new regime of sensory experience, a reflective performativity in its reception' (Hammond, 2004). Using the Hollywood frameworks that demand coherency and order and combining them with the European propensity towards more illusive, less defined experience, these narratives articulate small knowable worlds in all their complexity. While not denying the hegemony of Hollywood, Abrahamson and O'Halloran succeed in creating narratives that reflect cultural immersion in two traditions, revealing an evolutionary and developmental stage in new Irish cinema.

Chapter 5

A Modern Love Story - *Nora*

The Joyces moved to Switzerland, where he taught English and started a theatre to produce English plays. They were very hard up. One day when he was in the theatre rehearsing, a letter came announcing that a huge sum of money (£5000 or $5000) had arrived from an anonymous donor. Nora, all excitement, put on her hat, went to the theatre and, before all the company, announced their good fortune. Joyce always remembered that, in the midst of congratulations, the wife of an actor in the company turned to Nora and said with an edge in her voice: 'And so, Mrs. Joyce, you open your husband's letters'. (*The Irish Times*, 20 April 2000)

The history of Irish cinema might be characterized by *late arrested development*. As detailed elsewhere, although most European cinemas enjoyed a high level of indigenous film-making in the twentieth century, it was not until the 1970s and 1980s that film-making in Ireland began to develop. This period is described as highly innovative and political, with a range of notable interrogative films emerging, positioning Ireland for the first time within a film culture that expands beyond national borders and is more international in frame. While this era of Irish film-making has been well documented (Gibbons et al, 1988; McIlroy, 2001; McKillop, 1999; Pettitt, 2000), its impact on the second Irish Film Board and the films emerging during the recent past is what interests this study. A hiatus of six years would have a number of effects on Irish film-makers. Cathal Black, Joe Comerford, Johnny Gogan, Pat Murphy, Thaddeus O'Sullivan and Bob Quinn are film-makers most associated with the radical and avant-garde practices of the first wave, all of whom maintained roles within Irish film at some level before the reactivation of the Board, either by continuing to produce films in Ireland or abroad, agitating for public policy and advocating support for film culture, or by becoming involved in teaching and training in the various film courses that continued through the production vacuum. When the Film Board was re-activated, they returned to directing, producing a number of films, particularly in the earlier phase (*High Boot Benny, 1994*; *Nothing Personal*, 1995; *Korea*, 1995; *Navagatio*, 1997; *The Last Bus Home*, 1997). Pat Murphy's work is particularly significant in this context; by spanning both periods her films display a narrative development reflecting the evolutionary nature of new Irish cinema. In this chapter, through a close analysis of her most recent work, the nuances of narrative style and aesthetic approach is examined as a way of bridging these two phases of Irish cinema and thus counteracting the tendency to pit one period against the other.

Pat Murphy's film *Nora* (2000) is one of the most challenging texts to emerge in Irish cinema in recent times. Clearly regarded as a feminist film-maker from her earlier works,

Maeve (1981) and *Anne Devlin* (1984), this more recent film has defied labelling. What makes Pat Murphy's film *Nora* (2000) critical in scholarly terms is its divergence from Murphy's earlier work that was distinctly feminist in both form and content, revealing a trajectory reflecting key changes and developments within feminist film debates. Murphy's approach to the intellectual exploration of the relationship between feminism and nationalism in *Maeve* (1981) was modernist and avant-garde, while *Anne Devlin* (1984) could be seen as part of the feminist project that sought to reclaim female historical figures from oblivion, coinciding with the development of women's studies in 1980s' Ireland. Much has been written about these two films (Gibbons, 1986; Gibbons et al.,1988; McLoone, 2000; Pettitt, 2000), particularly because they fit the project of Irish cinema discourse since the 1980s. Murphy's earlier work emerged within a context of a developing interest and activity in feminist film studies in the 1970s and 1980s as well as being part of the radical first wave of Irish film.

Within the context of Irish cinema, *Nora* presents a particularly significant case study for two reasons. Firstly, Pat Murphy is a director more clearly associated with the first wave of Irish cinema and worked very much in the avant-garde and modernist movements. Her art college training is evident in the *mise-en-scène* of her early work and her ideological influences emerge clearly focused in the stories she tells. *Nora*, therefore, cannot be examined in isolation and must be seen as part of Murphy's repertoire. Secondly, *Nora* was co-written with Gerry Stembridge, a director notably associated with the second wave of Irish film. He wrote and directed *Guiltrip* (1995) and *About Adam* (2000), was scriptwriter on *Ordinary Decent Criminal* (1999) and was the creative force as scriptwriter and director on the television drama *Black Day at Blackrock* (2001). *Nora* suggests and signals the meeting point of the first and second waves, where these two phases of Irish cinema converge. *Nora*, through narrative analysis and theoretical examination, illustrates how the writer/director Pat Murphy has negotiated the move from one wave to another, shedding previous ideological and stylistic baggage that no longer functions within contemporary film, principally because the political 'moment' has changed. She constructs a narrative style that embodies a universal dimension, without fully endorsing the mainstream approach she previously challenged, echoing her earlier work while shirking outdated modes of representation. Gerardine Meaney states that

> *Nora* is an unusual instance in the tendency in recent Irish films, and films set in Ireland, to recount hidden histories. It tells a story outside the paradigms of official history, but also outside those of contemporary Irish film's construction of the past. A large measure of this derives from the chief protagonist herself. Nora Barnacle still has a quality of unexpectedness about her. Much of what is most surprisingly contemporary about her character as represented in the film is painstakingly accurate. (Meaney, 2004b: 7)

Nora is different, partly because it is difficult to label or categorize either as part of Murphy's *oeuvre* or within the boundaries of feminist film. Brenda Maddox's biography *Nora: the*

Real Life of Molly Bloom (1988) is part of the feminist project of reclaiming neglected female historical figures. Murphy takes this publication as her inspiration, thus following the feminist trajectory established in the 1980s, yet deviates from this path by steering the narrative address in a new direction. Its uniqueness is highlighted further when viewed within the context of the stylistic tendencies of contemporary Irish film. Murphy herself disclaims it as a feminist film because of the Joycean nature of the text, stating that

> [y]ou can never get to [Nora] separate from [Joyce]. You always have to use him as a way into her and that's one of the reasons *Nora* is not a feminist film in the way that *Anne Devlin* and *Maeve* are feminist films … [This film] is not trying to recuperate her and say that she was something else. (Murphy quoted in Meaney, 2004b: 70)

Revealed through the film structure that simultaneously embraces and subverts conventional narratives and paralleling some of the evolutionary trends within recent Irish cinema and feminist politics, this film signals key changes in discourse and aesthetics since the 1980s. Using many of the conventional mainstream devices of narrative at one level, Murphy's film can be described as a contemporary Irish love story. However, in subverting these structural dimensions, mainly through thwarting audience expectation, she articulates a radical discourse. A discourse of equality surfaces through this structure, albeit in a problematic and complicated way. Murphy refuses simple explanations of emotional states, exploring the themes of romance and love through a complex and conflicting paradigm of positivity and negativity. In contrast to the conventional love story, this film defies an assured position for the viewer.

Contemporary Irish love stories

> According to their typical narrative formula, a young boy and girl of marriageable age, beautiful and chaste, meet and fall in love suddenly and unexpectantly. But their marriage cannot take place because they are parted. There are shipwrecks, pirates, slavery, prison, miraculous rescues, recognition scenes, court trials, and sleeping potions. The story ends happily, with the marriage of the two lovers. This plot is, in other words, the original of the boy meets girl, loses girl, gets girl stereotype. (Clark & Holquist, 1984: 281)

The love story or romance tale is a dominant form in world cinema, storytelling, myth-making and many forms of narrative expression. Unsurprisingly, new Irish cinema presents a number of examples of the love story but, significantly, not in a homogenized form. Pat Murphy acknowledges that she did not initially set out to tell a love story, as her interest in James Joyce stretches back to 1977 when she was working on one of her first art pieces, *Rituals of Memory* (1977). Her enthusiasm for Nora Barnacle's story developed much later after reading Brenda Maddox's 1998 biography *Nora*. It was not until the early nineties, therefore, that she was inspired to make a film about Joyce's wife. As the film *Nora* evolved, it then became more about Nora and Joyce, and about their relationship in particular. According to Pat Murphy in an interview in *Film & Film Culture*

> I wanted to make a love story, partly because we're not really known for movies about sexuality and relationships and I'd never seen a really passionate love story coming out of Ireland that wasn't gloomy and thwarted and tragic. Nora is a distilled intimate portrait of a marriage, an exploration of what it's like to be in love and the task in making the film was to give a sense of a relationship which felt alive and dynamic *now* as well as representing a historical reality. (Thornton, 2004: 7–10)

Murphy sees the depiction of erotic love in Irish film as 'something forbidden and transgressional. No movie narrative seemed to be able to hold the notion that people could just be together, have this great passionate love affair and be together. There was always a level of punishment' (Meaney, 2004b: 14). As explored in Chapter 3, second wave films have considered the tropes of love and sexuality in a range of ways, and generically through romantic comedy, from restating traditional values (*About Adam*) to complicating notions of masculinity and femininity (*The Most Fertile Man in Ireland*). The articulation of the love story, in its more serious dramatic form, is the primary focus of examination in this chapter.[1] A survey of a range of recent Irish love stories reveals that the narrative strategies employed reflect a wide scope in detail and approach, visually and structurally, to accommodate a specific and narrow overarching generic frame.

Narratologists including Mikhail Bakhtin, Vladimir Propp and Northrop Frye have contributed to the development of anatomies or schema for various plot types within the realms of the fictional world and storytelling. Generally speaking, these approaches present 'a finite number of story frameworks underlying the infinite variety of narrative' (Herman, 2007: 43) in a range of 'types' or 'mythoi' – romance, tragedy, comedy and irony. Bakhtin, through a theory of chronotope meaning time/space, takes an essentially abstract and non-specific notion and 'shows how concrete spatio-temporal structures in literature – the atemporal otherworldly forest of romance, the "nowhere" of fictional utopias, the roads and inns of the picaresque novel – limit narrative possibility, shape characterisation and mould a discursive image of life and the world' (Clark & Holquist, 1984: 217). In this chronotope, which he calls 'adventure time', there are only two events: falling in love and getting married. In structural terms, the two events provide the boundaries as well as limits of plot formation. Between these boundaries the possibilities are unbridled, with many and diverse events taking place in the intervening time. If the chronotope is appropriated as a narrative prototype, and it has limitations as well as potential as a structural model, what marks the narrative capacity of contemporary Irish film in love stories as distinctive is their initial adherence and subsequent resistance to the template or formula. While all the stories structure themselves along the lines of 'boy meets girl', the reunification of the lovers after the initial separation often fails to take place. Instead, the love story is simply a device to tell a different story.

Ailsa (Paddy Breathnach, 1994) focuses on how the main protagonist, Miles Butler (Brendan Coyle), through his obsession with an American woman, Campbell Rourke (Juliette Gruber), puts his own relationship with his girlfriend Sara under pressure. Made distinctly in a low-budget, arthouse style it is closer to European art cinema than mainstream Hollywood narrative.[2] By concentrating and focusing the narrative on Miles and Campbell, the film resembles a *short film* stretched and structurally hindered despite its promise as an intimate piece. This film meaningfully defies the conventional template by choosing to objectify Miles' obsessional behaviour rather than Campbell, the object of his obsession. Miles' thoughts and actions are internalized and, ultimately, he destroys himself rather than the object of his obsession. In a similar way, *November Afternoon* (John Carney and Tom Hall, 1996) explores an unconventional relationship and subject matter that is generally seen as taboo, in a non-mainstream aesthetic. This film is about the incestuous relationship of Richard (Michael McElhatton) and Karen (Jayne Snow), brother and sister. Structured around events when they are together on a weekend away with her husband (Mark Doherty) and his American girl-friend (Tristan Gribbin), the story brings to the surface the sexual relationship between Karen and Richard over the past fifteen years. This psychological drama is brave in its attempt to explore such difficult subject matter; it does so at the level of the emotional turmoil that this complex action brings to its characters. Rejecting conventional closure, the story is unresolved when both couples return home to deal with the revelations of the weekend. *Ailsa* and *November Afternoon* are noteworthy thematically and aesthetically, contrasting with later trends in second wave films. Functioning as some of the few examples of second wave films that signal references to European art cinema, they span first and second wave by embodying stylistic and thematic characteristics of both. While the themes explored in these films are more adventurous and ambitious than many later 'love stories', the way they are cast is in a more universal realm than location-specific, a characteristic that clearly distinguishes more recent Irish film. In their adoption of unresolved or open endings, they reject the conclusion of Bakhtin's chronotope 'adventure time', negating the conventional mode of closure, displaying links to the non-conventional approach of earlier Irish film.

Clearly a metaphor for colonial tensions, Cathal Black's film *Love and Rage* (1998) uses the love story as a device to explore the relationship between landlord and tenant in a colonized state. Like Pat Murphy, Cathal Black is more closely associated with the first wave of Irish film (*Our Boys,* 1981; *Pigs,* 1984) yet he has also directed films in the later period. Following *Korea* (1995), *Love and Rage* rejects classical narrative, perceptible through its form and style rather than its content. Telling the story of Agnes McDonnell (Greta Scacchi), an independent land-owner living on Achill Island, Co. Mayo during the nineteenth century who falls in love with James Lynchehaun (Daniel Craig), an Achill native, it is a historical piece based on real-life events, providing the context for JM Synge's *The Playboy of the Western World* (1907). Their intense relationship results in a violent incident which leaves Agnes disfigured. Because Lynchehaun's assault on Agnes is regarded as a political act, he escapes imprisonment when he flees to the United States. Ten years later he returns to Ireland and, as he taunts Agnes at her house, she shoots him. The main narrative tension and rupture from expected norms is experienced, particularly around exposition and motivation. While Black resists the dominant form of storytelling, he does not replace it with a structure that can exploit the narrative potential of a strong female-led narrative. Neither a mainstream narrative, nor drawing on the European art movement with which Black is more commonly associated, this film is hindered by its production circumstances. While the film draws on a historical love story, it acts as an allegory for colonial tensions but, through narrative confusion, it is unclear what story it wishes to tell. This film is important in revealing the changes in production environment, not just in Ireland but across Europe, in the time between the first and second Film Boards. Black is more closely aligned to 'creative-led' than 'finance-led production'.[3] The new regime would mean that no film could receive total finance from the board (unless it was in one of the micro-budget schemes). Co-production deals, creeping into television production in the 1980s, are, by the 1990s, institutionally embedded throughout Europe.[4] Since 1993, and until the introduction of the micro-budget scheme, it was impossible to finance a film solely in Ireland: the global nature of film impacting firstly at the level of budget.

Another film taking its subject matter from historical detail is Syd Macartney's *A Love Divided* (1999). Based on the now-familiar episode in Fethard-on-Sea in 1957 seen as a turning point in modern Irish society, this story is about the couple of a mixed marriage who refused to accept the 'Ne Temere' rule of the Catholic Church.[5] Sheila Kelly (Orla Brady), daughter of a Protestant cattle dealer, and Sean Cloney (Liam Cunningham), a Catholic farmer, got married in a London registry office in 1949. They returned to Ireland marrying again in a Protestant church and finally in the local Catholic church where Protestant Sheila was obliged to sign the 'Ne Temere' agreement, ensuring her children would be educated in Catholic schools. When she refuses to see this through after the local Catholic priest takes it upon himself to enrol the eldest child in the local Catholic school, she flees to Scotland. She goes alone when her husband fails to question the authority of the priest and reject his instruction. This incident divided the Catholic and Protestant communities in Fethard-on-Sea at the time, when Sheila and her children returned home, and for many years after. Interesting as a historical detail in the church/state chapter of Irish history and the developments that took place in the middle of the twentieth century when much Catholic Church doctrine crossed into and regulated wider society, this film points to the tension within film narrative when exploring historical fact. What started off as a political film, led mainly by Gerry Gregg as its producer, in the process that is script development and production it changed, becoming, in the final version, a love story set against a political backdrop. Gerry Gregg's career as a current affairs producer in RTÉ and a documentary-maker is known for its political motivations.[6] As the film went through development, key figures along the way questioned its overtly political slant, and the portrayal of Catholics and Protestants in particular. When Stuart Hepburn (screenwriter on Scottish TV drama series

Taggart 1983–2009) was brought on as script writer, he saw his 'Scott[t]
way to counteract what the director Syd Macartney saw as a 'religiousl[y]
the latter preferring to 'come at it through the love story of Sheila and Se[]
other stuff a backdrop to that' (Owens, 1999).

What emerges in the final film version is a narrative that privileges the
it against the backdrop of a significant historical detail and narratively en[   ]ing Bakhtin's
theory of 'adventure time'. This example points to the difficulty the medium of popular film
and its particular narrative structure (mainstream, classical) has in dealing with historical
stories. Few films based on Irish historical events remain immune to a contentious post-
screening response and are rarely interpreted as purely entertainment. At the same time and
in spite of this difficulty, *A Love Divided* points to an apparent predilection for historical
films by Irish audiences, if its popularity among audiences is a reliable bench-mark. This
film was the third most successful Irish film of 1999.[7] The debates generated by films such
as *Michael Collins* (Neil Jordan, 1996) and *In the Name of the Father* (Jim Sheridan, 1993)
reveal history as a highly-contested discourse in Ireland's public sphere, through popular,
academic and intellectual debate. Similarly, the film *Nora* is complicated by the extra-textual
references that the Joycean industry has generated over time, entangling the film's reception
and fragmenting the audience. If the audience favours historical stories or stories based on
historical fact or real life circumstance, how then are writers and directors to approach the
material from a narrative point of view? Clearly, classical narrative structure squeezes the
story into a pre-determined shape of equilibrium, disequilibrium and, finally, equilibrium
which is not always appropriate to historical stories. On the other hand, audience reception
of Irish films which disavows mainstream narrative is not always positive, either because
these films are inaccessible, or narratively-flawed, a position which is supported not only
by critics' appraisal but also from box office receipts.

Contemporary Irish love stories are often more about the destructive nature of love, either
for psychological or historical reasons or about separating rather than uniting couples.
While these early films use the narrative device of romance/love story in an allegorical way
to deal with aspects of Irish culture and society, they were much less popular than their
more recent counterparts exploring what may be called the universal nature of love and
romance (*About Adam*, *Goldfish Memory* and *Intermission*). What distinguishes these later

films from their earlier counterparts is the portrayal of heterosexual and homosexual love
often in a positive and progressive light, at a superficial level anyway. Rather than focusing
on the 'boy meets girl' paradigm already mentioned, these narratives progress along a multi-
character plot akin to 1990s' independent American film, whereby the classical device of
protagonist and antagonist relating narratively in cause-effect is supplanted with a multi-
character set up. Chance and coincidence often generate the narrative advance. Not only
are these films moving away from what could be seen as 'Irish' preoccupations, they are
embracing a narrative style that would appear at one level to be ironic. However, despite the
apparent challenge to conventions, by the narrative closure of these three films, the 'boy and
girl' having metaphorically experienced 'shipwrecks, pirates, slavery, prison ... and sleeping

ions … the story ends happily with the [symbolic] marriage of the two lovers' (Clark & Holquist, 1984: 277).

However, when examined more closely, positive heterosexual relationships espousing progressive outcomes are often absent in contemporary Irish film. This makes Murphy's text all the more significant. Irish love stories do not ensure a happy ending – in fact, many stories centred around relationships are about negative properties that bind people (*Guiltrip*, Gerry Stembridge; *Snakes and Ladders*, Trish McAdam 1996; *Dancing at Lughnasa*, Pat O'Connor 1998; *Peaches*, Nick Grosso 2000). Framed against this back-drop, Pat Murphy's *Nora* presents a complex love story that narratively is more challenging than most of its second wave equivalents, revealing the value in Murphy's approach whereby she uses the conventions to support and subvert her story rather than slavishly allowing the codes to dictate the story direction and design. *Nora* both defies and tailors the various category norms to present a text that is simultaneously feminist and humanist, romantic yet unsentimental in an accessible narrative structure. She neither alienates the audience through an inaccessible form nor gives them the superficially-satisfying standard that ultimately makes one feel cheated. Instead, she presents a film that is 'easily digestible' on first viewing while commanding multiple re-visits for more narrative exploration.

Nora – An Irish love story

Narrative is an art of the opening and closing of gaps, and that in those gaps lie whole worlds that the art of narrative invites us either to actualize or leave as possibilities (Herman, 2007: 50).

Like Jane Campion with *The Piano* (1993), Pat Murphy moves beyond the traditions of feminism to create a film that is difficult to categorize. However, unlike *The Piano*, which relies on binary oppositions anchoring the narrative to a range of discourses, *Nora* explores themes of emotion such as love and desire and puts them through a range of discursive and representational processes. Without subjecting the narrative to a structure of opposition, the visceral is rendered rational and becomes reason for the audience's interpretation. In terms of narrative analysis, figuring out how this process works involves two stages: firstly, the narrative can be broken down along the lines of 'canonicity and breach', exploring how the writer/director uses familiar or ordinary contexts to explore unfamiliar or extraordinary events, stereotypic and non-stereotypic knowledge (Herman, 2002: 7). In the case of *Nora*, what is interesting is how Pat Murphy tells an extraordinary love story within the structure of the familiar Bakhtinian scenario of 'boy meets girl'. Secondly, narrative analysis reveals how the medium uses stories to organize and comprehend experience (Herman, 2002: 86): in Bordwells' term 'historical poetics'. In any narrative process, the viewer matches what they see and hear with 'pre-stored groupings of actions that they have already experienced'

(Herman, 2002: 89). The challenge is to cognitively map the storyworld conveyed (Chatman, 1999: 8), alongside perceptions, impressions and unconscious biases stored in the memory over time. Meaning is negotiated between the two. This becomes quite a challenge in telling Nora's story within the wider context of, and knowledge around, James Joyce.

Story, plot, narration and character are all part of a process, with distinctive functions in an overall structure. A story, for example, has a separate role from narration. Narration is the act of communicating the story. The same story can be told in many different ways. Similarly, a story can be plotted in a range of structures and forms. While story, plot and narration are distinctive parts of the process, narrative discourse (plot and narration) is how the story is communicated. Yet it is not that simple, as David Herman states: 'nothing is tidy in the study of narrative' (Herman, 2007: 40). Breaking narrative down into its component parts suggests an application of tangible processes. But 'narrative happens in the mind, with its empirical components – words spoken or printed, pictures on a screen, actors on a stage – transformed by cognitive processes that are still largely mysterious' (Herman, 2007: 40). This indicates the complexity of the activity. The first stage, therefore, of narrative analysis, involves breaking down a film into its component parts, revealing how it is structurally arranged and formed. The second stage entails interpretation of the story based on the narration of character and plot, combining explicitly-depicted action and events with an implicit form of suggested nuanced and implied activity.

According to Herman, 'plot is an even slipperier term than narration ... Plot is ... used to refer to that combination of economy and sequencing of events that makes a story a story and not just raw material' (Herman, 2007: 43). Aristotle's term 'mythos', which refers to plot, is the story fashioned and shaped into a structure of beginning, middle and end; for Aristotle plot is everything. Plot, therefore, is the way of bringing the story to its fullness in a given context. It refers to a coherent whole governing the sequencing of events in a story, or 'everything visibly and audibly present in the film before us' (Bordwell & Thompson, 1990: 57). According to Bordwell and Thompson, story and plot overlap in some respects and diverge in others – for example, the story is composed of 'inferred events' and 'explicitly presented events' while the plot is composed only of explicit events and non-diegetic material such as music and credits. The viewer, therefore, is presented with plot details that generally go undisputed, while the process of narrative involves taking these plot details and creating the story in the mind of the viewer. This is achieved by *inferring* events as the narration occurs through the demonstration of action details, and is sometimes disputed.

In this particular narrative, the story told is broadly familiar to the general audience. This can be a help or a hindrance, depending on the writer's and director's intentions, but at the same time, is not necessary to the comprehension of the story. The plot is, specifically, the events in the life of Nora Barnacle between 1904 and 1912, represented and unfolding through the character Nora. The narration, therefore, is what makes this story unique in its wider familiar context. It is the story of Nora told through the narration of the entity of character. Gerry Stembridge and Pat Murphy's story reveals the actions of the character Nora. When the character is very close to the action, they operate within the storyworld (diegetic space). Gerard Genette terms this type of character a homodiegetic narrator in contrast to a heterodiegetic narrator who stands outside of the storyworld (Herman, 2007: 42). In terms of the storyworld constructed, a homodiegetic narrator is a very reliable narrator. The character, as an agent of cause and effect, that occupies and operates within the diegetic space, therefore, is the narrator to be trusted. In this story, that is Nora, the character named.

Nora opens in 1904 when Nora Barnacle (Susan Lynch) runs away to Dublin from her native Galway and, from the outset, she is portrayed as an active, dominant character. In a set-up that conventionally wastes no time, Nora meets Joyce (Ewan McGregor) on a Dublin street. Evoking a small, localized milieu, Joyce knows that she is a stranger in town and guesses from her accent that she hails from Galway. Nora from the start is confident and assertive. When Joyce introduces himself and arranges a date but fails to ask her name, she calls after him, 'Hey James Joyce, don't you want to know my name? … My name is Nora Barnacle.' From the opening shot, when she is framed seated on a bench in Galway train station, to her declaration on a public street of who she is, Pat Murphy is privileging Nora in the narrative, giving her a central narrating voice. The use of voice-over and flashback to fill in the back-story further reinforces this.

The narrative journey in *Nora* is, on one level, standard and conventional. It follows the trajectory of development, upheaval and restoration as the characters overcome obstacles in reaching an equal plain. The narrative, in an innovative way, simultaneously plays with the potential of feminist narrative and mainstream classical while subverting both to proffer a radical discourse. Moving beyond traditional feminism, Murphy appears to be working towards a postfeminist discourse but also, in keeping with the Joycean theme, she articulates in a modernist way. [8] In doing so, she tells a story in narrative form that conveys a progressive message, revealed through the centrally-placed homodiegetic narrator. The narrative therefore requires the audience to take a leap of faith and move in a different direction from the previously received and perceived familiar Joycean 'story', particularly around Nora Barnacle, wife of James Joyce.

Because film is a storytelling medium and the nature of narrative determines how that story is told, biographical material presents a particular challenge to the writer and director. When the subject matter is the wife of one of the best known writers of the twentieth century, the challenge becomes fused with obstacles and controversy. In many ways, Murphy's approach defies expectation. She does not present a biopic that remains truthful to the facts, as this would be impossible in 90 minutes of screen time. Neither does she proclaim Nora as a figure ahead of her time, an off-shoot of the feminist project of reclaiming previously-forgotten female historical figures. Instead she chooses to focus the narrative on telling a story about the relationship between two people, through the agency of the characters Nora and Joyce. The narrative progression concentrates on the 'working-out' of the relationship, whereby the two characters journey through the stages of equilibrium, disequilibrium and, finally, equilibrium: the much maligned plot points of classical narrative. Where this narrative deviates from the conventional love story, however, and follows on from Murphy's earlier work, is by telling a love story that expresses a discourse of equality, speaking of gender relations in a positive, progressive and complex way. In constructing the narrative, the director rejects the structure that pits one character against the other, neither character dominating while one or other retreats. Instead, they maintain positions of symmetry yet still engage with the narrative obstacles – an interesting approach to the 'love story'.

Character / plot / narration

Central to the story told in this film is the sexual relationship between Joyce and Nora. On their first date Nora is shown as leading and pro-active in their sexual encounters. While it could be inferred that Nora was all too aware of the consequences of pregnancy outside of wedlock in Ireland at the time, and therefore was more in control when guiding their sexual encounters, this 'first date' scene sets the tone for the rest of the film whereby mutual sexual pleasure is a key part of their relationship. Meeting in a city-centre park, the passage from daylight to night suggests that their courtship takes place outdoors and over a long time. Evoking the cityscape, they descend steep steps leading to a secluded, dark alley, both framed equally by the camera. Here they start kissing. Nora reaches for Joyce's trousers and puts her hand inside. After bringing him to orgasm, she concludes the scene with the request, 'Do you have a hanky, Mr. Joyce?' Sexual guilt or fear is not associated with Nora at any point in the film: the first indication that Stembridge/Murphy are telling a different story. In contrast to Nora, the theme of guilt links to the character of Joyce, articulated later in the film when his mother's apparition visits him. His subsequent behaviour with their friend Roberto Prezioso also indicates a problematic response to his own sexuality, impacting on his relationship with Nora, forming part of the narrative of 'love story'. His emotional disposition is hindered by jealousy and control yet, within the narrative, these issues are confined to the agency of his character. Nora, while obviously affected by his emotional state, does not take on board his problems as her problem to fix. Although framing the narrative around the theme of positive sexuality, where its experience is the objective of both parties, Murphy does not negate the obstacles and challenges that shadow their relationship, complicating the depiction and thus requiring more narrative processing.

From the outset, the narrative of *Nora* is distinctive in its portrayal of women of this era. As the subsequent plot details reveal, Nora leaves her employment to run off with her lover, unwed, to continental Europe. Challenging preconceptions about early-twentieth-century Ireland, Murphy's text presents a refreshing modernist tale, one that attempts to give voice to female sexuality, a discourse that has been absent by and large in Irish film culture. While Gerardine Meaney points out that 'Murphy's work mirrors a current interest in the history of spaces of sexual dissidence and difference within Irish culture and society' (Meaney, 2004b: 8), Pat Murphy suggests that Nora Barnacle could not have been that unique, firmly believing that there were women who were able to form decisions and create their own lives despite societal norms and traditions: 'the way women do all the time'. By negating the 'woman ahead of her time' message, she tells a story that is far more representative than Irish narrative forms have suggested heretofore. Linking back to her earlier work, Murphy is unravelling a hidden history that has contemporary resonances about female sexuality.[9] *Anne Devlin* is similarly concerned with the common role women played in Irish historical rebellion, drawing on equivalent narrative devices, placing the female character and narration centrally within the storyworld.

The letters that Nora and Joyce exchange detail in a most intimate way their sexual relationship. While the letters that Nora wrote to Joyce are not available in the archives, Murphy does not doubt that they exist. The way Joyce writes, as if in dialogue, suggests that this conversation was two way. Using the device of letters to illustrate the closeness of their relationship, Murphy says that, in the movie,

> it's a time when they are physically separate, yet you are aware of an incredible closeness between them. I feel they used the letters to hold on to each other when they were physically apart. So the most sexualized parts of the movie in terms of their relationship is actually not when they're together, it's when they are apart from each other. That really interested me. (quoted in Meaney, 2004b: 70)

Negating the pillorying of opposites in this love story, the exchange of letters details both the positive and negative aspects of their relationship. Not only is the representation of female sexuality progressive and honest, the portrayal of a heterosexual relationship with all its complexities is what sets this film apart, revealing evolutionary and developmental shifts in Irish film. It parallels other narratives from this era in Irish film which position the private voice as radical and progressive, yet ordinary (*A Man of No Importance*; *A Love Divided*). Possibly an attempt to tell stories as a counter-force to the traditional representations of Ireland as sexually and socially repressed, these films represent a shift away from earlier preoccupations.

While the argument is that this film is a postfeminist text, a love story based on equality, this is not to say that it is a romance story without conflict. Clearly Joyce's jealousy, as it manifests itself for the first time when Nora attends the concert with his friend Cosgrave (Darragh Kelly), is an obstacle to their relationship and thus one source, possibly the main source, of conflict. Even though Joyce arranged the escort himself, seeing Nora with Cosgrave sends him into an irrational state of jealousy. By choosing to tell the story along these lines, Murphy is making Joyce's jealousy one of the plot obstacles to overcome as they develop in their relationship. However, the narrative, by maintaining Nora's character in a dominant position, clearly positions Joyce's jealousy as his flaw, his obstacle to overcome. Nora does not take it on board or identify with it, neither does she leave him as a consequence of this action. His emotional hang-up is not locked into a narrative power struggle. The character Nora, as constructed by Murphy, resists and prevents this happening.

Giving expression to the most intimate parts of their relationship through the key narrative devices of voice-over and personal letters is a trait of Murphy's style, experienced

Ewan McGregor in *Nora*, courtesy of Jonathan Hession, Photographer.

before in *Anne Devlin*. However, rather than confining such intimacies to the private sphere, Joyce's compulsive jealousy often catapults their privacy into the public realm. When Joyce returns to Dublin to open Ireland's first cinema, the Volta, his jealousy seems to grow and intensify. He writes a letter to Nora accusing her of being unfaithful. As she is reading it to herself, Joyce's brother Stan (Peter McDonald) asks, 'is there something wrong, Nora?' She hands him the letter and as he reads quietly to himself she says, 'read it out, read it out where he asks if Giorgio is really his son, read it out where he asks who else fucked me before he did.' She continues, 'people in Dublin are laughing at him for taking on a girl many men have enjoyed, nice is not it? That's your brother, the great writer!' Given that internal focalization is understood as a device revealing the interiority of the character, this sequence reveals the narrative strategy that places Nora as the central narrative voice, thus making this story *her* story. Murphy combines it with an approach that makes what is most private manifestly public by externally focalizing through Nora's dialogue. While voice-over and point of view are conventional ways of revealing interiority (Branigan, 1998), Nora speaking Joyce's words as she reads or recites *his* letters rather than him reading in voice-over, places her as the central 'reliable' narrator in this storyworld, unravelling his meaning and giving her experience predominance. Later, Joyce refuses to come back to her until she threatens to have Lucia baptised. When she receives the letter announcing his return, she says to Stan, 'I knew I'd best him at this writing game', once again achieving the narrative upper hand.

Despite living apart and having the destructive powers of jealousy impacting relentlessly on their relationship, Murphy portrays Joyce and Nora as managing to conduct a sexual relationship, Joyce masturbating in the projection room of his new cinema in Dublin while reading her letters and she doing the same, at the other side of Europe. Unlike classical narrative that portrays negative emotional states (i.e. jealousy) in polarized terms such as persecutor/victim, the film *Nora* manages to simultaneously represent the destructive force of jealousy alongside positive sexuality. What complicates the narrative structure of this film is the disavowal by Murphy of the simplistic polarization of emotional feeling that mainstream texts often perpetuate. In the 1970s, feminist film theory argued that the approach in Hollywood classical narrative cinema which relies on the confrontation of opposites (often along the lines of good versus evil) to express conflict, ensured that the patriarchal, bourgeois version of the social order and the status quo was continually restored and reinforced by the end of the film. The attempts to challenge this through feminist film-making sometimes had the effect of simply supplanting one dominant ideology with another. Murphy rejects the structure of opposites to create dramatic tension. Instead, she articulates a narrative exploring conflict by portraying two opposite states simultaneously, rather than pitting the two states diametrically opposite each other.

Jealousy and adultery are closely entwined as facets of the relationship that threaten to unravel it: problematic themes potentially destabilize the argument that this film is a progressive expression of equality. However, as Meaney states, '[t]here are large and fascinating differences of interpretation of the significance of adultery in the Joycean imaginary between [David] Lloyd and Murphy, which arises from their equally different interpretations of

Ewan McGregor and Susan Lynch in *Nora*, courtesy of Jonathan Hession, Photographer.

female sexuality. Murphy is very clear that Nora cannot be defined antithetically, as the opposite of repression or convention' (Meaney, 2004b: 60). Quoting Murphy as saying that '[s]ometimes people like Nora are represented in cinema and in literature as this earthy kind of sex goddess and that is just not all she is. It diminishes and limits her to propose that what liberates her from being a repressed, oppressed Irish woman is no more than the opposite of that image.' Examining the Prezioso affair in the film, Meaney argues that Nora's ultimate fidelity is to herself. In Murphy's reading of this episode, 'it is precisely because Nora refuses adultery that she maintains her sexuality and identity independent of her lover' (Meaney, 2004b: 61). In a similar way to the way she deals with female expression and identity in *Anne Devlin*, Murphy, by appropriating the feminist tool of silence, places the power with Nora in the way she chooses to respond to the Prezioso affair.

In storyworld terms, Nora and Joyce are portrayed at their happiest when they have nothing, are devoid of material possession. This is not an uncommon device of mainstream narrative: a romance/love story is often constructed in opposition to and superseding material wealth, a traditional moral that is widespread in fairy tales and myth-making. Linking poverty and happiness is a common myth perpetuated by Western society only recently challenged in Ireland, notably by Frank McCourt in his autobiographical novel *Angela's Ashes* (1996). So while the audience can recognize this as a familiar device from a range of sources, in film studies referred to as canonicity, what sets it apart and becomes breach, is the way it functions in this particular narrative as a plot device. Rather than celebrating their poverty as a state that lifts them to a higher emotional plain and deeper love, Joyce and Nora do the opposite. When Nora and Joyce are evicted from their apartment and Giorgio gets hold of Joyce's writings, scribbling on them with a crayon, rather than portraying this as a double catastrophe, Nora laughs it off. They meet in a hotel; Nora has already ordered and has champagne chilling on the side. Joyce greets her, and looking at the spread on the table, suggests in an offhand way that there is one month's salary before them. Nora shows him the defaced writings; he tells her that he has just handed in his notice at the language school, to which she replies, 'is it my turn for bad news?' informing him of their eviction. True to their form, she declares that 'we are staying here tonight'. Continuing a modernist aesthetic, Murphy says, '[y]ou go to the most expensive hotel, you buy new clothes and then you even stay in the hotel. I think it's very "them". I think it's quite a modern take on them … it's not about trying to slavishly recreate the period' (quoted in Barton, 2000: 12–15). Negating the trend in cinema towards 'heritage', where the aesthetics of the picturesque dominate, Pat Murphy says that the costumes are used as a kind of narrative: any sense of flamboyance is a gesture against poverty (Barton, 2000: 12–15). What Murphy constructs is a playful reflection on the theme of poverty, undermining its potential to dominate the narrative and inflect the story in a particular way.

At the end of the film when Nora and Joyce are re-united as a couple and decide to return to Europe together, Joyce says, broke again, 'I don't actually know how we are going to get back to Trieste, Stanley was supposed to send us some money.' Rather than being an obstacle to their future, it is incidental to their story. What is important is that they are united and the audience can only assume that the rest will fall into place. Murphy contextualizes the relationship as a 'unit' of Nora and Joyce, an interesting subversion of the dominant ideological approach that roots human behaviour to an external social or political context. As Harvey O'Brien states: '[t]he relationship issues between them and especially for Nora have been resolved satisfactorily as far as the narrative is concerned when the movie ends, and the rest of the adventure is for the viewer to pick up on by reading some books.'[10]

Plot / narration / story

As David Herman argues, structuralist notions alone cannot account for the immersive potential of stories. Story analysis must be more than the breakdown of plot and character along lines of action, arranged in a narrative sequence of cause-effect (or chance) relationship and occurring in time and space. The structural components are a means to an end: they are the building blocks in plot form towards story. The story is much more than the sum of the parts.

> Interpreters of narrative do not merely reconstruct a series of events and a set of existents but imaginatively (emotionally, viscerally) inhabit a world in which, besides happening and existing, things matter, agitate, exalt, repulse, provide grounds for laughter and grief, and so on – both for narrative participants and for interpreters of the story. More than reconstructed timelines and inventories of existents, storyworlds are mentally and emotionally projected environments in which interpreters are called upon to live out complex blends of cognitive and imaginative responses, encompassing sympathy, the drawing of causal inferences, identification, evaluation, suspense and so on. (Herman, 2002: 16–17)

The story, therefore, is a combination of depicted and inferred events, the inferences becoming interpretation of the story, addressing the question what is it about? In telling Nora Barnacle's story in a particular way, Pat Murphy presents to the audience a discourse of equality, a consequence of the love story she plots in narrative form. The scene illustrating Joyce questioning Nora about being pregnant reveals how this might work. 'The land-lady thinks you are pregnant', Joyce says from the bedroom door as Nora lies in bed at the other side of the room. Nora does not know for sure but suggests that the food is making her sick. 'Maybe you should write to your mother', Joyce says. 'What for?' she asks. 'For help', to which she responds 'I don't need her help'. Concluding the scene, Nora says, 'It'll be alright won't it, might not be, might just be the food, I can't keep it down', confirming her state while also looking for reassurance. The plot details, causal agents performing scripted actions, reveal the nuts and bolts of the story. In disavowing the audience a discourse of blame, Murphy presents this dilemma in a complex, human way, giving rise to a particular story. Joyce's initial reaction is denial and then he shifts the responsibility to Nora, expressed through his absences from her company and by spending a lot of time drinking. By rejecting the device of pitting one character against the other, rather than demonizing Joyce's behaviour, Murphy suggests that he, like Nora, is avoiding dealing with the issue. In Brenda Maddox's biography, *Nora: The Real Life of Molly Bloom*, the author shows how Joyce reacted to the news of Nora's pregnancy by writing to his brother Stanislaus, asking him to sit down with Cosgrave and study some books on midwifery as he and Nora were 'adorably ignorant' about the facts of childbirth. Pointing out to his aunt Josephine that he had not left Nora, as his cynical friends had predicted, he asked her to 'write Nora a letter of instruction' (Maddox, 1988: 57). In his own idiosyncratic way, through letters, he engages with the dilemma facing them and, with recourse to his friends, articulated at another narrative level in the film.

The relationship between Nora and Joyce is not easily interpreted for a number of reasons, but principally because the story is rooted in a much wider discourse. It could be interpreted as one of abuse, whereby Joyce is so consumed by jealousy that he is cruel and uncaring and highly destructive of their relationship. This has been suggested by some responses directed at the film and its director. Reminiscent of *Breaking the Waves* (Lars von Trier, 1996), where the main protagonist seeks sexual gratification through voyeurism, having set up his partner with others because he can no longer satisfy her, figuring out Joyce and Nora in story terms is far from straightforward. Just as von Trier's text can be read as misogynistic, the potential to negate the equality value of Murphy's film results from Joyce's jealousy and expectations around male/female relations. In Meaney's book, Pat Murphy is quoted as saying:

> one of the things that has been said to me, particularly in the United States, is why did you make a film about a woman who is being abused by this man and who stayed with him when she should have left. I kept trying to say this is not what abuse is … sometimes that's one of the situations where representation lags far behind and is not flexible enough to adequately mirror what women's lives were truly like. (Meaney, 2004b: 8)

Despite this inflexibility of form, and without going against the mainstream narrative grain, this film articulates a highly-nuanced radical human and emotional discourse. This is achieved by rejecting external rational explanations: instead, character motivation, whether rational or irrational, comes from within the individual through agency. While Joyce remains at a distance from Nora in the scene mentioned above, he does not reject her. His subsequent relationship with his son Giorgio, as portrayed in the film, along with the way they are shown to *co-parent* in a modernist yet not particularly responsible way, reinforce this. In fact, both Nora and Joyce are depicted as equally neglectful. Murphy, when asked about the portrayal of their parenting skills, explains that 'the dynamic is always between Nora and Joyce and the children are peripheral to that … The facts of Nora's life make a polarity between sexual expression and motherhood in the film inevitable' (Meaney, 2004b: 25). This is a love story between the two principle characters.

However, Nora does face her pregnancy alone. When Joyce eventually arrives home one night after Nora sends a neighbour to find him, they lie in bed together and once again

Susan Lynch in *Nora,* courtesy of Jonathan Hession, Photographer.

he suggests that she write to her mother for help. He accuses her of not being interested in his writing; her response is to recite, verbatim, something he has written. Murphy does not present Nora as victim, a sufferer or as persecuted, by Joyce, by circumstance or by her time. Nora, the character/agent, constantly re-asserts herself as an equal in the relationship, regardless of outside pressures or norms. By constructing the film in the way she does, Murphy articulates a discourse that is both contradictory and unifying. Through the moments of resistance Nora displays in the text, she asserts the position of 'equal dignity' central to the philosophy of modern, liberal humanism.

Joyce's jealousy takes increasing control of him as the narrative progresses. When he returns to Ireland to open the Volta cinema in 1909, taking Giorgio with him and leaving Lucia with Nora in Trieste, he does not return. While Nora does not follow him to Ireland, she does attempt to persuade him to come home, first by issuing him with a wedding invitation, and second by threatening to have Lucia baptised. When he returns, relations between them do not improve. Joyce tries to force Nora into an affair so that he can write about it but she resists, finally leaving him when he accuses Roberto Prezioso of having sex with Nora. Joyce tried to manipulate Nora into an affair but Nora refused to be controlled. Yet Joyce still uses it as a way of forcing a break up. 'Did you fuck my wife?' he shouts at Prezioso on the pier like somebody demented. It is after this incident that Nora returns to Galway. 'This is over now', she says as she displays the inner strength to walk away, returning to Ireland in 1912, an unmarried mother of two.

Even though she has left him, Nora stops off in Dublin to visit Joyce's publisher, as requested, to discover why his book, *Dubliners*, has not yet been published. 'Mr. Roberts, my husband wants to know why you haven't published his book.' 'It's very complicated, Madame, I will write again to your husband in due course.' 'You tell me now', she says directly. 'Well, they are not things one would wish to discuss with a lady.' 'Oh, you don't have to be afraid, myself and my husband have no secrets.' 'Well are you aware that one of the stories concerns a pervert?' 'Yes, of course.' 'There are also hidden meanings in these stories that you madam may not be aware of. For example, the most recent one, *The Dead*, frankly there is something dirty going on in that story if you ask me.' This blatant challenge to their personal and intimate relationship is revealed through a close-up shot of Nora. For a brief moment, what has been intensely private is revealed in public, sending Nora to a place she has heretofore resisted – separate from Joyce, suggesting a point of no return.

Continuing on her journey west to Galway, with the children dressed in sailor suits and straw hats and Nora wearing all whites, they could be mistaken for a well-to-do family setting off on a summer holiday. Her strength of character and state of mind, therefore, are exhibited and expressed through the clothes she and the children wear. Her inner character outwardly revealed through cinematic devices of production design, costumes and camera framing. As she steps onto the platform in Galway station, the camera holds a shot of the three of them until the children break loose and run towards their grand-parents. Although Nora is now a woman estranged from her children's father, facing into an uncertain and unknown future, the camera frames and holds her in a mid-shot, standing tall and then walking towards her parents and, through this movement and dress, assures the audience of her strength and confidence.

However, in classical narrative style, the film ends by supplanting the disequilibrium with resolution. Joyce visits Nora in Galway and finds her playing with the children on the beach. As Maeve Connolly points out:

> When they are together in her old bedroom, Nora's body language and appearance remains somewhat restrained. Instead of reacting to Joyce's provocations with her customary verbal outbursts she walks away from him, and stands outside on the street … But in sharp contrast to earlier scenes, her posture is upright and her subsequent return to the bedroom, and to the relationship, can be read as a deliberate choice. (Connolly, 2003)

Nora has shown that she has the strength to walk away but also to return to the relationship. She does so as an equal, aware of what lies ahead. The final scene visually evokes the romantic tale where the two lovers, reunited, walk off, hand in hand, into the sunset. Far from being a tacked-on ending to satisfy the demands for closure, Murphy plays with the classical and feminist devices that make this film difficult to classify.

Conclusion

Nora as a feminist film might be told in one of a number of ways: it could be a commentary on the social, cultural or political period of the time; it might tell the story of Nora, 'a woman ahead of her time', or Nora, 'victim of male dominance and abuse'. Alternatively, it could attempt to reclaim an important female historical figure. However, Pat Murphy deviates from this feminist project in the film *Nora* by telling a love story framed within the structure of a postfeminist tale, and the location, setting and backdrop of the film remain just that. Murphy does not attempt to be historically or chronologically true, even admitting that she is sometimes factually inaccurate. Her concern for truth in this film is for 'emotional truth' by telling a story about two characters who hold that love is the expression of equality, and the narrative is the articulation of their journey in that direction. Murphy's rejection of a structure that determines the actions of the characters as a consequence of wider society or norms is what shifts this film out of traditional feminism in the direction of a postfeminist discourse. The relationship between Nora and Joyce is constructed within the boundaries of the agents in the film – who they are and how they are defined. In Murphy's film, the relationship is delineated by the actions of the two characters – Joyce's actions push Nora away. She willingly leaves him as a consequence of his behaviour. When they are reunited, she decides to return to Europe with him. The relationship is an expression of who the two individuals are, not what society or fate determined them to be. As Meaney states:

[Their] relationship is not outside of society nor does it have the tragic destiny usually associated in literature and film with lovers who are at one with storms and the sea. While the couple are socially marginalized, the film also celebrates the way in which they find their way in and around society. (Meaney, 2004b: 66)

The film reveals elements that link it to various stages of feminist film as it developed and changed since the 1970s. The narrative reclaims a forgotten female figure and gives expression to a 'woman's story' but, by appropriating and subverting classical structures, it presents a contemporary story framed in a modern way. Far from being a heritage film which trivializes the past romantically, this film offers an experience that plays with familiar cinematic devices yet uses them ultimately to subversive ends. Furthermore, this film can be viewed as a bridge between the two phases of Irish cinema since the 1970s. Although not the function or narrative impetus of the film, *Nora* reclaims Nora Barnacle from historical oblivion, echoing Murphy's earlier film *Anne Devlin,* which recreated the figure of Anne Devlin as a politically-motivated rebel. By presenting Nora as much more than the wild, primitive girl from the west, the film succeeds in debunking many of the myths behind the image that is Nora Barnacle, wife of James Joyce. But it also offers a contemporary Irish love story articulating a modern discourse: one of equality. When read in this way, *Nora* can be seen as echoing some of Murphy's earlier preoccupations, while evolving and developing her *oeuvre* by reflecting contemporary feminist and female issues, through a treatment that is modern and progressive.

Notes

1. Joseph Moser in his article "Fighting within the rules: masculinity in the films of Jim Sheridan" (Rockett & Hill, 2004) quotes Jim Sheridan who states that there are 'no love stories in Irish literature ... In repressed ... broken cultures love stories have not prominence ... It's very difficult to do' (Moser in Rockett & Hill, 2004: 89). Sheridan attempts to redress this, and 'reconstitute affirmative figures of masculinity' (ibid). It appears, therefore that contemporary directors such as Sheridan and Murphy are concerned with changing the representations that have heretofore dominated Irish cultural texts and seek to offer progressive, more enlightened examples of national characters.
2. Other films that draw on the tradition of European art cinema include *All Soul's Day* (Alan Gilsenan, 1997), *How Harry Became a Tree* (Goran Paskaljevic, 2001) and *I Could Read the Sky* (Nichola Bruce, 1999), explored more closely in Chapter 6.
3. In an article entitled 'What's it all about?' by Brian Lynch, scriptwriter on *Love and Rage* in *The Irish Times* 9 Feb. 2002: 5 Lynch provocatively writes about the perceptions of the film as he awaits its release. '*Love and Rage* was shot in 40 days on Achill Island, in the house where the real life events happened, and on the Isle of Man. The logistics of this island hop were horrible. And all the while the money was vanishing like snow off a tambourine'. The article reveals the clashing of factors when an arthouse movie is made along industrial lines. Inevitably, creative input from financiers, although unwelcome, is a reality in this type of budget formation. 'All of [the Synge

references] would have been plainer had Cathal Black been able to shoot the script as written' writes Lynch, revealing the tensions between the creative force of an art form and the inevitable industrial nature of film production.

4. In a pre-screening interview with Cathal Black (November 2002) the director expressed a preferred method of working that would maintain creative independence even if it compromised the budget. This stand-point is generally associated with directors of the 1st wave, notably Bob Quinn and Joe Comerford.

5. This rule demanded that in a mixed marriage between Catholics and Protestants, the couple would undertake to educate and raise their children in the Catholic faith and religion.

6. Gerry Gregg has made documentaries that explore life in socially deprived areas (*Today Tonight – Finglas*, 1981) and has explored subjects such as the Gardaí; the RUC; Conor Cruise O'Brien. Michael Ross writes that 'Gregg has spent years going against the political grain, first in RTÉ as a current affairs producer, latterly as an independent film-maker. His politics are inseparable from his work, from *A Love Divided* to *Witness to Murder*, a Channel 4 documentary about massacre in Kosovo which won him an Emmy award', (Michael Ross, *The Sunday Times* (Culture), 12 March 2000).

7. It ranked 36 in the Top 100 performers of 1999 (*Waking Ned* (Kirk Jones, 1998) was at number 11 and *Dancing at Lughnasa* (Pat O'Connor 1998) was at number 30). Furthermore, it ranked second in its opening week, was screened in cinemas for 16 weeks and appeared in 30 screens in its opening week. Total gross £614,053, 0.84% share of box office total gross (source Irish Film Board).

8. Postfeminism is adopted here not as Susan Faludi sees it as backlash but as a continuation of feminism. According to Ann Braithwaite, postfeminism captures the state of feminism today, 'complete with all [its] difficult debates and animosities, [its] conflicts and contradictions, [its] pleasures and desires. [It is] not *about*, not *against*, feminism; not an appropriation or distortion, but a shift in central categories and questions; not a depoliticization or trivialization, but an active rethinking; not wholly new phenomena, but a way of articulating changes in and the evolution of feminism (Braithwaite, 2004: 27).

9. It is difficult to argue the case for a relationship of equality between Nora and Joyce given the extra-textual relations of this story. As Meaney points out, 'some viewers have been puzzled by Nora's decision to stay in what they see as an abusive relationship' (Meaney, 2004b: 8) and Murphy reveals that many viewers, particularly in the United States, wondered why she would make a film about a woman in an abusive relationship. It is only when the interpretation sets ideological influences aside to look at the work as constructed by the director that the story can be read along different lines.

10. See http://homepage.eircom.net/~obrienh/nora.htm

Chapter 6

Alternative Narrative Forms in New Irish Cinema

[T]he storyteller joins the ranks of the teachers and sages. He has counsel – not for a few situations, as the proverb goes, but for many, like the sage … The storyteller: he is the man who could let the wick of his life be consumed completely by the gentle flame of his story. (Benjamin in Arendt, 1968: 84)

Any consideration of alternatives to classical narrative cinema is hinged on exploring questions of narrative strategy and structure. According to Pam Cook, defining features of classic narrative structure include a linearity of cause and effect within an overall trajectory of enigma and resolution; a high degree of narrative closure; a fictional world governed by spatial and temporal verisimilitude and the centrality of the narrative agency of psychologically rounded characters (Cook, 1992: 212). Cinematic terminology, in its rigid form, tends to present non-mainstream film as 'other'. It is variously described as alternative, counter, art, avant-garde or underground, even though art cinema embraces a wide range of possibilities, varying from, yet encompassing, mainstream European cinema to radical avant-grade.

Art films are typically characterized by aesthetic and narrative norms different from classical narrative films. These films are made with a less streamlined and defined system of production, offering a flexibility not familiar in the studio system. The productions are often supported by government policies designed to promote distinctive national systems of identity and cultural activity. Yet art cinema is also sometimes conceived as commercial cinema, appealing to a more ciné-literate audience but within a defined range of what can be still conceived as mainstream. Some definitions of avant-garde cinema, different again from art cinema, would see the style as distinctly 'other' and conceived in two ways – as a parallel phenomenon to the mainstream tradition or as a reactive phenomenon against the dominant form. Very often, the project is about challenging narrative and realism. The production circumstances for this range are widely varied, as is their marketing and consumption. The historical evolution and trajectory is equally non-linear, making a singular account and snapshot difficult.

While each system has clearly defined characteristics, where the boundaries of distinction lie is more difficult to establish, particularly since the post-classical era when many of the certainties of classical cinema gave way to a multiplicity of alternatives, at the same time still clearly functioning in mainstream cinema. The alternative narrative systems are largely defined by their structural features, more so than a thematic exploration, and yet form and content are inextricably linked. Working in alternative forms is frequently about expression of form, but can also be about looking at a familiar motif in an innovative and fresh way. Very often the narrated events do not conform to the linear model and narrative closure may be problematic, uncertain or ambiguous. In alternative narratives, the fictional world can reject the spatial / temporal verisimilitude of the classical model and, in some examples, a narrative may entirely lack human agency to move it along (Cook, 1992: 216–7).

Although this is a useful definition at one level, to define alternative cinema practices by its omissions fails to account for an art form that has clear motivations realized through its narrative form. While Cook attempts a definition of arthouse film – continental European; auteur driven; defined by a certain type of exhibition outlet and a subjective verisimilitude – she still finds it difficult to avoid pitting as opposites. In short, she describes counter cinema as film practice which challenges dominant cinema, usually at the levels of both form and content. Other writers, including Peter Woollen writing in the 1970s and 1980s, see classic and counter cinema in opposition to each other. According to Wollen, counter cinema adds up to a cinema in which the linearity of causal relations between narrative events, narrative closure, spatial and temporal verisimilitude, and character identification is eschewed by the process of film narration (Wollen, 1988), a definition that once again describes it in opposition.

At the same time, counter cinema may be regarded as a matter of degrees, with some films more transgressive of the classic model than others, and for many practitioners in this field, it is in relation to the mainstream that they find their voice. Complicating matters further, the transgression that is the alternative, in turn, becomes mainstream once it is conventionalized through use. The classical model has been breaking down now for fifty years, leaving some European cinema more mainstream than that emerging from America. The binary opposition of European and American cinema, in narrative terms in particular, is as tenuous now as it was at the start of the twentieth century. Narrative is a structural construct in constant flux, either through evolutionary, innovative and experimental techniques or in a more nuanced fashion of shifting basic terms. Miriam Hansen (2000), in exploring the relationship between classical Hollywood and the avant-gardes in the 1920s and 1930s, theorizes classical cinema as a form of 'vernacular modernism': an aesthetic idiom encompassing elements of the American quotidian, which mediated competing cultural discourses on modernity and modernization (Hansen, 2000: 333–4). Cinema reflects the wider international changes that affected both Europe and America throughout the twentieth century, given expression in the narrative systems.

David Bordwell argues that by the 1960s a distinctive 'art cinema' mode of narration had emerged in America, characterized by films foregrounding narration (the process of storytelling) as much as narrative (the action itself), defined as post-classical. The term post-classical emerged to describe an epochal shift in Hollywood, reflecting the disintegration and displacement of classical narration and the studio system as the dominant forms of aesthetic organization within mainstream American cinema. Post-classical cinema is seen as an impure, less rigorous, highly flexible cinema, characterized by the coexistence of contradictory aesthetic strategies (classical editing, expressionism, realism) rather than a strict and exclusive adherence to the continuity system; by the extension, embellishment, playfulness, and mixing of its genres rather than by generic purity; and by an engagement with topical issues and controversial subject-matter even in its most conventional generic offerings. (Kramer in Hill & Church-Gibson, 1998: 291)

Since the 1990s, American independent cinema, it might be argued, is the site at which most radical and deviant film-making is happening (Sconce, 2002), starting with Richard Linklater's *Slacker* in 1991, continuing through the work of Quentin Tarantino (*Pulp Fiction*, 1994) and beyond. On the other hand, narrative technique that was once radical – jump cuts, crossing the line, speaking directly to the camera, all attempts at breaking the illusion – are now often seamless and so conventional that they bear no challenge to the viewer. For many critics, Hollywood's long-awaited renaissance finally occurred when the traditional qualities of American film-making were combined with the intellectual sophistication and stylistic innovations of the new directors and new waves of European cinema, in films addressing contemporary and specifically American subject matter. According to conventional narrative definitions, stylistic changes in classical narrative towards post-classical include

the introduction of aimless protagonists, the loosening of causal connections between narrative events, the foregrounding of stylistic devices in their own right, which serves to demonstrate the directors' artistic presence and intentions, and the refusal of unambiguous narrative closure, which invites the audience to speculate about the film's significance. (Kramer in Hill & Church Gibson, 1998: 306)

Post-classical, according to the discourse of historical poetics (Bordwell et al, 1985), describes a narrative system of codes incorporating key devices of European art cinema appropriated by New Hollywood, principally an increased use of the long take, deep-focus photography, staging in depth, alongside a move towards quasi-documentary style; in short a self-conscious, self-reflexive approach to narrative style. Bordwell neither conceptualizes as opposite nor sees art cinema as a radical departure, but rather a modification of classical norms of narration and style. Following Hansen's approach, he characterizes art cinema narration as a 'domesticated modernism', contrasting it with the more radical departures found in 'artisanal avant-garde'. These are films which are free to explore spatial and temporal form in the cinema outside of any obligation to tell a story, and an aesthetic movement that makes films – with or without any traces of narrative – of any length, ranging from a few seconds to many hours.

Popular cinema deviates from convention and delves into alternative form, but it does so within an institutional framework. This definition is similar to Rod Stoneman's vision for an Irish film industry. Describing Irish cinema not in industrial terms, he saw it as operating at an artisanal level of production and therefore playing to cultural strengths. Stoneman asserts that the main difference between the artisanal and industrial approach to cinema is located at the level of budget and style. The artisanal budgets are inevitably low and the style is one that emphasizes diversity as opposed to Hollywood's repetition (Stoneman, 2000). Furthermore, artisanal cinema encourages national cinemas to work together; a direction European cinema has gone since the 1980s, actively supported by a range of European Union funding schemes – Eurimages and the Media programmes in particular. Characterized as hybrid production, Stoneman sees the process involving various countries working together to create a wide range of different, yet modestly-budgeted films; a system that not only respects but promotes and encourages cultural specificity. While the effects of this approach could be seen as just another version of the euro-pudding phenomenon diluting creative autonomy to the point of narrative construction by committee, it is a worthy attempt at going beyond the industrial models handed down by Hollywood. On the other hand, negating the possibility of an industrial model in favour of an 'artisanal' approach surely limits the potential for commerciality and industry. Stoneman, in philosophical terms but also through policy, brought with him an approach to film production that was fostered and developed in the early days of Channel 4, and has remained the underlying tendency of the Board since.[1]

The picture emerging of contemporary Irish film, narrative and storytelling, reveals a divergence between policy and practice when the number of non-mainstream films produced in this period can be counted on two hands. Selecting films for analysis in this way is not only highly contentious but also quite difficult. While a series of films called 'Beckett on Film' could quite easily slot in here in terms of artistic style, it functions differently as an art event and, therefore, stands alone. The work of John Carney and Tom Hall brings together so many of the central themes and issues discussed generally in this book that their repertoire deserves a chapter in and of itself (see Chapter 7). What remains are a couple of individual and isolated films, that somehow slip through the net in the absence of a more structured policy, yet are significant markers for the development and evolution of new Irish cinema. The following discussion attempts to reveal the nature of experimentation in new Irish cinema across a selected range of films, within the context of narrative and storytelling.

I Could Read the Sky

I Could Read the Sky (Nichola Bruce, 1999), it could be argued, is the film most closely fitting a definition of avant-garde, generally posed in binary opposition to mainstream Hollywood cinema – 16 mm/35 mm; non-commercial/commercial; non-narrative/narrative; formalist/ political; abstract/representational. This definition lends itself analytically to take account of the fundamentals of cinema in terms of form and content, storytelling and structure as well as institutional factors. *I Could Read the Sky* is based on a 'photographic novel' produced by writer Timothy O'Grady and photographer Steve Pyke (1998), telling the story of Irish

Dermot Healy in *I Could Read the Sky*, courtesy of Nichola Bruce, director, and Enopticvisions.

All photos from *I Could Read the Sky* by Owen McPolin and Séamus McGarvey, cinematographers.

emigration to Britain. Based on the reminiscences of an elderly man, the novel comprises pictures of his life in post-war England (having taken the boat in search of work) alongside the memories of his life that he harbours of family and friends back in Ireland. The main character, Brady, played by Dermot Healy – a writer rather than a professional actor – is a labourer who travelled from the west of Ireland in the 1950s/1960s to work on the building sites of England. Sitting alone in his bedsit, the film weaves a story of experience, devoid of the dramatic arc that primes the audience for various emotional responses.

While delivering a story of a certain kind of life, the film transmits to the viewer an impression widely familiar but remaining in the shadows of Irish film narratives. The film is abstract, giving voice to themes such as memory, love, identity, loss and exile, and is representational in so far as it relates, in a narrative form of image and sound, the particular Irish experience of emigration to post-war Britain. It tells a story of masculine experience whereby identity was hinged on working, earning and providing but, in reaching these goals, the experience of exile deprived Irish men of those other aspects of male identity: intimacy, love and security. It conveys this theme and experience through narrative and non-narrative devices, including the poetic readings of Brady, where actor Dermot Healy recorded the words as a soliloquy, without any knowledge of how it was to be visualized. It is non-narrative through the layering of images, based on the source photographic novel, where a picture dissolves into another picture, achieving meaning by itself and in relation to its filmic circumstance.

While mainstream narrative production has evolved in a highly-streamlined way, production circumstances in avant-garde and art cinema vary widely. In fact, the production conditions are invariably fundamental to the nature of the film as a whole. The situation of this film brings together an interesting mix. Nichola Bruce, the director (*The Human Face*, 1991; *The Loved*, 1998) works mainly in video art and video installations while the editor Catherine Creed (*The Last Bus Home*, 1997; *The Ambassador*, 1998; *Crushproof*, 1998; *The Mapmaker*, 2001) is more associated with mainstream film-making. Given that the production was very effects-driven, it does not have a definitive narrative structure. In short, the objective of the production was to recreate human memory and deliver it in a final form of 35 mm. Arriving at that point required combining many narrative layers in a form of 'memory sequences', putting together recorded footage of the main character, Brady, combined with archival footage of Bruce's own memories, which existed already on different formats – Super 8; 16 mm; Hi8 and DVC. The final film renders human memory by creating a narrative through the film-editing process, involving a multiplicity of material and formats, sometimes shot for the production and other times pre-existing, having been recorded for other purposes. This creative endeavour was achieved in an edit suite in London, making the editor the equivalent of the cinematographer in another, more mainstream production.

For Catherine Creed, Avid technology, one of the industry standards for non-linear editing, was vital to the process. While, ordinarily, the editor would work on a production from the outset, the nature of this narrative drama meant that Creed did not come on board until the post-production phase. When she did, her first task was to view and archive 'walls

I Could Read the Sky, courtesy of Nichola Bruce and Enopticvisions.

and banks of tape and film'. Creed described the task as like finding a needle in a haystack. Used to mainstream film work, Creed started by organizing and cataloguing Dermot Healy's performance – a way of establishing a familiar footing within the narrative structure. Onto this narrative stratum four or five more layers could be built, by way of creating the memory sequences. According to Creed, she had to 'learn to let go of my narrative, linear tendency. I worked with non-linear editing and had to grasp this idea of creating memory through these layers – trying to insinuate thoughts – and that was a huge battle for me. I found that very, very difficult. I even think I tried to hold on to it, to make the old man's story linear in terms of time …… I really had to let go of everything I'd been taught' (Creed, 2000: 36–41).

Not only was the film hugely ambitious in narrative terms, it was quite complicated technically. The old formats – Super 8, 16 mm, Standard 8 and Hi8 – had to be transferred to Beta SP. The memory sequences were, by and large, shot on DVC Pro and DVC and the main narrative thread, Dermot Healy's scenes to camera, were shot on 35 mm. Complicating further, the contractual obligation was to deliver in the widescreen format of 16:9 aspect ratio. Far from being a straightforward experimental piece, this narrative required quite complex creative and technical matching. The special effects had to be completed in a software package by another specialist to allow for colourizing, draining colour or creating soft edges on some of the images – in some sequences on four or five layers. According to Creed, Bruce had not only a clear artistic vision for her film but also excellent organization skills. The layers of soundtrack were equally intrinsic to the visual and verbal narrative layers, making the production process more involved. The final transfer to 35 mm is described by Catherine Creed as 'nerve-wrecking' but the combination of the artistic vision and what the technology could achieve in expert hands managed to hold up, and the working relationship between director and editor ensured the final outcome. A conventional production involves complex management of people and departments whereas this production required an intricate integration of multiple formats. Both have the potential to implode at many moments within the process.

What the production detail of this film illuminates is the complex process involved in working within the avant-garde, art cinema or the non mainstream and, at the same time, revealing some of the misconceptions around these terms and how the film-maker functions within this form. *I Could Read the Sky*, at a technical level, combines 16 mm with 35 mm and is both non-commercial and commercial. It has parts that may be described as non-narrative but, by and large, is a narrative film; it is both formalist and political in its broadest sense. The visual and narrative pleasure in viewing the text results from its abstract and representational nature, delivering initial immediate pleasure as well as posing a challenge and demanding repeat visits. Without the technical complexity that was necessary to deliver the ambitious artistic vision, this film would not resonate on the level it does, thus demanding its consideration as more than a little-known and isolated film within new Irish cinema.

Nichola Bruce presents a very motivating narrative and thematic study in the context of recent Irish film, yet, to all intents and purposes, her work remains a stand-alone piece. Primarily about the emigrant's experience, it explores themes more associated with films

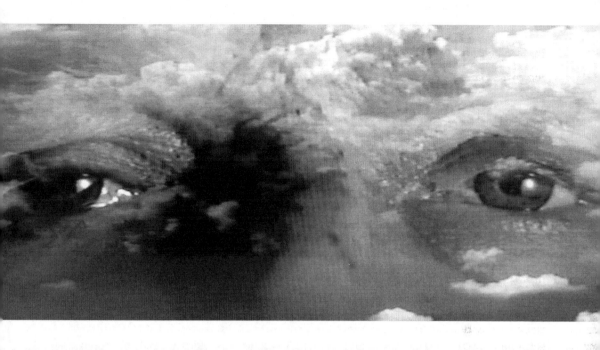

I Could Read the Sky, courtesy of Nichola Bruce and Enopticvisions.

produced in Ireland in the 1970s and 1980s, featuring stories of memory and regret. Yet it puts a new and subtle interpretation on this experience, one that goes to the heart of the experience in a deeply poignant way. It does so through the account of one man's life experience as he sits alone in his London bedsit – his adopted habitat but not his home. The theme of emigration and the emigrant's experience is a complex yet little told one. The upbeat romantic portrait in *Gold in the Streets* (Liz Gill, 1996) could not be further removed from *I Could Read the Sky*, at a thematic, visual or narrative level. Tapping into the mood of 1990s' Irish film, of up-beat, youth-oriented, hopeful narratives, *Gold in the Streets* grapples with the challenges facing emigrants chasing the American dream. After a fun-filled summer in Little Ireland, New York, Liam (Ian Hart) faces the challenge of adapting from holiday mode to new-found reality, without the shadow of remorse for the homeland.

The story of Irish emigration is interesting on two levels. While it has received scant treatment in visual texts through the decades, those narratives exploring it are noteworthy and lasting on a critical plane, if little known at a popular level. Philip Donellan's documentary *The Irishmen* (1965) tells the story of male Irish immigrants to Britain in the 1950s and 1960s. Focusing on their marginal status in post-war Britain, where despite their utilitarian function in re-building the towns and cities, they will never be fully integrated, it could be a documentary about Brady's peers. A BBC documentary that was never televised, it travelled the less mainstream route of festival exhibition. On the other hand, *Deeply Regretted By* (Louis Lentin, 1978), an RTÉ television drama adapted from a Maeve Binchy short story, tells the story of a man living a double life, working year-round in London to support a growing family back in Connemara, returning home only for holidays. When he dies, a second family comes to light in Britain, revealing his way of coping or counteracting the loneliness, filling those empty emotional spaces while away at work. A similarly-themed narrative but told in a conventional way, bilingually through Irish and English, Tom Collins' *Kings* (2007), which he adapted from the stage play, *The Kings of the Kilburn High Road* by playwright Jimmy Murphy, constructs a tale of friendship, loss and isolation among a group of men who had embarked on an adventure many decades before, only to experience dreams unrealized and promises broken. They reunite 30 years later to mourn the death of their friend, Jackie. Structured around the habitual mourning event, the Irish wake, it comes to pass that many of their dreams and ambitions were never realized. This story of enduring male friendship despite the obstacles is told through the use of flashback to illustrate the lost youth of these men.

A much earlier film, *On a Paving Stone Mounted* (Thaddeus O'Sullivan, 1979), displays many parallels with *I Could Read the Sky*. The film's narrative, like the one told by Nichola Bruce, tells the story of the emigrant's journey. That journey, punctuated by involuntary trips home to funerals, is 'a confusion of anticipation, memories and experience'. Rather than existing in the adopted world, the emigrant creates a harbour of memories from the homeland: memories and images that are fabricated and changing. Like Nichola Bruce's *I Could Read the Sky*, O'Sullivan's film is concerned with memory and how the mind is selective. This is a story about the pain of emigration and exile and, in telling its story, the film negates the familiar points of identification. According to Marc Karlin, denying us the comfort of indulging in the bard's traditional art, the film, like the migrant, travels backwards and forwards in time. Using a subjective camera, in the guise of witness, confessor and searcher, the film wanders through the Diaspora finding no stories, just their source: a ceaseless parade of characters coping with the condition of being Irish. (Karlin, IFI archive, nd)

In the unfolding narrative, which Karlin describes as a refusal on a point of political principle to tell a story, the audience is engaged in a very unusual way. The film, like *I Could Read the Sky*, is rich in visual detail, highly nuanced in exploring its theme but remarkably parallel in its message. Both films attempt to evoke a state of mind, but avoid the traditions of storytelling involving conflict and tension, easily done if the story was one of pitting opposites. Neither film romanticizes 'Irishness' nor blames the British – rather, an experience is conveyed in existential terms.

I Could Read the Sky is filmed in the style of a personal diary, drawing a structure that recounts a life told rather than documenting the events in a linear narrative form. Because this film is an adaptation of a photographic novel, rather than a filmed version of its original source, Nichola Bruce creates the events in layers of images that tell the story. The voice-over recounts fragmented memories of a time passed while the visuals collaborate by evoking the emotion through colour and texture; the relationship is constructed and glued within a dissolve. Potentially a story of sentiment and sadness, Bruce prevents this resonance by layering the narrative to constantly progress the theme in a relationship of time and space, yet negating the pleasure and security of continuity editing. The film appropriates the narrative device of montage over *mise-en-scène* to explore ideas and notions, feelings and emotions. The use of voice-over and speaking directly to the camera allow the main character address his audience, yet it eschews an intimacy – avoiding romanticization. Hence, the film evokes a mental and physical state, described by Brady, the film's main character as 'anguish, fond memory, despair and disgust and the sweaty terrors of digs and pub life'. The old man's experience as an emigrant is a journey common to the Irish experience, but the feelings of dislocation, alienation and remoteness could be a universal sense of displacement by people travelling and exiled from home, anywhere. Instead of inter-cutting fragmented memories in flashback, which might be the conventional approach, Nichola Bruce uses dissolves to superimpose images reflective of this on Healy's face. The entire film takes place in the head of the main character Brady. Bringing the past alive through a combination of voice-over and direct address to the camera, the images superimposed evoke and construct a narrative of memory. Dermot Healy was working off a script, unaware of the images that would be overlain later; the performance is a stand-alone narrative, knitted later into a multi-layered sequence.

The film, in deviating from the dominant conventions of recent Irish film, evokes a mythical state based in memory and dream yet conveys a sense of realism through some documentary techniques. Telling the audience how ill-equipped the Irish emigrant was in the alien environment of industrial Britain of the 1950s and 1960s, Brady reveals his skills and abilities as if recounting his résumé – 'I could thatch a roof. Knew the song to sing to a cow when milking. Cut turf. Work the swath turner, the float and thresher. Read the sky. Remember poems.' Yet these were perceived as useless skills in the new territory and environment in which he found himself. Recounting what he could not do explains more poignantly the real sense of alienation and dislocation – 'I couldn't eat a meal lacking potatoes. Trust banks. Wear a watch. Ask a woman to go for a walk. Drive a motor car. Wear a collar in comfort. Acknowledge the Queen. Drink coffee. Follow cricket. Speak with men wearing collars … Stop remembering.' When they find their purpose, recounted by his friend played by Stephen Rae, 'we build the railway, the roads, the buildings but we leave no trace', it suggests that they exist ghost-like, necessary to a project of modernity but not acknowledged or remembered for it. This inability to be remembered, to create a new remembered experience, suggests that the emigrants' legacy in Britain particularly at this time remains a unique one, acknowledged somewhere: in the ether.

The memories are presented in a warm glow of yellows and oranges, like old sepia-toned photographs in a family album. The happy memories are rooted in childhood and often located in one event – traditionally a wedding, visually conveyed through music and dance. The sad memories are of his parents – the death of his mother when he dug her grave, his missing brother and his father. Such is their centrality to this story, memories are presented as tangible and holding a solid form. Although referring throughout the film to the sadness and loneliness of the experience evoked – 'I believe this sadness can never leave me' – the narrative evades sentimentality, mainly because of the narrative style adopted. The production circumstances and intentions of the director mean that the central theme is conveyed as experience, neither romantic nor sentimental. Nor is it cruel or harsh. Each day is new, he starts fresh – 'I walk now, with nothing alongside me … all my pasts vanish as I go … there's a time for forgetfulness and there's a time you know what to do … in the morning light I let it go' – never putting down roots for fear that memories will sprout.

In many of the films framed thematically around the emigrants' experience, the central narrative thrust is about memory and loss. *I Could Read the Sky* explores this theme in the context of the Irish experience through its representational narrative of familiar events, traditions and experiences (the wake, the funeral, the journey home), yet simultaneously conveys the universal theme of the displaced, whose memories are rooted to a paused moment in time, depicted in the abstract discourse of music sequences, choice of colour and dissolved images (blackberries, the goose, the stone wall). Each narrative is interchangeable: the representational evokes a local and universal experience while the abstract conveys Irish symbols yet are not restricted to this interpretation alone. Brady's life exists in two parts: his memories which link back to a previous existence he cannot let go of or re-capture, while his life as an emigrant is devoid of memories. The experiences that reminiscences come to be based on require roots, and Brady's experience in Britain exists without roots. The narrative suggests that the life of the emigrant is forever frozen in time; the emotional life shut down. The momentary experience of love, when he meets Maggie in a London pub, is whipped away when she dies soon after. The film weaves a tale of recollection, based on a perceived lost life, told now from a point of fleeting existence.

Not only are these stories particularly poignant now, given the level of global migration, the direct experience addressed, it could be argued, is rooted in a past era. Not only, it seems, is the moment right for these experiences and memories to be told and received, the nature of recent changes of a global and technological nature suggest that such isolated and lonely experiences are confined to a specific time and place. Can such experiences ever be felt the same way again, be central to the emigrants story, in a globalized, modern urban world? It might be argued that life experiences are drifting more to a centralized place of universality, becoming less defined and specific along cultural or national lines, due to the advance of technology and the experience of the global village. What feelings and emotions replace this loneliness in an era of e-mail, internet and cheap travel? What is keenly created in these few narrative pieces (*I Could Read the Sky*, *The Irishmen*, *Deeply Regretted By*) is the uniqueness of the 1950s'/1960s' experience of the émigré, in some instances so particular to a place and time.[2]

Although this film rejects the familiar story-weave, recounting its theme and style is impossible without placing them in narrative terms. Peter Lennon, reviewing the film, says, 'only gradually does a storyline emerge: a simple one of a lost homeland, slavish work, a crippling accident, a love found in a pub' (Lennon, 2000: 12–13). The romantic episode is illusive and fragmentary, portrayed like a fragile memory, 'quenched one day when, walking towards him … she collapses and dies. Like everything else in Brady's life, it is too fragmentary an episode to linger over sentimentality for too long'. Describing *On A Paving Stone Mounted*, Stephen Dwoskin says the film is rich in detail, with a balanced sense of timing, 'and if, in writing, the film's story seems linear, the film's way of telling it is never linear … it uses the film's own language to tell, to ponder, to question, and, most of all, to understand this one man's story, and his journey' (Dwoskin, Irish Film Archive, nd), a description equally befitting Nichola Bruce's *I Could Read the Sky*. Two important points emerge from these films. Ireland's experience of emigration, when explored in film, often rejects the conventional approach to storytelling, principally because such linear narratives do not lend themselves to the conveying of impressions, dreams and memories. Yet this diasporic experience is one worth recounting, if only because of its central position within the Irish experience. At the same time, the primal response and need for story to be fashioned into a comprehensible and managed structure, to be received, digested and experienced, still dominates the process of film-making. But such is the experience of a range of narrative structures across mainstream film for contemporary audiences that choosing an alternative should not be such a rare occurrence. Why it is, therefore, must be more a matter of institutional policy within the structures of commissioning than the narrative expression of film-makers and narrative interpretation of audiences.

All Souls' Day

Memory and loss form the central narrative theme of Alan Gilsenan's *All Souls' Day* (1997), articulating its story in an experimental form. A low-budget film, it is notably unconventional for a first feature, and yet what is interesting about Alan Gilsenan's *oeuvre* is his mobility within narrative forms: almost like a calling card for high-concept narrative film, *Zulu 9* (2001) displays a confidence and mastery of conventional spatial/temporal relations, through its execution of a dramatic, tension-filled plot-driven story; *Home Movie Nights* (1996), a series made for television and screened on RTÉ, tells personal family histories through home video and film footage, a popular series at time of broadcast for family audiences. Also known for a range of documentaries (*The Road to God Knows Where*, 1990; *Prophet Songs*, 1991; *The Asylum*, 2006; *The Hospice*, 2007; *The Yellow Bittern: the Life and Times of Liam Clancy*, 2009), Gilsenan has demonstrated an eclectic approach to telling stories. Few Irish directors move across forms, formats and genres with such ease.

Similar to *I Could Read the Sky, All Souls' Day* uses a range of formats – Super 8, Super 16 mm, video, film and audio tape with extra-diegetic music tracks – to tell a fragmented, fractured, formally-experimental narrative about memory and loss. Framed within the verse of Oscar Wilde's *The Ballad of Reading Gaol* (1897), the film is at its most fluent when it deviates towards formal experiment. Unlike the unity of form and content in Nichola Bruce's work, this film presents an awkward narrative tension in its exploration of the notion of memory and how it distorts over time. Described by its director as an amoral tale, the film recounts the relationship between its two main characters, Jim (Declan Conlon) and Nicole (Eva Birthistle). Gilsenan views this film in the context of guerilla film-making: a practice that 'allows the imagination run free of the constraints of conventional film-making' (Battersby, 1997: 14–15). The film is about the meaning behind memories and images from the past; for Gilsenan, 'memory and distortion tend to be more truthful than the things presented with rigid clarity' (Carty, 1998: 12). This position is articulated and reflected through the film's address, which moves between the exact and the vague as its tale unfolds.

All Souls' Day tells the story of Jim and Nicole's love affair, which ended tragically in death: Jim is now serving a sentence for her murder. Seven years on, Madie (Jayne Snow), Nicole's mother, visits Jim in prison to find out exactly what happened. The story unfolds, told in flashback, combined with voice-over and non-conventional techniques such as direct address to camera and home-movie footage, blending in collage-form archival and low-budget formats, culminating in an ensemble piece. Contrary to its guerilla status, it uses many of the conventional narrative techniques of anticipation, enigma and mystery, priming the audience to search and expect resolution. Just as Catherine Creed sought a conventional format, before leaving it behind, to make sense of the alternative structure in the editing process of *I Could Read the Sky*, in viewing *All Souls' Day*, the nature of story expectation and narrative coherency demands that sense be made of it. For Gilsenan, this is possible at the level of individual viewer; a liberating experience if one is up for the task. However, when certain seeds of conventional narrative are planted, is it possible to maintain confidence in constructing one's own narrative, resisting the urge to follow a sequence piece with certain justified expectations? Such seeds of anticipation are first sown at the beginning of the film when *The Ballad of Reading Gaol* is referenced – 'all life is a limitation', in Oscar Wilde's words. The narrative purpose of Wilde's epic poem is unclear if it is not simply to evoke a tradition of storytelling, poetry and ballad in the Irish experience. While such traditions have formed an over-arching narrative guidance for many Irish films (*I Could Read the Sky*; *Maeve,* Pat Murphy 1981), its purpose here is unclear. Creed initially used convention to understand its opposite and, by her own admission, she cast aside her deeply-held narrative convictions to go with Bruce's vision. Despite Gilsenan's experience across a range of narrative approaches, a reluctance to let go completely ultimately hinders the film.

Questions of truth and how they relate to memory form the central narrative motivation alongside issues of life and death and the ageing process. The film's title suggests the multi-functional significance of 2 November, when the religious calendar marks the memory of the dead and the seasonal calendar suggests the advance of winter as things die or go to sleep. It requires a painstakingly-crafted production process to evoke many themes, often around notions of identity, and construct a complex web of situations in a multi-layered narrative, as Pat Murphy's *Maeve* did in 1981. Even though *All Souls' Day* developed organically and evolved through this complex process, rather than reaching clarity it leaves a trail of confusion, particularly in the relationship between form and content. If aesthetically the film deviates from the conventions and norms of recent Irish cinema, many unanswered questions remain around its central story, leaving room for multiple interpretations or confused reception. Certainly the philosophical thematic of life and death can be taken from the film. The issue of abuse, which surfaces at various levels as characters interact, remains oblique; what is fabricated and what is real remains obscure.

Luke Gibbons discusses the trope of memory in film and literature and sees it as part of what makes up the Irish psyche as a post-colonial construct. He argues that there are 'different registers of memory, one that is contained and legitimized within the confines of the monument and the museum, and the other having to do with the endangered traces of collective memory, as transmitted by popular culture, folklore, ballads, and so on' (Gibbons, 1996: 172). In *All Souls' Day*, memories unfold and secrets are laid bare in the search for truth and redemption, but not necessarily to a point of clarity. Gilsenan explores similar themes about memory and even loss but the fractured relationship between form and content ultimately hinders its potential radical address. Instead, unsure about character role, function and motivation in many narrative details and aspects of characterization (the mother, the father, the boy-friend, the priest and the man in the dunes), the audience can react negatively. Some respond to the film by viewing is as misogynistic (Linehan, 1998): a label that attaches easily, not necessarily justified but not readily dislodged when there is confusion around narrative explanation. The portrayal of motherhood is contentious, particularly as it is linked to the ageing process in a negative light. The danger lies in reading the significance of Nicole's death as inevitable, according the narrative text. Women ascend in youth but motherhood is a negative, declining state.

On the other hand, reading against the grain is often the route to a radical discourse and critique. The formal experimental approach to narrative suggests the film is pondering two fundamental conditions of human existence: living and dying. Jim says at one point, 'I wasn't trying to save her sanity, I was trying to dive into her madness.' Representations of the elements such as fire suggest life in full flight, and yet the ageing process is never far away, depicted in the old woman – sagging, drooping, wrinkling. The use of home-movie footage and flickering light intercut with the representation of the body suggests the fragility and fleetingness of human existence. The narrative atmosphere switches from a guilty resignation to an energetic possibility, the lighting alternating between tungsten and day-light. Never on sure footing with the meaning articulated, which is unclear, vague and foggy, the film requires a great leap of faith to avoid a negative interpretation.

The narrative discourse of storytelling, poetry and ballads, evokes traditions that suggest no one truth but multiple levels of expression and interpretation. This film dabbles in an experimental form (mixing formats, resisting conventions of narrative and negating one fixed point of address), but neglecting to have its theme and voice clearly worked out means that it drifts in a puzzling rather than experimental way between different narrative addresses. While Nichola Bruce achieves a unity within the fractured and experimental nature of her piece, Gilsenan's fails to hang together, even in a fragmented way. The framing of Wilde's *Ballad* adds little to the overall coherence – if anything it simply raises questions. Does the good angel win out, did the man kill the thing he loved and who is the brave man with the sword?

Ailsa

Ailsa, originally conceived as a one-hour film for television, adapted from a short story by Irish writer Joseph O'Connor, like the other two films, was shot on an artisanal format, Super 16. Irish film production achieves a technical proficiency on a par with most other European cinemas, through some of the key personnel working on this film - Emer Reynolds as editor (*I Went Down*, 1997; *The Asylum*, 2006; *Small Engine Repair*, 2006), Ned McLoughlin as production designer (*Korea*, 1995; *Love and Rage*, 1998; *Accelerator*, 1999); and Cian de Búitléar on camera (*I Went Down*, 1997; *Blow Dry*, 2001; *Man about Dog*, 2004). The story told centres around the obsession of main character, Myles Butler (Brendan Coyle) for an American girl, Campbell Rourke (Juliette Gruber), compulsively watching her and monitoring all her moves. When she disappears, he opens her post and pays her bills so as to not arouse suspicion. Campbell moves away temporarily and gives birth to a baby girl called Ailsa. When she indicates her imminent return with her husband and baby, Miles commits suicide. The narrative follows the conventional format of direct voice-over address to the object of the obsession. Yet, the choice of narrative device has consequences for the identity and point of view of character. While voice-over is used to recount details of enacted story information, when simply describing the feelings of the protagonist the film audience is in danger of becoming disengaged. While it works well as a literary device, it often fails to transfer to screen in narrative terms. Where this film deviates from many of its new Irish counterparts is in its visual style, whereby it 'overtly [positions itself] within the aesthetic of the European art film' (Barton, 2004: 180), deriving 'its narrative arc from the force generated by the juxtaposition of random events in a quotidian world' (Gillespie, 2008: 64).

Gillespie states that 'through all these events, Breathnach's film shows a wonderful trust in its viewers. Although the narrative painstakingly reveals the details of Myles's life, its tone remains dispassionate … It represents but does not judge Myles's mental degeneration' (Gillespie, 2008: 64). Certainly, in the films that deviate in form and content from mainstream narrative structures, the audience is accustomed to engaging on a different level. In the case of *All Souls' Day,* deviating at the level of form only yet priming the audience for certain common expectations of story content leaves the story illusive. *Ailsa,* conforming at the level of form, thwarts expectations around content. Despite Gillespie's assertion otherwise, there is no certainty that 'each audience member interprets why Myles behaves as he does and what one should think of it' (Gillespie, 2008: 64). While there are no definites around audience engagement and expectation, traditionally a non-mainstream or avant-garde approach meant interrogating form and content. Audience pleasure derives from the challenges posed by the narrative at various levels.

According to Laura Mulvey, the relevance of avant-garde to a developing radical aesthetic is threefold: it consciously confronts traditional practice, often with a political motivation and it works in a way that aesthetically challenges. The approach adopted here alters relations with modes of representation and expectations in consumption (Mulvey, 1979). While examples of 'alternative narratives' in recent Irish cinema reach these objectives in varying degrees, the context for contemporary Irish film is very different from the filmic landscape Mulvey was describing in the 1970s. Certainly the absence of a political motivation for recent Irish film has been noted by many writing about this period (McLoone, 2000; Barton, 2004). Although Martin McLoone recognizes that while the films themselves cannot be taken as political texts, they can be engaged with 'politically', Ruth Barton, in acknowledging the space, albeit limited, for avant-garde practice, is less enthused – 'even Bruce's film lacks any polemical political engagement' (Barton, 2004: 93). If alternative practice is measured according to criteria set down in different political and economic times, it is doomed to fail. In post-classical cinema, there are different ways to deviate from the norm and diverse ways to conform. Sometimes the deviations are less radical than those texts that apparently conform. For new Irish cinema, innovation in narrative form is not always found in the most obvious places.

How Harry Became a Tree

Rod Stoneman outlined his vision for Irish cinema in terms of 'artisanal cinema' back in 1993. Even though this approach was not a radical departure then, tying in with the direction many European cinemas were going as a result of active policy developments formalized through European funding mechanisms, few Irish films embraced it in all its complexity. *How Harry Became a Tree* (Goran Paskaljevic, 2001), through its narrative structure and complex genealogy, is an ambitious narrative for our times and one that reflects recent trends in European cinema. As has been argued elsewhere, the influence of Hollywood has been felt throughout contemporary Irish cinema, with only a handful of productions looking in the other direction: towards Europe. *How Harry Became a Tree* can be described as a mainstream arthouse film, a film that fashions a simple idea in a complex way, resisting the formulaic story arc structure without denying the narrative its dramatic purpose.

How Harry Became a Tree, far from being yet another example of a euro-pudding, is a hybrid form, Irish-produced by Liam O'Neill, directed by Serbian Goran Paskaljevic, based on a Chinese fable *Lao Dan* adapted by Yang Zhengung, and formed into a screenplay telling an Irish story by Stephen Walsh with Goran Paskaljevic. The story is acted out by an almost-exclusively Irish cast. With such a complex genetic pool, it is a wonder that the film manages to balance many and distinct voices: clearly an Irish film, culturally specific to a place and time in post-Civil War Ireland, yet resonant of an aesthetic familiar in the eastern part of Europe. Remarkably it does not bland out as a story set anywhere, about nowhere and nothing in particular. Although situated in Ireland in the 1920s, the film's Serbian director Paskaljevic saw it as a parable on the life of Slobodan Milošević, the Serbian dictator central to the war crimes committed in Kosovo in the 1990s. Although not an avant-garde film, it is told in a tradition of arthouse common to mainland Europe. For a director like Paskaljevic, insulated from the dominance of Hollywood cinema, it is easier for an alternative and culturally-distinctive aesthetic to develop and be expressed. Because of Ireland's close relationship with the US on many levels, it is not surprising that many Irish films display a visual style not out of place in the suburban multiplexes of any American city.

How Harry Became a Tree, therefore, is a light at the end of the tunnel of cultural imperialism, and an example of how creativity can be harnessed from a mixed range of backgrounds to tell a story that resonates on many different levels for diverse and separate audiences. At the level of story, this film is about Harry (Colm Meaney) who, disappointed and let down by love, has decided to lead his life through the emotion of hate. Set in a fictional place called Skillet, Ireland, in 1924, it is situated in the immediate aftermath of Civil War Ireland, where resentments linger on both sides and old hatreds are at work above and beneath the surface. Harry, believing that a man is measured by his enemies, picks George (Adrian Dunbar), local business-man, shop owner and pub proprietor, as his enemy. When Harry's son, Gus (Cillian Murphy) asks 'what he has ever done on you', Harry replies, 'nothing'. The narrative follows this irrational tale of hatred through the growing negative relationship that Harry manufactures between himself and George. When he seeks out George's niece, Eileen (Kerry Condon), as a match for Gus, George says 'make me an offer'. Not having much to offer, Harry pledges half his field of cabbages, muttering to himself as he manufactures offence, 'you take Annie's cabbages, George high and mighty O'Flaherty', seeking retribution by breaking the heads of the cabbages and allowing George's half to rot. On a surface level, this film contains all the conventional tropes of Irish film: the lonely widower rearing his only son in a tiny, isolated farm, poverty-stricken materially and emotionally; drink-fuelled events in the local pub providing release; and never-ending rain.

Colm Meaney in *How Harry Became a Tree*, courtesy of Liam O'Neill and Paradox Pictures.

Yet all these habitual symbols of Irish film – rural Ireland, the dominant father, the Civil War – are re-imagined and presented in a fresh and alternative way. Telling the story of irrational and manufactured hatred without the heavy hand of overt and dogmatic overtones allows the resonance of Irish history to float to the surface without becoming preachy and strait-laced. This is achieved through an alternative approach to narrative, aesthetic and visual style. The story is bizarre – a black comedy, inflected with the absurdism of Flann O'Brien and Samuel Beckett, and a hint of the legacy left by a tradition of Serbian Dadaism in avant-garde Belgrade going back to the 1920s. The film reveals what a director coming from a strong cinematic and art tradition can bring to a conventional and mainstream cinematic milieu. The film reveals a mythic, almost fairy-tale quality – a new outing for the post-Civil War theme much beloved of Irish narratives.

According to Gerry McCarthy, 'some cultures have calendars hard-wired into the brain. They take human capacity for superstition and magical thinking – widespread even in supposedly rational societies – and channel it into a web of anniversaries and commemorations' (McCarthy, 2001: 31–2), suggesting a link between Serbia and Ireland and the tendency of both cultures to focus on the past. The theme of collective memory, whereby old grudges are harboured and allowed to fester and rule for generations, is at the heart of the tale, familiar in what was deemed 'civil war' politics.[3] Just as this divide was fading out, and Irish people were asserting political allegiance based on more rational beliefs and opinions, the Balkan states were plunged into a bloody Civil War – the events of which led to Goran Paskaljevic's exile.

Yet, the theme of irrational hatred is neither ridiculed nor trivialized in this narrative but given a thoughtful treatment. Harry's mission is ascribed the seriousness of any other idea that requires deliberation, strategy and execution, with a hint of absurdity. What adds substance to this tale is the deep loneliness felt and the inability to emotionally deal with one's fate or destiny, again a common trope of recent Irish film. Harry talks to his wife and deceased son at their grave, just like the young boy Harry and his mother did in *The Boy from Mercury* (Martin Duffy, 1996). Grief-stricken and lonely like Brady in *I Could Read the Sky*, Harry's energy is projected towards an irrational, bizarre and absurd task. He is not to be laughed at but felt for empathetically as he tries to come to terms with his life and the cards dealt to him, albeit in an irrational, ridiculous way. Far from being a moral tale for a post-conflict situation, this film does what film does best: it provides an outlet for the expression of an emotional state. In this instance, grief is explored through the allegorical tale of hate and, rather than presenting solutions or offering an ideological treatise, the film allows the audience to empathize with a situation that is just too difficult to express or comprehend rationally. This applies to Ireland's tragic distant past as well as Serbia's recent one. The film skilfully brings together Balkan and Irish themes yet avoids 'blanding out' – sometimes a side-effect of transnational narratives. Far from offering pat solutions as the tale unfolds, it descends into a deeper and unavoidable tragedy: fruits of the story-seeds sown. Although all details of historical events are absent from the film, it functions as a tale of personal tragedy in keeping with the great dramatic traditions of old, yet resonates on a level that speaks to

Pat Laffan and Colm Meaney in *How Harry Became a Tree*, courtesy of Liam O'Neill and Paradox Pictures.

a cultural and national milieu. In this way, Stoneman's approach to 'artisanal film', although only minutely realized, demonstrates how contemporary European cinema might withstand the advances of the globalized form of Hollywood by telling local tales in a universal way, stories from the periphery that are accessible at the centre.

How Harry Became a Tree represents the current status of alternative film – carving out a narrative space away from the dominant global forms, at the same time not reacting against them as a way of creating extreme narrative forms only accessible to *cinéastes*. Changes in narrative form over the past twenty years, in American and European cinema, means there are multiple possibilities for alternative cinema. Far from preaching to the converted, this film allows its narrative to unfold subtly and the audience to take from it what it will. At the same time, there is no avoiding the pleasure of the absurd and bizarre in the fable set in comic mode, as well as the visual style that is neither monotonous nor lacklustre. Most importantly, this film links Ireland aesthetically to its European neighbours, more so than almost all other recent Irish films, if in imagination alone.

Notes

1. Cathal Black's *Korea*, while in narrative terms tells a conventional story of a relationship between father and son in 1950s' Ireland, its pace and visual style link it more to the first wave than the emerging new Irish cinema. Similarly, Joe Comerford's *High Boot Benny* (1994) works within the dominant first wave trope of Northern Ireland and the 'Troubles', exploring the notion of responsibility and blame. Comerford and Black are directors more associated with the political and radical first wave and through these narratives, link the two phases. As has been argued here, these links become more tenuous as the 1990s progress. *Helen* (Christine Molloy and Joe Lawlor, 2008) is regarded as an arthouse movie. Its narrative pace is slow and stylized, the mug shot sequence, circular tracking camera and use of a non-professional cast give it the trappings of artisanal cinema. According to Scott Townsend, 'despite its lyrical aesthetic, the film initially appears to follow a traditional blueprint, but as it reaches its conclusion it gradually becomes apparent that Lawlor and Molloy have no interest in providing simple gratification or easy answers. *Helen*'s denouement makes it clear that these brave, talented film-makers are more interested in what makes sense for their characters than serving any kind of story structure. Ultimately, it is this quality that makes *Helen* a film that will frustrate and fascinate in equal measure.' (Townsend, 2009). The only point of consensus arising from this range of non-mainstream film is that the audience rarely remains indifferent.
2. While Donnellan's film documented the terrible lives of these emigrant men back in 1965, only as recently as 2007 a campaign entitled 'The Forgotten Irish' was launched to raise money through the activities of philanthropists for the Irish who migrated to Britain after the Second World War and sent home their earnings from construction jobs on the building sites of most major British cities. This history of the Irish in Britain is a story untold in many narratives.
3. This refers to a tradition in Ireland only broken with the election of Mary Robinson as President of Ireland in 1990, whereby people had voted according to long-held family allegiance to one or other of the two main political parties. This political practice stemmed from the Civil War of 1922/1923 when families were divided along the axis of pro- and anti-treaty, sowing the seeds for the construction of Irish political identity for many decades to follow.

Chapter 7

Narrative Diversity and Range in New Irish Cinema

If myths then can be both functional or dysfunction[al], if they can either move an audience toward cultural individuation or away from it, what mythic visions do we need as humanity moves into the next millennium? ... Rushing and Frentz assert that such myths would invite cultures, while 'still maintaining their uniqueness,' to 'expand their identities outward into a more global, even universal consciousness.' [Joseph] Campbell reaches a similar conclusion regarding the shape of myths in the future. As he explains, 'when you come to the end of one time and the beginning of a new one, it's a period of tremendous pain and turmoil. The threat we feel, and everybody feels – well, there is the notion of Armageddon coming, you know' and this requires 'myths that will identify the individual not with his local group but with his planet'. (Mackey-Kallis, 2001: 238)

When considered closely within the context of recent Irish cinema, the work of film-makers John Carney, Kieran Carney and Tom Hall might signify the direction Irish film has been going over the past fifteen years. Their range of stories and films are emblematic of the tropes and styles of new Irish cinema since the re-activation of the Irish Film Board in 1993. The cinematic trajectory of this writer/director team over a ten-year period beginning in the mid-1990s is illustrative of the defining features of this period. Starting in 1996 with an alternative approach to an incestuous relationship (*November Afternoon*, John Carney and Tom Hall 1996) to the brief relationship with a multi-million-dollar Hollywood budget (*On the Edge*, John Carney 2001) until returning to the low budget artisanal approach to film (*Once*, John Carney 2007), the *oeuvre* of this trio reflects the ebb and flow of recent Irish cinema as it develops and evolves into the new millennium. In this concluding chapter the central concerns of this book – to elucidate on narrative and style in recent Irish film – are brought together and focused on the diverse range of films, stylistically and thematically, in this body of work. These films facilitate an examination of key questions central to contemporary Irish film, from a narrative, aesthetic, political and economic perspective, while also addressing concerns facing all small countries and their negotiation of indigenous film in the era of 'globalization'.

The films of Carney, Carney and Hall in many ways encapsulate and reveal the dominant themes and issues raised already in this study. These films display a concern with many of the expected topics of a national cinema: the investigation of social issues and taboo subjects such as incest (*November Afternoon*), paedophilia (*Park*, John Carney and Tom

Hall 1999), adultery (*Just in Time*, John Carney & Tom Hall 1998) and suicide (*On the Edge*) within the context of social phenomena such as the 'Celtic Tiger' (*Bachelors Walk*, 2001/2, Carney, Carney and Hall) and migration (*Once*).[1] However, the narrative and aesthetic approach framing and structuring these films is less about the specific in terms of identity and more about the broader human preoccupation of individual themes: a tendency in recent Irish film already identified. Hugh Linehan observes that '*November Afternoon*, *Park* and *Just in Time* all explore what goes on beneath the surface of suburban respectability and the themes – unfaithfulness, incest, child abuse and rape – chime with many Irish concerns of the 1990s without seeming issue driven' (Linehan, 1999). Rather than using these themes and issues to offer clear and direct representation of recent Irish society, Carney and Hall's approach to the story themes and styles in terms of filmic address (acting, music, formal expression) is what is most compelling. It is not simply enough to discuss the themes and issues represented – these narratives are much more than that. The approach demands that the basic elements of film be examined – actors, music, plot and story – in order to get beneath the surface of this range.

Part of the critical approach involves assessing whether the films achieve some of the directors' intentions in order to identify authorial purpose/auteur approach. The caution around intentionalism is not to take statements by writers and directors as fact. Instead, they are used to identify patterns in the work regardless of differing production environments, or to identify narrative consistencies despite varied themes and subject matter, and assess developments in the range over a period of time. Furthermore, it is useful in discerning how visual style reveals key themes and how the approach to the filmic medium is uncovered according to narrative traits. In pointing out that those against the 'intentionalist principle' say that we can never know what an author intended, while often claiming to know what readers perceive and interpret, Paisley Livingstone asks 'if it is possible to know something about other reader's constructive operations, why would author's storytelling aims constitute a special and insurmountable problem?' (Livingstone, 1996: 169)

Looking more closely at the work of Carney, Carney and Hall, key questions emerge, particularly in terms of acting and performance. How are the relationships configured on screen? What does this configuration owe to an artistic vision? How is it affected by the limitations and possibilities within the production environment? Are these films concerned more with character than plot, with theme than issue, with existential questioning rather than social and cultural context? Who are the films' characters addressing, on-screen and off-screen? In exploring themes such as incest and paedophilia, is the thematic exploration confined to an address between screen characters or does it implicate the audience? Through the narrative approach, is the 'issue' being interrogated in its multi-faceted complexity or is it driven in an overtly ideological way? These are questions preoccupying critics and commentators on film, but ultimately relate to the nature of storyworld construction. It is the way they are addressed and how they are framed that makes for diverse interpretation.

Narrative theme

Narrative analysis, according to Paisley Livingstone, is not about chasing up the 'belief set of a fictional author who tells a story as known fact; rather, [it is] interested in what the actual author decided was to be the case in the story he or she was inventing and trying to communicate' (Livingstone, 1996: 164). The director and scriptwriter make decisions about what story to tell and how to tell it. These decisions are inevitably informed by a range of circumstances including, but not limited to, personal belief systems, artistic influences and social, political and cultural environment. Concentrating on narrative sheds light on at least the first two: the areas that this study is interested in. Thus the 'what' in the research question concerns the narrative themes that preoccupy the writer/director as they construct a series of films, while the 'how' refers to the structure, strategy and devices appropriated to articulate these concerns, ideas and imaginings.

The narrative themes expressed through this range of films goes to the heart of many themes that Irish society has been grappling with and coming to terms with over the past fifteen years, played out in the public domain and spilling into the fictional realm. The themes that films such as *November Afternoon*, *Park* and *On the Edge* explore are not uncommon for a small, indigenous, national film industry framing its mission, however informally, as 'telling stories to ourselves about ourselves'. The themes of suicide, incest and paedophilia have gone from being hidden and suppressed to occupying central stage in public discourse in Ireland, either through court proceedings, official reports, individual accounts or statistical information. However, the parallels between these forms of narrative expression and those appropriated by Carney and Hall stop just there. While this type of subject matter is often viewed in terms of 'issues', forming conventional tropes in kitchen-sink drama, soap opera and social-realism film, the treatment given in this body of work is quite different. While some recent Irish films have sought to hang narrative stories on issues and themes with the emphasis on plot-driven narrative (*Accelerator*, Vinny Murphy 1999; *Crushproof*, Paul Tickell 1998), Carney and Hall use the device of characterization to explore the theme in its humanistic complexity. The actors become agents rather than ciphers. The net effect is less a social comment and positioning of the issue remarking on the nature of Irish society but, rather, in the case of each of the 'issues', a complex, sometimes uncomfortable, certainly unconventional treatment. Yet, these narratives emerge from a time and place at a specific moment and are not therefore decontextualized from their wider environment.

November Afternoon, the first film to be co-directed and co-scripted by John Carney and Tom Hall, tells the story of two couples spending the weekend together in Dublin city. John (Mark Doherty) and Karen (Jayne Snow) are married and living in London. They come to Ireland for the weekend and meet up with Karen's brother Robert (Michael McElhatton) and his American girlfriend Cathy (Tristan Gribbin). Shot on a shoestring budget in black-and-white grainy video, it evokes the style of 1960s' New York underground and the work of John Cassavetes in particular, as well as paying distinct homage to the French New Wave's Jacques Rivette and Eric Rohmer, for example. While parallels can also be drawn with the work of

Woody Allen and 1940s' film noir, *November Afternoon*'s approach is less dialogue-driven; rather, the emphasis is on performance – a key auteurist device that features across the body of work. Shot on the streets of Dublin, this film sets the tone for institutional defiance that surfaces and impacts on most of the narrative approaches in this body of work.

As the narrative unfolds, the audience learns of an incestuous relationship that Karen and Robert have been conducting for fifteen years and, far from pitting it in a dominant/recessive or victim/abuser alliance, both are complicit and consenting. The dramatic tension is played out as they try to disengage from the dysfunctional bond they both admit is wrong. As in the conventional depiction of relationship break-up, one of the characters is keener to hang on while the other is willing to go. Carney and Hall complicate the narrative trajectory by constructing Karen as the driving narrative force behind the socially inappropriate affair. While Robert has indicated a willingness to cut loose, Karen cannot let go yet knows she should; even though married with a child, she has more to lose. The film concentrates on exploring the taboo relationship rather than looking at it as a clandestine act, yet the dramatic tension hinges on being 'caught'. For a first film, it displayed a strong narrative command and deftness and an original take which resists cultural trends. To a degree, the model was repeated in *Just in Time* (1998), a 52-minute drama for television produced under the Real Time scheme (RTÉ and IFB). This drama also places an intimate relationship under the microscope. A middle-aged couple, facing a disintegrating marriage, encounter a friend in the country cottage they co-own when he brings his lover for a clandestine affair. As the main couple explore and face their challenging relationship, Frank (Gerard McSorley) comes close to confessing his own extra-marital affair back in London. Like *November Afternoon*, this film explores the internal workings of a relationship in trouble and the various attempts at setting it right.

Park, a little known film shot on DV, partly in real time and in colour, offers one of the most problematic texts in recent Irish film, presenting a critical challenge to its representation of paedophilia. Shot in flashback, this film tells the story of Catherine (Claudia Terry) recounting a day skipped from school when she encounters and is befriended by Adam (Des Nealon), old man and park keeper, in the local park where she was supposed to meet her friend who did not show. Similar to the later film *All Soul's Day*, discussed in Chapter 6, it hinges on the narrative theme of memory, truth and dreams in the context of an abuse story, with the psychiatrist acting as investigator seeking out the truth. Because, like *November Afternoon*, it rejects the abuser/victim narrative strategy where one is pitted against the other along hierarchical lines, it makes for both confused and uncomfortable viewing. No easy or pat solutions are offered; it explores the notion of trauma and how it is individualized in circumstance.

This film presents a complex interpretation of the paedophile character – not demonized but shown as delusional in his self-perception. The narrative recounts how Catherine remembers the events without the device of point of view. In recalling the events as the day unfolded, her account is anything but straightforward. Neither false memory nor fabrication, the trauma of remembering is subtly conveyed. The psychiatrist prompts questions, forming the dramatization of how Catherine recollects. Rather than presenting a plot-driven account of the events, this narrative reveals how the story is recalled eight years later from Catherine's perspective, suggesting and evoking, without stating, the emotions associated with someone abused. It pays particular attention to the theme of guilt and the feelings of complicity. In approaching the story in this way, this film is not easy viewing, giving the impression of a documentary told in fictional format. Because it eludes the highs and lows of a conventional narrative that strategically places plot points within its story arc, it fails to acquire the status of a film like *The Magdalene Sisters* (Peter Mullan, 2002) or even *Song for a Raggy Boy* (Aisling Walsh, 2003), films not dissimilar in dealing with an aspect of Ireland's recently revealed history of institutional abuse. While these films made their mark in another way, more socially directed, *Park* is an accomplished psychological study. Catherine's perspective is one of guilt: not an uncommon experience following abuse, resulting from a whole range of reactions to what happened. Adam's delusion makes him repellent without creating a character that is grotesque or eccentric. In this way, his behaviour is neither excused nor negated, while Catherine's response is complex and credible. This film is ambitious and intricate by virtue of its subtlety, tackling very difficult subject matter by resisting the conventional narrative temptation to create dramatic conflict through oppositional characters. Like many of Carney and Hall's films, the performance element is central to how the narrative is executed; in this case, the outward performance of the interior or psychological state of the abused and the abuser is what designates the style.

Aesthetic and performance

Understanding character construction and how the actors interpret this through their performance is central to an appreciation of this body of work. Getting a handle on character in narrative terms is aided by some philosophical approaches, listed in the writings of Paisley Livingstone. As already mentioned, Livingstone's objective in his construction of character analysis is to defend intentionalist principles.

> But for there to be an actual event or episode of characterization, some actual agent or agents must perform the right sort of representational action, intentionally producing a representation of some agent or type of agent with the intention of thereby representing that agent or agent type ... Characterization ... should be understood as a species of intentional action. (Livingstone, 1996: 150–1)

In defending the intentionality of characterization, Paisley argues that no matter how closely and deeply drawn they are, fictional characters never represent empirical characters.[2] Appropriating a philosophical defence through the writings of Theodor Adorno, who states 'the very precision of their representation may be what removes them even further from empirical reality, so that they become aesthetically autonomous' (quoted in Livingstone,

1996: 155), Livingstone suggests that fictional performance functions at a different level from representation and verisimilitude. The narrative variation between novel and film, for example, allows characters to be represented through internal thought (the former) and action (the latter), both explicated through gestures, looks and expression. In both cases, the character constructed is not a replication of a real-life person, ever, but the agent through which an emotional experience, structured within the frame of represented empirical reality, is brought to life.

What makes cinematic representation and performance different is the close resemblance characterization can have to what we perceive as reality but in a digestible and explanatory way, explaining in emotional terms some aspect of humanity or experience. Its representational nature is purely interpretative, according to the way the writer, director, cinematographer, etc. sees the world, presents it and intends it to be received. Film narratives interpret human behaviour, often without explaining or offering solutions, through actor performance, camera and editing technique. In exploring a theme or topic, Carney, Carney and Hall tease it out according to agency and not issue. This is achieved through actor performance, action and dialogue. Rather than using the narrative to explore the issue of incest, paedophilia or suicide, through actor performance these issues are given an exploratory treatment in a humanistic and emotional way, with little reference to the social or cultural environment out of which they emerge. Of course situated in a social and cultural milieu, invariably Irish, middle class and urban, it is not so much a comment on this as on the human emotional experience of the story.

John Carney and Tom Hall's second feature, *Park,* restricts its storyworld mainly to one place, which is defined and contained within the boundaries of the city-centre park where most of the action unfolds. The physical limits imposed on the storyworld contribute to a claustrophobic atmosphere on one level, echoing the emotional tale being told. However, within this tense and constricted imagined world, the sense of space is fluid, creating a world that both contracts and expands. Through the use of a very long tracking shot whereby the school-girl, Catherine, is followed through the park by the park keeper, Adam, yet not in an overtly, predatory way, the vantage point for the viewer is neither assured nor fixed. The girl is not presented as feeling under threat and the narrative inhabits an atmosphere of relative calm – in story terms working to the benefit of the abuser. Hugh Linehan observes that 'the strongest and most disturbing part of the film is that original, central sequence, in which Terry [Catherine] and Nealon [Adam] circle each other against the lush, green backdrop of the park. It's sometimes dreamlike, sometimes terrifying and sometimes quite funny, with Nealon a pathetic, comical but deeply threatening figure' (Linehan, 1999). The costumes and props alongside the performance create an image that is subtly disturbing. Nealon, with his trousers worn high on his waist and his jumper tucked tightly in, is presented to the audience as a disturbing character, but not as such from the girl's point of view. It is a film unpleasant to view because of the way the actors personify the characters: Adam befriending Catherine, chatting and casually walking alongside her, then leaving abruptly – destabilizing and unsettling. He invades her personal space, acting silly and like a fool but still not perceived as a threat. The impression left through the personification by actor Nealon is one of unease, impersonating a 'character', the embodiment of individual traits and peculiarities drawn by the narrative. In this instance he is eerily delusional, 'my mammy always said I was the most handsome boy in town', he says to Catherine as he preens himself vainly, suggesting a threatening force to the audience, but not in the eyes of the other character on screen.

This approach to performance and acting is established in *November Afternoon* from the outset. From the opening sequence, as the narrative unfolds through the introduction of characters, before the revelation of the central plot, each frame is set up around character movement. Either the characters occupy the frame in a highly fluid way or they move into and out of the frame. Performance is central to how this narrative unfolds, as illustrated in the scene when the characters are stuck in gridlocked traffic. The sequence follows a series of close-up shots of each character as the story is yet to be revealed. This film, it might be suggested, uses the film frame 'theatrically' to evoke unease, tension and restlessness, not through what the characters say or see but, rather, how they perform, what they do. Alongside this fluidity of performance within the frame, subtle clues are dropped, anticipating revelations yet to come, recalled later when their meaning becomes clear. Rather than opting for the conventional and narratively 'easy' option of flashback, Carney and Hall create the sequence of memories and the past through circular camera movements and dissolves, as the characters recount their memories of childhood.

The shift in narrative device changes notably when the story of incest is revealed. Much more static framing is adopted to articulate the unease of relationship between the various participants and how they are connected – John and Robert, Cathy and Robert, Robert and Karen – not so much fluid but restricted and constrained. The approach to performance and aesthetic devices tracks the mood and theme as they change along the narrative trajectory. For a first feature, *November Afternoon* displays an accomplished experimental approach to narrative construction. Working within an arthouse aesthetic, Carney and Hall move freely between mainstream and innovative narrative devices. The film explores the boundaries, the norms and the deviations within a range of relationships. In a counter-Hollywood approach, none of the variations are privileged as ideal (marriage, romance or incest). Nor are they demonized outright. The story is presented through a distinctive style of performance, *speaking voices and moving bodies*, with each relationship carrying emotional pros and cons. As Paisley Livingstone says,

> [there is] something powerful about the cinema's depiction of people, something having to do … with the special role played by perception. Filmmakers can often, if they so choose, employ the cinematic apparatus in such a way as to provide the spectator with sounds and images that depict the physical appearances of a performer in a manner that no verbal narration could ever achieve. (Livingstone, 1996: 156)

While Livingstone makes these statements in the context of teasing out what equipment the spectator needs in order to perceive and interpret a given sequence, it requires an advanced level of narrative skill by the director to show through character behaviour a human situation that is received and perceived on an emotional level.

Deviating from the alternative norm

According to this analysis, the film that 'slips' in its narrative purpose of delivering agents that impact purely in emotional terms is the Hollywood-studio-supported production *On the Edge*. In *November Afternoon* and *Park*, the narrative theme is delivered through what the characters say and do/see and hear, through their performance of scripted action. However, a number of alternative devices are appropriated in *On the Edge*, making it a very different narrative approach. The theme of suicide is given an ironic treatment in keeping with developing trends in European and American independent film since the 1990s. The effect of an ironic tinge is in contrast to that achieved in *November Afternoon* and *Park*, where the 'issue' resonates in a much more serious light. The use of irony lifts the issue, in this case suicide, from its weightiness, presenting it in a light-hearted way. While it entertains at a comic level, it maintains the audience at an emotional distance from the characters. Either challenging perceptions or expectations by turning stereotypes and perceived norms inside out, this film presents an alternative representation of a psychiatric institution and characters with mental illness.

Particularly interesting from a production perspective, these films suggest the contrasting approaches to work practices between an indigenous, low-budget film and one that has a Hollywood studio with a big budget behind it. The lack of autonomy in the latter is well documented while the limitations of the former are widely accepted. This dichotomy was explored in Chapter 6, revealing the tensions brought to the surface depending on the balance of power as financial input impacts on creative independence. The evolutionary process of *On the Edge* that saw the title shift from the distinctive and provocative *The Smiling Suicide Club* to the nondescript and instantly forgettable *On the Edge* reveals the strain between taking a risk and remaining safe. John Carney maintains that there was little interference by financiers from Universal Studios in the production process. He was largely left alone until post-production, when the institutional device of test-screenings had a central part to play in shifting and altering narrative strategy.

The distinctive auteurist device of tracking shot, already identified in *Park* as an establishing approach to narrative and a typical mark of visual style, is adopted here. The provocative opening scene tracks Jonathan (Cillian Murphy) as he marches up the church aisle to the coffin containing his father, knocking loudly as he proclaims 'still dead'; the music shifts from heavy tones suggesting grief and sadness to excitement and possibility as he departs the church. Requiring no explanation of the main character following this sequence, the narrative modifies with the need to 'explain' the motivation behind Toby (Jonathan Jackson), when he recounts the story of his brother's death and how he caused it in a car accident. While the spectator can rationally receive the tragedy of the story, in film narrative terms 'telling' rather than 'showing', makes it difficult to empathize emotionally. On the other hand, the explicit and measured development of the scene involving self-harm brings the emotional impact of such activity to the surface through the action and performance. The unfolding 'love story' is incongruent, again through its confinement to a level of telling rather than showing, whereas the depiction of the growing friendship between Toby and Jonathan is both convincing and moving. Whether these narrative glitches that breach storytelling norms, whereby some aspects of the story are delivered at an empathetic level whereas others demand a rational understanding and acceptance, are as a result of the tensions behind the scenes between John Carney (writer and director) and Universal Studios is open to speculation. In an interview with Derek O'Connor in *Film West* John Carney, describing the finished film as 'a slow-burning film with long dialogue scenes, and what we've tried to do is shoe-horn that into [what] is a fast funky kids spunky film', sees it as over-edited. Admitting little interference by the studio in the production phase, it was the process of test-screenings that led the film to be edited, deviating from the initial 'intention' of the director. Following this experience, John Carney returns to the more artisanal approach to film-making with his next feature, producing the Oscar-winning low-budget movie *Once*.

In keeping with this approach to performance aesthetics developed over time, one of the more memorable scenes of recent Irish film and television appears in the television drama series *Bachelors Walk* (2001/2). The drama centres around the lives of three bachelors who live together in a Georgian house on Dublin's Bachelors Walk. In a typical narrative battle between residual and emergent cultures (Tulloch, 1990), this drama shows how the fruits of 'Celtic Tiger' Ireland have bypassed the lives of the three main protagonists, in many ways. None are particularly successful in their chosen field: solicitor Michael (Simon Delaney) has no clients, Raymond (Don Wycherley) struggles as a writer while Barry (Keith McErlean) goes from one off-the-wall business idea to another, without any success. Neither are any of them fulfilled romantically. However, they are a likeable trio, resisting the trappings of Ireland's boom, clinging on to the comfort-zone of a 1980s' recession-styled life.

The drama aesthetically constructs an imagined Dublin where you can still get free on-street parking without a clamper in sight, and going for afternoon pints in Mulligan's on Poolbeg Street is an impromptu and regular occurrence. The series was both critically and commercially successful for Irish audiences, particularly those craving nostalgia for a bygone era. Written and directed by all three, John & Kieran Carney and Tom Hall, *Bachelors Walk* concludes the first series with the iconic scene depicting the characters lounging around in Raymond's sitting-room, the expanded space of high-ceilinged, impressively-proportioned Georgian architecture. Slowly breaking-down in tears as the reality of their failed careers and doomed love affairs sinks in, to the maudlin tones of a Tom Waits number, the emotional display fills the space. Rather than ending on a high note or a cliff-hanger as most television dramas tend to as a way of ensuring a follow-up series, the directors held their nerve and defied narrative expectations of an upbeat, happy ending. Allowing the characters to perform non-traditional roles and confounding stereotypes of masculinity, what emerges is a soppy and sentimental ending not only to the series but to an imagined Dublin much beloved of a pre-M50 generation. These films display an auteurist approach to acting and performance in particular, but they also reveal the tensions and differences within a narrative structure depending on the production deal or set-up. While the interference from a studio-supported film can be overstated, if this range is anything to go by it appears that more creative autonomy and independence is achieved in the smaller, low-budget approach to film. This identifies one of the key obstacles for most small, indigenous film industries, attempting to establish and consolidate and face down Hollywood's might.

Artisanal meets mainstream

Once, John Carney's feature film from 2007, embodies many of the idiosyncratic features of recent Irish film and in many ways symbolizes the direction the Irish Film Board has been going since its re-inception in 1993. In the true spirit of artisanal film, *Once* was shot on a minuscule budget of €180,000 over seventeen days with a crew of twelve and two small digi-cameras – the digital format chosen for stylistic as well as budgetary reasons. It combines the use of hand-held cameras, shaky movement and jump cuts evoking the aesthetic of the French New Wave in particular. Defying institutional processes, the production dispensed with the services of many of the roles defined by the studio system, allowing movement through the city, unobtrusively, of a small group of cast and crew. Like the approach adopted by Lenny Abrahamson in *Adam & Paul*, the crew did not have to shut down streets and re-direct traffic in order to capture a scene. Shooting outside of the institutional parameters of a 35 mm production – big trucks, trailers, complex layers of bureaucracy and expanded crews – allows for a more intimate approach to cinematography. The crew are forced to use what is available directly to them on the street, with passers-by becoming unwitting performers – the effect being one of artisanal, sometimes low production values. The absence of 'gloss' in favour of a muted visual style is in keeping with the aesthetic drive behind the process.

Yet this is not an example of *cinéma-verité*. Echoing the iconography of *Bachelors Walk* and retreating further into a nostalgic Dublin, there are no visual representations of ipods, cappuccino bars, mobile phones, etc. – these deliberately concealed outside the frame. It evokes a residual culture of pre-'Celtic-Tiger' Dublin: the main male character (Glen Hansard) is a busker and works in his father's 'hoover' repair shop while the main female (Marketa Irglova) is a flower seller, cleaner and *Big Issues* trader, neither of whom are professional actors.[3] In terms of characterization, Hansard and Irglova are simply referred to as 'guy' and 'girl' in the credits, the narrative intimacy confined to *them* rather than shared with the audience. The narrative shirks the notion of authenticity at two levels, neither evoking, *verité*-like, an 'authentic' representation of contemporary Ireland, nor fitting the 'heritage' expectation common to Irish films reaching an international audience. The only nod towards a contemporary Dublin is the immigrant family and friends that form part of the story, and yet this depiction confines their living space to Georgian Dublin, conjuring up images of a bygone era similarly evoked in *Bachelors Walk*.

Marketa Irglova and Glen Hansard in *Once,* courtesy of David Cleary, Photographer.

The film is a story about musicians, starring musicians and featuring their own music. Telling the tale of the two characters falling in love through the innovative (for an Irish film) and over-arching narrative device of music, composition and performance, the film is unusual in eschewing the usual plot points of a love story. Not a musical in the traditional sense of the word, the film features music and singing moving in and out of the storyworlds. Sometimes evoking a documentary feel, the film's narrative moves from a diegetic (emerging from within the storyworld) approach to a musical performance to extra-diegetic (outside of the storyworld), unified all the time through music yet visually shifting in time and place. Writing on musical genres, Rick Altman identifies the altering of conventional narrative devices such as causality and motivation, which are replaced, in the musical, by 'the audio dissolve' and the 'video dissolve'. The audio dissolve superimposes sounds moving from one portion of the soundtrack to another (from conversation, for example, to music and song), while the 'video dissolve' serves to connect 'two separate places, times, or levels of reality' (Altman, 1987: 63–74). In *Once,* the songs and lyrics become a narrative device to convey story and plot detail, supported by the visual shifts in space and time. In one such sequence, Glen Hansard, as main character, performs one of his own songs, which is inter-cut with visuals of his ex-girlfriend in happier times. Shirking the conventional device of flashback, this sequence is presented like a music video yet seamlessly knits into the fictional narrative. Hansard's character and his ex-girlfriend (Majella Plunkett) perform one song for the audience watching the film, the other for the camera within the film. The grainy-documentary feel of the home-movie footage alongside the performance of a whole song allows the narrative to stretch the fictional potential in an interesting and innovative way. In other parts of the narrative, music is appropriated to act as the 'voice' in a voice-over, displaying more of the conventional devices appropriated from the genre, and used experimentally in the context of recent Irish film.

In terms of Altman's typology of the musical form, *Once*, which is seen as 'dual-focus' in structure privileging neither main character, could safely be categorized as 'the show musical' in which 'creating the couple is associated with the creation of a work of art (Broadway show, Hollywood film, fashion magazine, concert, etc.)' (Altman, 1987: 126). In this instance, a range of personally- and jointly-composed songs leading to an ensemble recording is what links this film to the Hollywood template, yet transposed to a local setting. Large chunks of narrative space are given over to performing whole songs, unsurprisingly for the musical. However, documentary-like, many of the performed songs are written by one or other of the main characters, not as part of the storyworld but in real life. This approach to documentary is fused with the highly conventionalized approach to musical genre. The scene at the back of the bus, where Hansard recalls the potted history of his doomed love through the improvised lyrics of a number of country-western songs, firmly roots this film in the musical tradition emanating from the Hollywood studio system, coinciding with Altman's template, yet its narrative pace is much more low-key and local. This film defies the Hollywood and Bakhtinian approach to romance when the couple part company at the end of the film, resisting the tacked-on traditional ending. Once the music is composed, performed and recorded, there is no need for the couple to stay together; not always an unfamiliar device of the musical.

Music is central to the films of Carney and Hall, unsurprising given John Carney's role as guitarist in the Irish band *The Frames,* founded in 1990 with Glen Hansard. Each of the films discussed here has a particular musical identity, yet the approach in *Once* is more complex in its diegesis and the only example of a musical. *November Afternoon* has a distinctive jazz score, playing a narrative role that positions the plot in a specific social/cultural milieu, while *Park* and *On the Edge* confine music largely to the extra-diegetic layer of narrative construction. *Once* stands out from this body of work in seamlessly knitting music and performance into the narrative as a way of telling the story, evoking mood and advancing the plot while also providing spectator pleasure similar to that derived from musical performance. Because the music has a genesis beyond the storyworld of the film, the narrative not only suggests a documentary feel but is very much rooted to artisanal cinema.

The sleeper phenomenon

While this book is concerned specifically with a narrative analysis, and *Once* is a key film for this discussion, another aspect to this film sheds light on the wider world of cinema and the positioning of Irish film therein. One of the criticisms of contemporary Irish cinema, particularly in its first ten years, was its failure to identify and promote the production of 'hit films'. A critical definition of a national film industry is its ability to produce 'sleeper hits': low-budget films that exceed all expectations for success. 'Sleepers' are defined as films from directors who already have a degree of success on the national and international stage, through the exhibition outlets at international film festivals, for their short and feature films (O'Regan, 2002: 102). *Once* has been described in America as the 'sleeper' hit of the summer of 2007. Is achieving this status a coincidence, a lucky break or well-deserved recognition? Turned down by the Edinburgh and Toronto film festivals and with a lukewarm response from a general audience in Irish cinemas, it was spotted at the Galway Film Festival and picked up for the Sundance Film Festival. When screened at Sundance, renowned for its promotion of independent films, it was a surprise hit. Word of mouth spread among festival-goers and extra screenings were demanded. The distribution company Fox Searchlight acquired *Once* for US theatrical distribution and its success took off from there. Made for the paltry sum of €180,000, it grossed over $9 million dollars at the US box office, was nominated and won an Oscar for best original song in 2008.

The 'sleeper' phenomenon is an interesting one – in business terms an enigma, impossible to predict and raising more questions than answers about film form. Tony Stafford, Head of Acquisitions at Fox Searchlight, says that inevitably it is important for an audience to respond well to a film, but sometimes it also needs the critics' focused testimony and emphasis. According to Stafford, there 'are some films which have a certain marketable element attached to them. *Once* was not one of them. *Once* absolutely needed critics to say it is adorable, delightful, one of the best films I've seen all year – those kinds of things. It had that sense of authorship, but it needed a push.' (Orpen, 2008: 15). While the success of a film like *Once* can be described accordingly, it is difficult to account for its 'sleeper' status in a scientific and material way. It took almost fourteen years and well over one hundred films for Ireland to produce what most national cinemas rely on, on a more frequent basis. *Once* is the film that gives new Irish cinema the 'sleeper' credibility: a low budget film, from an already well known director with a Hollywood production under his belt, shunned on many fronts before being 'discovered' to international acclaim. Stafford describes *Once* as having an 'incredible sense of authenticity of its world and its characters. Audiences responded to that. Character, place, dilemma, song, music, emotion, romance, love' (Orpen, 2008: 15). Stafford is not suggesting that this film presents us with an 'authenticity' in relation to Irish culture or an expected and perceived 'authenticity' according to foreign audiences; what he points towards is the *authentic* relation with its own storyworld. A critical mass of productions emerging from a stable film environment that nurtures and promotes talent over time ought to ensure sporadic, if not more frequent, 'hits'. Within the narrative parameters of Hollywood models combined with local inflections, the storyworld created in this film succeeds in pushing new Irish cinema into the international arena. But should this be the primary objective of a small national cinema?

At a domestic level, the impact recent Irish cinema has made on the local audience often goes unnoticed and unrecognized. While Barton is correct in pointing out that few Irish films from the recent period made any impact on the international stage, it is not totally correct to state that 'their performance in the home market has also been in many instances unremarkable' (Barton, 2004: 179).[4] Of 61 films listed by Barton, between 1994 and 2000, 52 received a theatrical release and while some had very few viewers (*Ailsa* – 429; *Words Upon the Window Pane* – 693; *A Further Gesture* – 953), 20 received almost 100,000 viewers (*The Last of the High Kings*; *Accelerator*) with some receiving 250,000 (*The Boxer*; *When Brendan met Trudy*; *Some Mother's Son*) and others around half a million (*The General*; *Angela's Ashes*; *Circle of Friends*).[5] More significantly, *Garage* took in €400,000 at the Irish box office, recouping its costs as did *Adam & Paul,* which accumulated €450,000 domestically.[6] These figures suggest that the meaningful achievement of this period is the relationship between the films and the local, domestic Irish audience, who displayed strong support in box-office terms for many recent Irish films.

The most obvious feat during this period is the yield of cinematic harvest: over one hundred and forty features reached completion between 1993 and 2008. With the changes in the cinematic landscape over the past ten years, through technological innovation and the growth of conglomerations, contemporary Irish film-makers are less protected from market forces than their predecessors, having to consider the audience and the market from the outset. At the same time, there are many more distribution options than there were fifteen years ago (Clarence Pictures; Abbey Films; Buena Vista International (Ireland)) for new Irish cinema, and more possibilities to be innovative. Ed Guiney and Andrew Lowe (Element Films) set up a distribution company, Guerilla Films, specifically to release their own film, in this case Lenny Abrahamson's *Garage*, taking it to European markets and further afield. Simon Perry, current CEO of the Irish Film Board, envisages greater distribution with the installation of digital equipment in cinemas and through new digital platforms – video on demand, getting movies through the PC, internet and so on (Orpen, 2008: 32). One of the key accomplishments of this time is establishing local connections with subject matter, oral and visual expression. This has been achieved by the shift in narrative focus but also through increased and diverse outlets for exhibition. Far from being the preserve of *cinéastes*, new Irish cinema's habitat is just as likely the omniplexes of suburban Ireland as the arthouse cinemas of the metropolis.

However, the flip-side to this is that many of these films founder on the international stage. Productions which were well received in Ireland (*I Went Down*; *About Adam*; *Intermission*) failed to attract widespread audiences abroad, arguably because the narratives, aesthetics and productions function on a small scale. While there have been some notable exceptions (*The Magdalene Sisters*; *The Wind that Shakes the Barley*, Ken Loach 2006), the pattern whereby Irish films released to a local Irish audience hold their own at the box office at least sufficiently to recoup marketing and distribution costs was not an arrangement repeated on the international stage. One of the criticisms of recent Irish film is its 'small-scale nature': films that fit more easily into television slots than cinematic distribution. Ireland is not unique in producing small-scale films, an observation Martin McLoone makes about British film in the mid-1990s (McLoone, 1996: 76–107), and clearly an advantage for the local, domestic market. On the other hand, the changing face of distribution and the multiplicity of outlet-type suggest that this could be an advantage. While the connection between film text and local audience has been established and consolidated over a fifteen-year period, it is only in recent years that foreign markets are becoming more accessible. With the fragmentation of the audience across a range of exhibition platforms, this approach may well become an advantage.

Moving away from the partnership with the Carney brothers, Tom Hall's recently-directed *Wide Open Spaces* (2009) submits itself to this dominant feature of recent Irish film. Scripted by Arthur Mathews (*Father Ted*, 1995–1998) and starring Ewen Bremner (*Fool's Gold*, 2008), Ardal O'Hanlon (*Father Ted*) and Owen Roe (*The Ambassador,* 1998; *Ballykissangel*, 1996–2001), *Wide Open Spaces* deviates from the characteristic style, already discussed, of *November Afternoon*, *Park* and *Bachelors Walk*. In fact, this film has more in common with many other features supported by the Film Board in the past fifteen years, characterized by specifically-local humour and set-up, as discussed in Chapter 2. Described by Allan Hunter (2009) as 'a melancholy, miserabilist buddy comedy with a fondness for strained eccentricity', this film tells the story of Myles (Ardal O'Hanlon) and Austin (Ewen Bremner) who, forced to work off a debt, help to convert an old tin mine into an Irish-Famine theme park for local entrepreneur (Owen Roe). Many parallels can be drawn between this film and *I Went Down*: theme (paying off a debt); location (rural non-descript landscape); humour (eccentric and idiosyncratic); and narrative (sketch-like, circular). Broken down elementally, this film's narrative is hindered in ways similar to many other recent Irish films already identified in this study. While the acting, writing, cinematography, editing, visual style and iconography of many recent Irish films is undoubtedly accomplished and comparable internationally, the sum of the parts in narrative form is often the point of enervation. *Wide Open Spaces* resonates on many levels with recent Irish film, particularly in terms of dominant narrative strategy. And like many of these films, it received a local theatrical release. However, even with some international deals, it is difficult to imagine it placed outside of a small arthouse and *cinéastes'* circuit, despite its mainstream approach.

The limited success in foreign markets of Irish films during this period may be explained by Rebecca O'Flanagan (former Development Manager at the Irish Film Board, 2000–04). She states that once distributors have recouped their costs in Ireland, they are less inclined to embark on a costly marketing campaign in an unknown foreign territory where they are unsure of the success potential. In this context it could be argued that these films did not necessarily fail; rather, they were not given the range of opportunities needed to succeed in the international film market. However, this does not account for the films that failed to impact on foreign audiences when given the chance. According to Rod Stoneman, '[new] Irish cinema established a good relationship with its home audience, good returns for most theatrical releases, high levels of video hire and purchase and strong ratings on television … fifty per cent of the Irish population had watched *The General* and twenty-five per cent *The Magdalene Sisters*, at a point when it was only available theatrically' (Stoneman, 2005: 257), echoing the assertion that contemporary Irish film's ultimate achievement is its performance at home.

Unlike British and Australian film industries that rely on and achieve a certain number of 'sleeper' hits ensuring their continued presence and survival on the international film stage, often on an annual basis (*Four Weddings and a Funeral*, Mike Newell, 1994; *Strictly Ballroom*, Baz Luhrmann 1992), it remains that Ireland has not reached notable levels of success in international distribution and exhibition, with films assisted by the Irish Film Board failing to overcome all the obstacles, as sleeper hits do. While the British film industry has a much longer tradition and more developed infrastructure than Irish cinema, the Australian situation, although having a longer life starting in the 1970s, parallels Ireland in many ways. It could be said that those directors who placed Irish film in the international arena in the late 1980s, giving rise to the re-activation of the Irish Film Board in 1993, are still the directors most associated with Irish film: Neil Jordan and Jim Sheridan. Aside from a few notable exceptions (Lenny Abrahamson, Paddy Breathneach, John Carney, Pat O'Connor, Damien O'Donnell to name a few), Irish directors and Irish films emerging from within the Irish Film Board structure are little known beyond national borders or outside of those groups with a vested cultural or critical interest.

So while contemporary Irish film-makers tell more global, universal stories now than they did before, and Irish audiences respond favourably to this by supporting these films at the local box office, the narratives, aesthetics and productions appear not to be universal or global enough for the wider international audience. A film like *Accelerator* had a successful run at the suburban Omniplex in Tallaght, an area of Dublin experiencing many of the social problems the film explores, suggesting that the characteristic feature of second wave films, combining a local story within a global narrative, is connecting with the audience. Is the audience attracted by the local inflections or the universal address, or a combination of both? [The universal nature of these stories appeals to the domestic audience, exposed mainly to American films, if the box office figures cited are to be read positively, but, it could be argued, the cultural-specificity within the narratives: idiosyncratically-Irish humour (*I Went Down*; *Intermission*; *Wide Open Spaces*), identifiable local actors (*The General*; *Dead Bodies*; *Disco Pigs*) and recognizable locations (*About Adam*; *Accelerator*; *Goldfish Memory*), is too provincial to travel.]

Although many would claim that Ireland is a country with more affinity to the literary than the visual, accomplishments within the medium of film over the past fifteen years suggests that this is changing. New Irish scriptwriters are influenced by the visual medium, by fractured narratives and by the changes brought about technologically. At the same time, the work of the Irish Film Board reveals that storytellers are still concerned with themes that seek to answer, or at least explore, key and fundamental philosophical questions about the nature of humanity: subject matter that is not the preserve of nationality or ethnicity but has the potential to cross borders and impact on an international community, fragmented nationally yet united culturally. The narrative forms are sometimes variegated and influenced by current or recent international trends; the content often re-imagines ancient myths and tales.[7]

New Irish cinema continues to consolidate yet is developing in different ways: the most notable changes since 2000 include the launch of the micro-budget (*Deadmeat*, Conor McMahon 2004; *Starfish*, Stephen Kane 2004) and low- budget schemes (*Goldfish Memory*; *Dead Bodies*; *Adam & Paul*; *Headrush*). The Catalyst Project launched in 2007, which is promoted as a risk-taking strategy giving opportunities to new talent through 'ultra-low budgets', funds production and training on a limited number of productions (*Eamon*, Margaret Corkery 2009). While many Irish films throughout the 1990s failed to get a theatrical release (*High Boot Benny*, Joe Comerford 1994; *Frankie Starlight*, Michael Linsay-Hogg 1995; *November Afternoon*, John Carney and Tom Hall 1996; *My Friend Joe*, Chris Bould 1996; *Spaghetti Slow*, Valerio Jolango 1996; *Separation Anxiety*, Mark Staunton 1997; *Sunset Heights*, Colm Villa 1998; *Night Train*, John Lynch 1999), more recent indigenous Irish films have been exhibited in the multiplexes of Ireland (*Circle of Friends*; *Accelerator*; *Intermission*; *Adam & Paul*; *About Adam*; *Man About Dog*; *Dead Bodies*; *The General*; *I Went Down*; *The Magdalene Sisters; Garage; Kisses* (Lance Daly, 2008); etc.) reaching larger and more diverse audiences than their first-wave predecessors, due to a combination of more accessible forms and the developing distribution stage of the process. All films produced now can expect at least to screen in some of the cinema-houses of Ireland followed by a DVD/Video distribution – many getting a television screening.

The period between 1993 and 2008 is distinctive historically as a phase in Irish cinema that sought to put distance between itself and its predecessor by approaching the medium of film in a new light, formally and thematically. The re-activation of the Irish Film Board in 1993 presented the film industry with an opportunity to 'catch up' with other national cinemas: this it has achieved in many aspects of the production process. The aesthetics, the narratives and the stories emerging in the years between 1993 and 2008 reveal that Irish cinema functions within a medium that combines an international shape with national elements – principally by integrating universal, global approaches to narrative and theme while firmly rooting their elemental expression in a local and often idiosyncratic milieu – thus knitting Irish film into the fabric of Irish culture more so than before.[8] While Irish cinema has developed in a positive way, shaped by an approach to film that is wide-ranging as opposed to specialist, it has not remained immune from international trends and practices. Most of the challenges facing Irish film are not unique to this country but are common to all national cinemas that seek to exist in what is a global entertainment industry, competing with block-buster movies that often have marketing budgets exceeding the spend on production. With the effects of technological change lodging permanently into the filmic process and the audience continually fragmenting, the Board has responded by initiating new schemes, already launching the next phase of Irish film. While this study reveals the narrative tensions within contemporary Irish cinema hinging on the relationship between the local and the global, how these approaches to storytelling are negotiated within emerging structures driven by new technology and organized under different budgetary strategies introduced by the Board, will influence the direction of Irish cinema in times to come.

The body of work, written, produced and directed by John Carney, Kieran Carney & Tom Hall, illustrates the complex nature of working in film in the twenty-first century. Experiencing a wide range of writing and directing possibilities and scenarios across Hollywood studio productions, small indigenous film and television drama, this production group is clearly most at ease within the local framework, giving concrete and tangible support to small local cinematic possibilities in the era of globalization. This team of writers and directors displays an experimental approach to both form and content while proving that this is often more achievable within a low-to-medium budget, with institutional support at a national or local level. The artisanal approach to film-making, experienced many times through the history of cinema when various movements emerged at particular historical junctures, remains a necessary part of both local and global cinema. Not sufficient to reflect all needs within a national cinema, it is certainly a vital component of what makes up the world's stage of film today. It is by no means the only form of film that gets people talking but, in a small national cinema that cannot compete with the global apparatus of Hollywood, it facilitates the continued practice of film-making that touches, unites and/or disperses a community locally or globally but keeps the artistic machine of visual storytelling in motion.

Notes

1. *Zonad* (2009) marks a departure for John and Kieran Carney into comedy with their adaptation from a short film of the same name that they produced in 2003. This film tells the story of an escaped convict, an overweight alcoholic dressed up in red vinyl, who fools a whole Irish village into thinking he is a visitor from outer space. Pre-release reviews of the film were very positive as it awaits a theatrical release sometime in 2010.

2. The 'intentionalist fallacy', which gained ground with the dominance of psychoanalytic theory in film studies since the 1970s, remaining intact ever since, has been usefully challenged by Paisley Livingstone (1996:149–75) in *Post-Theory: Reconstructing Film Studies*.

3. Glen Hansard's only previously acting role was as the character Outspan in *The Commitments* (Alan Parker, 1991).

4. Ruth Barton includes viewing figures, where available, for Irish films with part or complete Irish financing (not all are Film Board films) in the appendix of her book *Irish National Cinema* (2004: 191).

5. Some films recouped their costs and many others came close to it, through domestic and international sales (*Circle of Friends; The Magdalene Sisters; About Adam; Intermission; Adam & Paul*). Another commercial success was Ken Loach's film *The Wind that Shakes the Barley* (2006) which took in about €1.8 million at the Irish box office and around $21 million for international sales.

6. *Adam & Paul* made approximately €250,000 in international sales. These figures are courtesy of the films' distributor, Element Films (Oct. 2009).

7. *Trojan Eddie* (Gillies MacKinnon, 1996), for example, re-works the ancient tale of the Fianna – *Toraíocht Diarmuid agus Gráinne* – into a modern, contemporary drama situated within the settled and travelling communities in Ireland.

8. While Ireland's national theatre, the Abbey, stumbled through its centenary celebrations in 2004 amid internal bickering and poor box-office returns, *Adam & Paul*, an Irish film, was seen by 80,000 people at the cinema. The implications of this contrast must lie with the current population's response to what it deems national cultural matter, choosing a story that is not determined only by national issues, incorporating universal themes but resonating locally all the same.

References

Altman, Rick (1987) *The American Film Musical*, Bloomington: Indiana University Press.

Arendt, Hannah (ed.) (1968) *Illuminations, Walter Benjamin – Essays and Reflections*, New York: Schoken Books.

Aristotle. *The Poetics*, Translated by Theodore Buckley (1992) Buffalo: Prometheus Books.

Bal, M. (1999) *Narratology, Introduction to the Theory of Narrative*, Totonto: University of Toronto Press.

Barthes, Roland (1975) *The Pleasure of the Text*, Oxford: Oxford University Press.

Barton, Ruth & O'Brien, Harvey (eds.) (2004) *Keeping it Reel, Irish Film & Television*, London: Wallflower Press.

Barton, Ruth (2000) 'The Smaller Picture? – Irish cinema, funding, figures and the future'. Unpublished Conference Paper. University of Wales, Bangor.

Barton, Ruth (2004) *Irish National Cinema,* London: Routledge.

Battersby, Eileen (1997) 'You can all me Alan – Thursday Interview with Alan Gilsenan', *The Irish Times,* 20 November: 14–15.

Baudrillard, Jean (1988) *America*, New York: Verso.

Bell, Des (2004) 'Practice makes perfect? Film and Media Studies and the challenge of creative practice', *Media, Culture & Society*, (26) 5 September.

Berger, Arthur Asa (1992) *Popular Culture Genres: Theories and Texts,* Thousand Oaks, CA: Sage Publications.

Bordwell, David (1990) *Narration in the Fiction Film*, Madison: University of Wisconsin Press.

Bordwell, David & Carroll, Noel (eds.) (1996) *Post-Theory: Reconstructing Film Studies*, Madison: University of Wisconsin Press.

Bordwell, David and Thompson, Kristin (1990) *Film Art: An Introduction*, New York: McGraw-Hill.

Braithwaite, Ann (2004) Politics of/and Backlash', *Journal of International Women's Studies*, Vol. 5, June: 18–33.

Branigan, Edward (1998) *Narrative Comprehension & Film*, New York: Routledge.

Campbell, Joseph (1949) *The Hero with a Thousand Faces,* New York: Pantheon.

Carroll, Noel (1988) *Mystifying Movies*, New York: Columbia University Press.

Carroll, Noel (1999) *Philosophy of Art, A Contemporary Introduction*, London: Routledge.

Carty, Ciaran (1998) 'Maverick Movie Maker', *The Sunday Tribune (Magazine)*, 2 February: 12.

Carty, Ciaran (2000) 'Good Things Come in Threes', *The Sunday Tribune.* 22 October: 19.

Carty, Ciaran (2001) 'Fertile Imagination', *The Sunday Tribune*, 2 October: 5.

Chatman, Seymour (1999) *Coming to Terms: the Rhetoric of Narrative in Fiction and Film*, Ithaca: Cornell University Press.

Cheshire, Godfrey (2001) 'Let's have More Playfulness', *The Irish Times,* 16 July: 9.

, & Holquist, Michael (1984) *Mikhail Bakhtin,* Harvard: Harvard University Press.

)05) 'Edward Said and the Cultural Intellectual at Century's End', *The Irish Review*, inter.

ty (2004) 'The Films of Gillian Armstrong', paper delivered during a symposium on Contemporary Australian Cinema on *Senses of Cinema* web-site, http://archive.sensesofcinema. com/contents/00/9/symposium.html. Accessed 25 November 2009.

Connolly, Maeve (2003) *An Archaeology of Irish Cinema, Ireland's Subaltern, Migrant and Feminist Film Cultures (1973-1987).* Unpublished Doctoral Thesis DCU.

Cook, Pam (1992) *The Cinema Book*, London: BFI.

Cooper, Mark Garrett (2002) 'Narrative Spaces' in *Screen* 43: 2.

Corcoran, Farrell (2004) *RTE and the Globalisation of Irish Television*, Bristol: Intellect.

Creed, Catherine (2000) 'Cutting the Sky', Interview by Jeanine Hurley with Catherine Creed, *Film Ireland* pp. 36–41.

Crosson, Sean & Stoneman, Rod (2009) *The Quiet Man … And Beyond*, Dublin: The Liffey Press.

Currie, Gregory (1995) *Image and Mind: Film, Philosophy and Cognitive Science*, Cambridge: Cambridge University Press.

Deleyto, Celestino (2003) 'Between Friends, Love and Friendship', *Screen* (44) 2: 167–82.

Doolan, Lelia (1993) 'In Interview with Johnny Gogan', *Film Ireland* (36).

Dwoskin, Stephen (nd) *On a Paving Stone Mounted*, Production notes, filed in the Irish Film Archive, Irish Film Institute, Dublin (np).

Dwyer, Ciara (2001) 'Sisters are doing it for themselves', *The Sunday Independent* 28 January: 2L.

Dwyer, Michael (1995) 'Review of *A Man of No Importance*', *The Irish Times*, April 21: 15.

Dwyer, Michael (1999) 'Report Diagnoses Illness of Irish Film Industry but Risks Alienation with "Cure"', *The Irish Times*, 5 August.

Eliot, T.S. ([1932]1999) *Selected Essays*, London: Faber and Faber.

Elsaesser, Thomas & Buckland, Warren (2002) *Studying Contemporary American Film*, London: Arnold.

Evans, Peter William & Deleyto, Celestino (1998) T*erms of Endearment: Hollywood Romantic Comedy of the 1980s and 1990s,* Edinburgh: Edinburgh University Press.

Feagin, Susan (1988) 'Imagining Emotions and Appreciating Fiction', *Canadian Journal of Philosophy*, Vol. 18, Number 3, September: 485–500.

Foster, Roy (2001) *The Irish Story: Telling Tales and Making it up in Ireland*, London: Penguin.

Frye, Northrop (1957) *Anatomy of Criticism*, London: Penguin.

Gibbons, Luke (1996) T*ransformations in Irish Culture,* Cork: Cork University Press in association with Field Day.

Gibbons, Luke, Hill, John & Rockett, Kevin (1988) *Cinema & Ireland,* London: Routledge.

Gillespie, Michael Patrick (2006) *The Odyssey of Adam and Paul: A Twenty-first Century Irish Film* in muse.jhu.edu/journals/new_hibernia_review/v012/12.1 Accessed 25 November 2009.

Gillespie, Michael Patrick (2008) *The Myth of an Irish Cinema,* Syracuse: Syracuse University Press.

Ging, Debbie (2002) 'Screening the Green: Cinema Under the Celtic Tiger' in P. Kirby, L. Gibbons & M.Cronin (eds.) *Re-inventing Ireland, Culture, Society and the Global Economy*, London: Pluto Press.

Ging, Debbie (2004) 'The Lad from New Ireland: Marginalised, Disaffected and Criminal Masculinities in Contemporary Irish Cinema', *Film & Film Culture*, Vol. 3.

Grodal, Torben (2008) *Embodying Visions*, Oxford: Oxford University Press.

Hammond, Mike (2004) 'Vernacular Modernism – Film, the First Global Vernacular?' in *Fourth Symposium of Screen Studies* Group, University of London, http://muse.jhu.edu/login?uri=/journals/history_workshop_journal/v058/58.1hammond.html. Accessed 25 November 2009.

Hansen, Miriam (2000) 'The Mass Production of the senses: Classical Cinema as Vernacular Modernism' in Christine Gledhill & Linda Williams (eds.) *Reinventing Film Studies,* London: Arnold Publishers.

Hauke, Christopher and Alister, Ian (eds.) (2001) *Jung & Film: Post-Jungian Takes on the Moving Image,* Cambridge, MIT: Cambridge University Press.

Herman, David (2002) *Story Logic: Problems and Possibilities of Narrative,* Lincoln and London: University of Nebraska Press.

Herman, David (2007) *The Cambridge Companion to Narrative,* Cambridge: Cambridge University Press.

Hill, John (1986) *Sex, Class and Realism – British Cinema 1956–1963,* London: British Film Institute.

Hill, John & Church-Gibson, Pamela (1998) *The Oxford Guide to Film Studies,* Oxford: Oxford University Press.

Hunter, Allan (2009) 'A Review of *Wide Open Spaces*', www. http,//www.screendaily.com/festivals/edinburgh-reviews/wide-open-spaces. Accessed June 2009.

Irish Business and Employers Confederation (1995) *The Economic Impact of Film Production in Ireland,* a report, IBEC.

Irish Film Board (2008) Expenditure Review of the Department of Arts, Culture and the Gaeltacht.

Karlin, Marc (nd) *On a Paving Stone Mounted,* Production notes, filed in the Irish Film Archive, Irish Film Institute, Dublin (np).

Kearney, Richard (2002) *On Stories,* London: Routledge.

Kerrigan, Gene (1993) 'Sound, Light and Some Action', *The Sunday Independent,* 4 April.

Ketteman Kerstin (1999) 'Cinematic Images of Irish Male Brutality and the Semiotics of Landscape in *The Field* and *Hear My Song*', in Mac Killop, (ed.), *Contemporary Irish Cinema: From The Quiet Man to Dancing at Lughnasa.* Syracuse: Syracuse University Press.

Lennon, Peter (2000) 'Where are all the cows gone?', *The Guardian (Friday Review),* 20 October: 12–13.

Linehan, Hugh (1999) 'Snakes in the Grass', Interview with John Carney and Tom Hall, *The Irish Times* 27 November: 3.

Linehan, Hugh (1998) 'Cutting Edge Cinema', *The Irish Times (Sound & Vision)* 20 February.

Livingstone, Paisley (1996) 'Characterization and Fictional Truth in the Cinema' in David Bordwell & Noel Carroll (eds.). *Post Theory: Reconstructing Film Studies,* Madison: Wisconsin University Press.

Lothe, Jakob (2000) *Narrative in Fiction and Film,* Oxford: Oxford University Press.

Lynch, Brian (2002) What's it all about?' *The Irish Times* 9 Feb: 5.

McCarthy, Gerry (1999) Interview with Gerry Stembridge in *The Sunday Times.* 9 May: 6.

McCarthy, Gerry (2001) 'Interview with Goran Paskaljevic' in *Film West,* Vol. 45: 30–32.

McIlroy, Brain (2001) *Shooting to Kill: Filmmaking and the 'Troubles' in Northern Ireland,* Steveston Press.

McIlroy, Brian. (ed.) (2007) *Genre & Cinema: Ireland & Transnationalism,* London & New York: Routledge.

McKeone, Marion (1995) 'Irish film has cutting edge', *The Sunday Business Post,* 17 December.

McKeone, Marion (1998) 'Celluloid Diplomat, Rod Stoneman, Chief Executive of Irish Film Board', *The Sunday Business Post,* 18 January.

McKillop, James (ed.) (1999) *Contemporary Irish Cinema: From The Quiet Man to Dancing at Lughnasa,* Syracuse: Syracuse University Press.

McLoone, Martin (1996) *Big Picture, Small Screen: The Relations between Film & Television*, Academia Research Monograph.

McLoone, Martin (2000) *Irish Film: The Emergence of Contemporary Cinema,* London: British Film Institute.

McMahon, Stephen (2001) 'Sperm on the Rampage in Belfast', *The Sunday Business Post*, 28 August: 8.

Mackey-Kallis, Susan (2001) *The Hero & the Perennial Journey Home in American Film*, Philadelphia: University of Pennsylvania Press.

Macnab, Geoffrey (1994) 'Review of A Man of No Importance' in *Sight & Sound*.

Maddox, Brenda (1988) *Nora: The Real Life of Molly Bloom*, London: Hamish Hamilton.

Mamet, David (1994) *A Whore's Profession, Notes & Essays*, London: Faber & Faber.

Meaney, Gerardine (2004a). '*Nora*, Biography, Biopic, and Adaptation as Interpretation' in *Film & Film Culture*, Vol. 3.

Meaney, Gerardine (2004b) *Nora*, Cork University Press.

Monahan, Barry (2006) *Adam and Paul* in www.estudiosirlandeses.org/Issue1/FilmReviews.pdf. *Accessed 30 November 2009.*

Mulvey, Laura (1975) 'Visual Pleasures and Narrative Cinema', *Screen* 16 No. 3: 6–18.

Neill, Alex (1993) 'Fiction and Emotions', *American Philosophical Quarterly* 30: 1–13.

Neill, Alex (1996) 'Empathy and (Film) Fiction' in Bordwell, David & Carroll, Noel (eds.) *Post-Theory, Reconstructing Film Studies*, Madison: University of Wisconsin Press.

Neill, Alex (1999) 'Appreciation and Feeling', Journal of *Aesthetics and Art Criticism* 57: 67-71.

O'Regan, Tom (2002) 'Australian National Cinema' in Alan Williams (ed.) *Film & Nationalism*, East Brunswick, NJ: Rutgers University Press.

Orpen, Michael (2008) '*Once* I acquired an Irish film – Interview with Tony Stafford', *Film Ireland* Issue 121, March/April.

Owens, Kieran (1999) 'Stuart Hepburn and *A Love Divided*', *Event Guide*, 12–15 May.

Parker, Phil (2000) 'Reconstructing Narrative', *Journal of Media Practice* 1: 66–74, Intellect.

Pettitt, Lance (2000) *Screening Ireland, Film & Television Representation,* Manchester: Manchester University Press.

Power, Paul (1994) 'Review of *A Man of No Importance*', *Film Ireland*, June/July, Issue 41: 40.

Propp, Vladimir ([1928]1968) *The Morphology of the Folktale*, Austin: University of Texas Press.

Quinn, Bob (2000) 'Recycled Rants', *Film West*, Issue 42, Winter: 26–30.

Rimmon-Kenan, Schlomith (1993) *Narrative Fiction: Contemporary Poetics*, New York: Methuen.

Rockett, Kevin (2004) *Irish Film Censorship*, Dublin: Four Courts Press.

Rockett, Kevin & Hill, John (eds.) (2004) *National Cinema and Beyond,* Dublin: Four Courts Press.

Sconce, Jeffrey (2002) 'Irony, Nihilism and the new American 'smart' film', *Screen* 43, 4, Winter.

Sheehan, Helena, (1988) *Irish Television Drama*, Dublin: RTE.

Smith, Gary (ed.) (1988) *On Walter Benjamin: Critical Essays and Recollections*, Cambridge, Mass: MIT Press.

Stalker, John (1988) *Stalker: Ireland, 'Shoot to Kill' and the 'Affair'*, London: Penguin.

Stoneman, Rod (1993) 'Irish Film', *Screen International*, 10-16 December No. 937.

Stoneman, Rod (2000) 'Under the Shadow of Hollywood, The Industrial Versus The Artisanal', *Kinema*, Spring.

Stoneman, Rod (2005) 'The Sins of Commission 11', *Screen*, Vol. 46, No. 2, Summer.

Tan, Ed. S. (1996) *Emotion and the Structure of Narrative Film*, New Jersey: Lawrence Erlbaum Associates.

Thompson, Kristin (1999) *Storytelling in the New Hollywood*, Cambridge: Harvard Univei..,

Thornton, Niamh (2004) 'Interview with Pat Murphy', *Film & Film Culture*, Vol. 1: 7–10.

Tierney, Michael (2001) 'Interview with Gerry Stembridge', *Film West*, Spring, Issue 43: 14–17.

Todorov, Tzvetan (ed.) (1982) *French Literary Theory Today: A Reader*, Cambridge: Cambridge University Press.

Townsend, Scott (2009) 'Review of *Helen*', *Film Ireland*, May/June.

Tracy, Tony (2008) 'Interview with Simon Perry' in http://www.estudiosirlandeses.org/Issue3/IrishFilm&TV2007/pdfTheYearinIrishFilmandTV2007.pdf. Accessed 26 November 2009.

Traynor, Des (2001) *'Review of About Adam'*, *Film Ireland*, Issue 79, Feb./March: 43.

Tulloch, John (1990) *Television Drama, Agency, Audience and Myth*, London: Routledge.

Vogler, Christopher (1999) *The Writer's Journey*, London: Pan Books.

Wilson. Jake, 'Love's Catastrophes', paper delivered at Contemporary Australian Cinema – A Symposium, compiled by Fiona A. Viella, http://archive.sensesofcinema.com/contents/00/9/symposium.html. Accessed 26 November 2009.

Wollen, Peter (1988) *Signs and Meaning in the Cinema*, London: British Film Institute.

Wood, Jason (2007) *100 Road Movies*, London: BFI Screen Guides.

Zimmermann, Georges Denis (2001)*The Irish Storyteller*, Dublin: Four Courts Press.

Index

Feature Films, Documentaries, Short Films and Television Shows and Series